Destiny and Human Initiative in the Mahābhārata

McGill Studies in the History of Religions,
A Series Devoted to International Scholarship

Katherine K. Young, editor

Destiny and Human Initiative in the Mahābhārata

Julian F. Woods

State University of New York Press

Cover image: Corbis Images

Published by
State University of New York Press, Albany

Printed in the United States of America

For information, address State University of New York Press,
90 State Street, Suite 700, Albany, NY 12207

Production by Judith Block
Marketing by Fran Keneston

Library of Congress Cataloging-in-Publication Data

Woods, Julian F.
Destiny and human initiative in the Mahābhārata / Julian F. Woods.
p. cm.
Includes bibliographical references and index.
ISBN 0-7914-4981-5 (alk. paper)—ISBN 0-7914-4982-3 (pbk. : alk. paper)
1. Mahābhārata—Criticism, interpretation, etc. I. Title.
BL1138.26 .W66 2001
294.5′923046—dc21 00-057356

10 9 8 7 6 5 4 3 2 1

Contents

Preface

The Mahābhārata (or "Great [War between] the descendants of Bharata") has probably had a greater impact on the mind of India than any other religious or philosophical text. It appears to have been composed, in metrical stanzas designed to be recited or sung, sometime between the fourth century B.C. and the fourth century A.D.[1] The prevailing view is that the poem passed through the three stages of:

1. oral composition and recital;
2. written compilation by a group or school of priestly savants, or even by a single poetic genius;
3. final stage of transmission involving supplementary accretion and interpolation by different hands.

However, the details of this process will likely never be known.[2] What comes down to us, however, is a remarkable compendium of ancient lore, containing all manner of mythical, legendary, didactic, and folkloric material—including an abridged version of the Rāmāyaṇa (the second great Indian epic) and, of course, the famous Bhagavadgītā or "Song of the Lord."[3] The modern "Critical Edition" used here is based on a review of over one thousand manuscripts, mostly written in Sanskrit, a language belonging to the Indo-European linguistic group. It is viewed by the editors as "a modest attempt to present a version of the epic as old as the extant manuscript material will permit us to reach with some semblance of confidence."[4]

Although the work clearly has affinities with European epics and sagas as Georges Dumézil and others have shown, it also differs from them in a number of respects.[5] It differs, firstly, in terms of sheer size. The various texts consulted contain up to two hundred thousand lines of verse, longer than all of the extant European epics combined—eight times as long as the *Iliad* and the *Odyssey* put together. It differs too in its encyclopedic scope. In an oft-quoted verse the poem itself claims that "whatever is here of dharma (rules of human conduct), *artha* (material prosperity), *kāma* (sensual enjoyment), and *mokṣa* (liberation, that is, from bondage to the other three of life's goals) may be found elsewhere. But what is not here is nowhere else" (I.56.33 and XVIII.5.38).

However, perhaps the most significant difference with respect to Western epics is the continuing allegiance the poem commands to this day as the most popular and influential of the canons of modern Hinduism. It is regarded, and indeed regards itself, as one of the *saṃhitas* (collections) associated with the four Vedas, in effect a "fifth Veda" (I.1.19).[6]

The purpose and function of the text is clearly designed to be more than exemplary or even didactic; the intent is therapeutic in seeking to prompt the mind to a greater awareness of spiritual truths, and ultimately, to lead it to the joy that springs from the presence of God.[7] As readers-listeners we are challenged to change ourselves through confrontation with the "names and forms" of the world *(nāmarūpa* in Sanskrit), the kaleidoscopic panorama of life itself, viewed through the allegories and images of the poet. This method of fostering spiritual insight and emotional calm and control, leading to liberation or freedom *(mokṣa),* is taken for granted by subsequent commentators.[8]

No English translation can do justice to the original Sanskrit, owing to the great cultural distance separating classical Indian thinking on these matters from our modern notions of autonomy, self-determination—and "freedom of will." I have therefore inserted in parentheses the more important Sanskrit terms behind the relevant English text, and have appended a "Glossary of Sanskrit Terms" to further assist the inquiring reader. Sanskrit words are highlighted in italics, and are capitalized when they appear at the beginning of an English sentence or constitute a proper name (including the personified forms of Dharma, Kāla, and the goddess Earth). However, terms already in common English usage such as karma, Yoga, and dharma, are given without italicization when they appear alone within, or in conjunction with, an English sentence. English terms for the Divinity in His Supreme aspect (referred to by the masculine He, His, etc.) are also capitalized in contrast to the lower forms of the divinity such as the divine incarnation (avatar).

When given without a prefix, reference numbers point to the volume, chapter, and verse numbers of the nineteen-volume Sanskrit Critical Edition published by the Bhandarkar Oriental Research Institute in Poona.[9] Bhagavadgītā sources include both the reference to the Critical Edition and to the better-known chapter numbers of this famous dialogue. The occasional reference to other Sanskrit sources is prefaced by the name of the source text, the only exceptions being the Gītā commentaries by Śaṃkara (SBG) and Rāmānuja (RBG), respectively. I would also like to direct the reader to the "Glossary of Proper Names," which is designed to clarify the identities and relationships of the various characters mentioned in what follows.

Translation from Sanskrit into English was much facilitated by the well-respected translation of the Sanskrit Critical Edition by J. A. B. van Buitenen (unfortunately only the first five books and the Bhagavadgītā).[10] Text within square brackets has been added in some instances to improve clarity or readability or to add a comment. Translation from French and German secondary sources is entirely my own unless otherwise stated. Of course I bear full responsibility for any weaknesses that remain with regard to the translations and other matters.

I would be remiss if I did not acknowledge the encouragement and assistance of Dr. Katherine Young of the Faculty of Religious Studies of McGill University. In fact, were it not for her continual urging, this endeavor would have been stillborn. Her own *puruṣakāra* has been truly remarkable. I am also greatly indebted to Dr. Jan Brzezinski who assisted in checking the translations. My sincere thanks must also go to the Shastri Indo-Canadian Institute for their financial support during my sojourn in India, and to all the fine scholars and librarians at the Bhandarkar Oriental Research Institute in Pune, in particular to Prof. P. G. Lalye, formerly professor and head of the Sanskrit Department, Osmania University, Hyderabad, India. Finally, I would like to thank my wife Jutta for her patience and long-suffering through days of semiseclusion, punctuated by long and passionate discussions on the different aspects of this enterprise. I am eternally grateful that she was able to stay the course.

1

Introduction

The Theme in Historical Perspective

The history of philosophical and religious speculation about the vicissitudes of human life is characterized by two principal lines of thought. There is the more optimistic view that men and women, though dwarfed by the immensities of the Cosmos, nevertheless have what it takes to change society and themselves, and to "conquer Nature." The opposite, and more pessimistic, view is that human beings are forever the victims of circumstances beyond their control, hostages to an implacable and irrevocable fate.

These two positions, or rather attitudes to life, are seen in the writings of both the West and the East. In classical Greece, Plato saw clearly how most of us are lost in the shadows of our own prejudices and passions *(ekasia)*. He nevertheless believed that the human soul can escape this unhappy condition through an epistemological ascent to the vision of the Good: "the cause for all things of all that is right and beautiful, . . . the authentic source of truth and reason."[1] Contrast this to the world of fifth-century tragedy, as Clytemnestra stands over her murdered husband and the chorus chants: "Alas, it is the will of Zeus, Who caused and brought it all to pass. Nothing is here but was decreed in heaven."[2] Christianity retains the eschatological hope, albeit with a sense of impotence in the face of the power and glory of God,[3] or of one's ultimate demise without the saving Grace of Jesus Christ.[4]

In India, too, these two traditions have a venerable antiquity. In the early Ṛgvedic hymns, human beings are largely subservient to the whims of the gods, who are praised for the favors they bestow in exchange for the sacrifice *(yajña)*. This attitude is also evident in the expiatory sacrifices designed to mollify the wrath of the god Varuṇa, or to remove guilt, often expressed as some kind of defilement or disease. This humble dependence on the gods changes dramatically, however, when the priests gain control of the gods by their knowledge of the ritual. A new sense of power thus emerges in the Brāhmaṇas, reinforced, in part, by a magical tradition that received orthodox approval in the Atharvaveda.[5]

Dramatic as these changes were, the new ritual knowledge still left the human agent at the mercy, as it were, of external forces. The secret of the cosmic power had passed into human hands, but only to a priestly caste *(varṇa),* not to the average man or woman. The desires *(kāma)* themselves are one's own, but they are fulfilled not directly, but mediately through an esoteric knowledge of the general order of the world over which one would otherwise have little or no control. Private actions would appear vain, impotent, or even illusory when set against the inexorable tide of events. Although accountable for what one does, there would be little to inspire confidence in one's inherent abilities to shape one's own destiny. Lacking is the depth and coherence of inner life that would point to the existence of an autonomous, self-directing center of willing and doing; what we would call a "person."

Such a situation does little justice to the creative potential within human nature itself, which lends dignity and uniqueness to the individual person, and hardly provides an adequate explanation for moral responsibility and human conduct in general. To the extent that one attributes one's actions to external agencies, one is determined by them, and thereby diminished. To the extent that one attributes these same actions to oneself, one is at least potentially free to choose one's own ends, to be called to account for what one does, and to accept some responsibility for the conditions of one's own life.

In ancient Greece, a similar clash of ideals gave rise to the tragic situation of the hero who faces an impasse *(aporia)* demanding an agonizing choice on which his entire fate depends. He is never actually free to choose between these two possibilities—only to recognize the tragic path he has to take, and, in so doing, to understand the purpose of his life. This conflict was never pushed to such extremes in classical India, but the human agent nevertheless remained suspended, as it were, between the external forces that bear down upon him and a margin of free choice that finds its latest and most developed expression in the moral causality of karma, the doctrine that the conditions of life are the inevitable fruit of past behavior, whether in this or in some previous life. The natural corollary of this more human centered view is that humanity is capable of determining the shape of its future all by itself, without the need to propitiate the gods—or the sacrificial experts among the Brahmin priests. This opens the way for the individual human subject to become the center and source for his or her own self-development as a spiritual being.

The first textual evidence of a movement in this direction was the appropriation, by Varuṇa, of the role of dispenser of divine justice (for example, Ṛgveda I.24.9). Other gods subsequently assumed this function. This line of development eventually led to the idea of the Divine Grace of Viṣṇu or Śiva as a reward for the conduct of the devotee. The conflict was never completely resolved, but as a general rule, we find that the ascetic (and generally more orthodox) traditions lean toward the goal of individual self-mastery through self-knowledge, while for the devotional cults, justice is often meted out by the Supreme Divinity according to the karma of the devotee. The karma doctrine eventually gained the ascendancy, even in the *bhakti* cults, and "Leaving out the rank materialists who are very few and far between, the entire structure of Indian culture from one end of the country to the other is dominated by the ideology associated with the doctrine of karma."[6]

The Mahābhārata is an ideal sourcebook from which to study human agency and conduct in the Indian context. Here, in fact, is an entire gamut of ideas on the subject from those reminiscent of the early Vedas to the role of divine Grace and the mature doctrines of karma. The earlier notions are echoed in the attribution of all power to the gods. Indra is credited with assigning "to all beings their strength, glory *(tejas)*, offspring, and happiness. When satisfied, the king of the gods distributes all good things. He denies them to evil-doers but grants them to the good (lit. 'those established in virtue')" (III.218.9–10). The favors of the gods are also considered vital for certain purposes; Arjuna must propitiate Indra and Śiva to secure divine weapons; Ambā must perform austerities *(tapas)* to get the support of Śiva for killing Bhīṣma (V.188.7–13). More common is the orthodox Brāhmaṇic perspective of the many passages comparing the Brahmins to the gods (for example, III.197.20; XII.329.13; XIII.129.2). Several passages even describe them as the gods of the very gods—*devānāmapi devatāḥ* (for example, XII.60.41, XIII. 35.21, and XIII.136.16–20). There are hints of a power struggle between the gods and the "forest sages" or *ṛṣi* (XIII.6.25). And the gods are finally reduced to the powers of the senses, which, of course, the yogi must control (for example, XII.120.44; XII.316.16).

E. Washburn Hopkins was the first Western scholar to recognize different strata of ideas in the Indian epic literature by contrasting the karma theory with one in which "man owes what he gets, not to his anterior self, but to the gods. What the gods arrange is, in any case, whether good or bad, the appointed lot; the "arrangement," *viddhi,* is fate. If the gods bestow a "share," *bhaga,* of good upon a man, that is his *bhāgya,* "luck, divinely appointed," *diṣṭa.* As divine, the cause is *Daiva,* which later becomes fate, and is then looked upon as a blind power, necessity, chance, *haṭha.*"[7]

Focus of the Analysis

These terms and ideas are of particular interest since they lead directly to the focus of the present work, which seeks to explore the powers and possibilities of human action in the Mahābhārata. Attention is directed not only to the act itself but to the motive (or "desire") behind it, and to its potential effects on the actor and on the world. The issue constituted a major philosophical conundrum prompting lively debate at numerous points in the epic. Modern discussion on this topic would likely be framed in terms of Destiny and "Free Will." However, it becomes increasingly evident as the story unfolds that the actions of the protagonists have little in common with our modern sense of either "will" or "freedom." Not only has the Sanskrit language no direct counterpart for "will"; the "freedom" involved is not of any function or faculty of the ego (such as a "will"), but of the human spirit—a very different matter. Epic freedom (or *mokṣa*) points beyond what we might recognize as the human "person" to a freeing of the bonds that bind that person to the things and beings of the world itself. The word most commonly employed to describe a motivated action in these epic debates is *puruṣakāra* (lit. "that which is done by a human being"), a term that is more akin to our concept of "human initiative" than to Free Will as such—hence its choice in our title. It is generally matched against the opposing forces of *Daiva* ("that which comes from the gods"), a term we may roughly translate as "Destiny."[8]

On the one hand, human life and the course of history are seen by many epic characters as governed exclusively by *Daiva* (and the other external forces noted by Hopkins), or by *svabhāva,* a term that suggests something inherent *(sva)* in the nature *(bhāva)* of a thing that makes it act as it does. "Human effort" or *puruṣakāra* is inconsequential, ephemeral, or even futile in the face of the overwhelming tide of events, whether these are the result of sociopolitical conditions, or natural forces beyond the power of the individual to change. Such a position is exemplified by the blind king Dhṛtarāṣṭra, so much so that Georges Dumézil, for example, takes him to be "the very image, if not the incarnation of Destiny, Bhaga."[9] All the king can do is to see in his thoughts the destruction of the Kurus: "This, I think, is the law of the course of time *(kāla)* that goes on for ever: all are fixed to the wheel like its rim; there is no escaping its effects" (V.50.58). Many other characters in the epic speak in the same vein in their troubled moments or when they feel powerless against overwhelming odds. However, Dhṛtarāṣṭra not only expresses these sentiments; he is overwhelmed by them to the point of actually becoming the chosen instrument of *Daiva*.

And yet, paradoxically, the epic also carries a commanding message that the lives of both individuals and societies may be changed for the better through human initiative *(puruṣakāra)* in accordance with the dharma, the moral order sanctioned by religious tradition. This is, indeed, the teaching that Kṛṣṇa is at pains to convey to Arjuna in the Bhagavadgītā section of Book VI. Kṛṣṇa himself always acts for the welfare of the worlds *(lokasaṃgraha)* and he urges Arjuna to do the same. Action not only can but *must* be taken in fulfillment of one's dharma. Arjuna must "get up and fight!" And he is finally urged to make up his own mind about what he should do (VI.40/BG.18.63).

Such encouragement and sanction by the Lord himself suggests that this more positive outlook is not the exuberance of youth or the ignorance of the blind but is justified by the very conditions of existence. However, there is little consensus on the degree to which human initiative *(puruṣakāra)* can change or stem events that unfold as if governed by a greater divine force with a will of its own. Moreover—and this will also claim our attention, there is still some question as to whether the work of the human agent flows from a truly personal decision in the first place. This creates a constant tension between the two opposed poles.

The most revealing summary of the prevailing state of learned opinion on this score is provided by Vyāsa himself, the reputed author of the text, when he states that

> Some authorities in the science of action point to human initiative *(puruṣakāra)* [as the cause of events]. However, other learned scholars say [that it is a matter of] destiny *(Daiva)*, [while] the materialists [say that] nature *(svabhāva)* [is responsible]. But yet others [maintain that] human initiative, action (karma) and destiny are [nothing but] the naturally-occurring product of [previous] mental states. These three [factors] are inseparable, without distinction. [It is argued] "it is like that: it is not like that" how the world comes into being.[10]

This clash of view is somewhat disconcerting at first sight. Vyāsa, however, immediately follows with the assurance that "[It is only] 'those who take their stand in action' *(karmastha)* [who] are of differing opinions (*viṣama* = not uniform [that is, in their opinions]). 'Those who take their stand in the truth' *(sattvastha)* look upon all things with an equal eye *(samadarśin)*."[11]

This brings us to another radical opposition that occurs throughout the epic, and indeed through all great works of Indian literature, namely, the contrast that is often drawn between the confusions of ordinary men and women and the truths entertained by the person of wisdom who is able to reconcile all opposites in a unitary vision. As V. S. Sukthankar has noted, this literature is "infused with the idea of penetrating behind the phenomena to the core of things, and they represent but so many pulsating reflexes of one and the same central impulse toward seeing unity in diversity, toward achieving one gigantic all-embracing synthesis."[12] What the real truth is, in this case, is not given directly in the quotation just cited. However, it offers the suggestion that the differences therein expressed are perhaps not mutually exclusive, but point to an underlying vision of human nature, action, and purpose, accessible only to "those who take their stand in the truth" *(sattvastha)*.

Reconciliation of these two views can thus serve as a goad in our attempt to determine the respective roles of these powers, their relationship to classical Indian beliefs about karma, and their implications with respect to self-determination and human freedom. It becomes increasingly clear as we proceed, however, that this can be done only in the context of the epic's unique concepts of human nature, and in taking account of that very special "final" freedom known as *mokṣa*. For, as the Bhagavadgītā suggests to us, this "final freedom" is not possible without a quantum shift in self-identity in which the human ego, together with its sense of agency, is "sacrificed" in favor of a larger system of identity, described in the Bhagavadgītā as "the self of the self of all beings." In the last analysis, therefore, *puruṣakāra,* based on ideas of "I" and "mine," is fated to dissolve with the dissolution of the ego, to be replaced by devotion to the higher purposes of the Cosmos. These "higher purposes," or *Daiva,* are represented in the epic by Kṛṣṇa, the incarnation (or avatar) of God who has descended to earth to restore the moral order (dharma). *Daiva* thus emerges as the driving force behind the cycles of human history and society, and indeed of the Cosmos as a whole. It is experienced in our own lives as the various obstacles that hinder the fulfillment of "desire" *(kāma)*. And in terms of the karma theory, it is the inexorable "fate" resulting from the desire-prompted initiatives of the past.

This ubiquitous pressure from above leaves the reader with the feeling that our all-too-human striving for material and spiritual betterment, and for the well-being of society, is ephemeral or somehow unreal. But its value for the epic author(s) is never in doubt. *Puruṣakāra* is universally promoted and prescribed, and is most dramatically exemplified in the person of the king. Without initiative, drive, and the energetic pursuit of worthy goals, both the king and his kingdom are lost. On this point the epic is quite clear. The king cannot simply abandon his worldly responsibilities in the manner of a renunciate, but must act in the world with the right attitude. This means giving up all thought of personal gain in the interests of the welfare of the community, something that can only be done by cultivating a spirit of detatchment and devotion to Kṛṣṇa. In this manner, all human behavior, including the inhuman violence and "sacrifice" of the battlefield, may be transformed into a new devotional path leading to the ultimate "freedom" of *mokṣa*. What appears as a dissonance between *Daiva* and *puruṣakāra* may thus be more conceptual than real. The real conflict, if there is one, is between the two distinct visions of human existence in which these notions find their place. These are represented, in the language of the epic, by "those who take their stand in action," and by "those who take their stand in the truth" respectively; the truth that the ego and its sense of agency is ultimately a mental fiction—a case of mistaken identity.

In order to illustrate how "those who take their stand in the truth" of things *(sattvastha)* are able to reconcile the conceptual inconsistencies experienced by us ordinary mortals (that is, the *karmastha*), we must clarify the levels of meaning bound up with these notions of *Daiva* and *puruṣakāra*. How far do they penetrate to the very roots of human action itself? Does the initiative come only from the human agent or from both within and without, the same character appearing now as agent, source, and efficient cause of action *(puruṣakāra)*, and now as acted upon, engulfed in a force from beyond that sweeps all before it *(Daiva)*? Or does this divine causality only come into play once the human action has been initiated, to block, counter, or divert its effects? In short, how do the lives of the human protagonists fit into the activities of higher beings on higher planes? If human beings are moved by a higher design like a machine *(yantra)*—as suggested by Kṛṣṇa in VI.40/BG.18.61, what freedom can they really enjoy to shape their own destinies and those of the societies in which they live?[13]

The Epic Context

The epic context for these ideas is a great fratricidal war between two sets of cousins, the Pāṇḍavas and the Kauravas, for control of the dynastic succession. For the epic, however, this conflict is simply an episode in the perennial battle of the gods and the demons for the control of heaven, temporarily shifted to the Earth where incarnations ("sons" and "daughters") of these same gods and demons are continuing this battle for supremacy. The growing ascendency of the demon hordes is marked here below by the gradual moral entropy of human society. This situation can only be reversed by the Creator Himself (since evil at this level is invariably more powerful than good), who engineers a renewal of society through the complete destruction of the old order. The human battle lines are drawn between the hundred sons of the blind King Dhṛtarāṣṭra, the eldest of whom is Duryodhana, and the five sons of Pāṇḍu (of whom Arjuna is the main actor). Kṛṣṇa, the incarnation of the highest Divinity, acts as Arjuna's friend and charioteer, though nominally remaining neutral in the conflict. The battle itself may be interpreted as a fitting metaphor for the human struggle "on the field of dharma" between a lower nature and a higher nature acting as a proxy for the spirit (Kṛṣṇa) who takes no part in the action. To what extent the story is purely symbolic, or is based on the facts of history, must remain a moot point.

Clearly, a thematic analysis such as this is only possible if the epic can be read as a synthetic whole (rather than as a haphazard assemblage of disparate materials). This has long been a major bone of contention among Western scholars. But here is not the time or place to enter into the fine points of this continuing controversy. However, I will clarify my own position at the outset by saying that I incline to the view that, while there are clearly all manner of accretions to the core elements of the plot, the epic does, in fact, constitute a *symbolic* whole. By this I mean that doctrinal or sectarian differences do not obscure what amounts to a common vision of the human journey and of the purpose of this life on Earth, presented in a mythological key. This will emerge as we proceed, and will be given concrete expression in chapter 9. I find myself in substantial agreement with Madeleine Biardeau in this regard. The interested reader will find a more complete exposé of scholarly attitudes on the integrity of the epic in the Appendix.

2

Hermeneutical Perspectives

A work as vast as the Mahābhārata may be read in a variety of ways, and this chapter will introduce the views of certain major commentators that have guided our own reading of the poem. Most of the traditional Indian commentators lean toward a particular philosophical position, and we will be mentioning at least two of these in due course to highlight different aspects of our chosen theme. The story as a whole lends itself to interpretation on a number of levels. A good example of the traditional Hindu view is that of Madhva (a well-known thirteenth-century religious figure), who proposes a three-level reading of the poem:

> The meaning of the "Bhārata," in so far as it is a relation of the facts and events with which Śrī Kṛṣṇa and the Pāṇḍavas are connected, is called *āstīkādi* (historical). That interpretation by which we find lessons on virtue, divine love, and other ten qualities, on sacred study and righteous practices, on character and training, on Brahmā and the other gods, is called *manvādi* (religious and moral). Thirdly, the interpretation by which every sentence, word, or syllable, is shown to be the significant name, or to be the declaration of the glories, of the Almighty Ruler of the Universe, is called *auparicara* (transcendental).[1]

A similar three-dimensional interpretation of the Mahābhārata is offered by V. S. Sukthankar, the first editor of the Critical Edition, in a well-known series of four lectures given in 1942. He reads the story on the mundane level as the realistic account of a fierce fratricidal conflict involving the epic characters. He goes on to interpret this war of annihilation on the ethical level as the conflict of dharma and *adharma,* of the principles of good and evil, justice and injustice. At this level the contending parties are incarnations of gods *(devas)* and demons *(asuras)* and the war ends in the victory of the gods and of dharma. However, beyond these struggles of dharma and *adharma,* Sukthankar also sees a third or "transcendental" level. This is the perennial struggle between our higher and lower natures, a struggle that can only be resolved in our own minds. He captures what he believes is the basic thrust of the epic by contrast with modern science:

> Modern scientists are interested in breaking the Atom, which we are told is a solar system in miniature, in order to release the captive energy for the exploitation of Nature. The Ṛṣis of ancient India were interested in breaking the tangled knot of personality, which is the very cosmos in miniature, in order to release the captive energy for the sublimation of Nature.[2]

Today, there is general agreement that the significance of the text lies in its symbolic rather than in its historical import. In short it has come down to us as "myth" rather than as fact (though probably based on the intellectual and social issues of its own time). And like any good myth, the epic is able

> to function like a perfect prism through which are refracted simultaneously all the possible ways of regarding the problems encountered in the myth. The first level we encounter is the narrative, usually quite a good story, though often with a rather predictable ending. Closely related is the divine level, which concerns mythology as it used to be understood by scholars of the classics: the metaphorical struggles of divine powers and personalities. Above this is the cosmic level of the myth, the expression of universal laws and processes, of metaphysical principles and symbolic truths. And below it, shading off into folklore, is the human level, the search for meaning in human life. Great myths are richly ambiguous and elusive; their truths cannot be filed away into the scholar's neat categories.[3]

Madeleine Biardeau, the well-known French scholar who has spent most of her long career researching the text, goes so far as to claim a "mythical necessity" for the Mahābhārata story, reading the war as a sort of Vedic "sacrifice" of the decadent moral and social order *(adharma)* for the rejuvenation of society and for the establishment of a new path to salvation for the warrior caste (in particular the king). In her view, the seizure of the throne of Hāstinapura by Duryodhana (incarnation of the demon Kali) is simply the culmination of a social malaise originating in the progressive breakdown of the traditional functional relationship between the *Kṣatriyas* and the Brahmins, the two pillars of epic society. Thus she traces what, in the traditional Indian context, amounts to a progressive reversal of the natural order of things down the generations starting from the reign of Śāṃtanu—whose very name evokes the renunciation of the Brahmin (*śānti* = "peace"), and the Brahmin Parāśara (the destroyer), the father of Vyāsa. We follow her further here, to obtain a taste for the story itself as well as for the symbolic light she sheds on it.

That king Śāṃtanu himself marries a princess (Satyavatī) born from a fish is itself suggestive of disorder (*mātsyanyāya* or "rule of the fish," is the Indian "law of the jungle" where the big fish eat the little fish). Bhīṣma—the *pitāmaha* or (honorary) grandfather, must also bear his share of the responsibility. Though a *Kṣatriya,* he opts for a higher dharma reserved for the Brahmin by renouncing both the throne (that is, *artha*) and his marriage rights *(kāma)*. The result is that he cannot fulfill the duties incumbent upon his royal status, which would have involved marrying the princess Ambā, and providing a legitimate heir to the throne. The responsibility for this is delegated to his Brahmin half brother Vyāsa.[4] The succession is thus defective from the start, and his nephew, king Pāṇḍu, finally abandons his duties to devote himself to the traditional royal vices of lovemaking and the chase, leaving the blind Dhṛtarāṣṭra (his half brother) to covet the kingdom in his absence. There follows the extraordinary situation of the generation of the protagonists in which the god Viṣṇu (in the form of Vyāsa, his Brahmin representative) engineers the birth of the demons *(asuras),* while the god Śiva (in the form of the irascible sage Durvāsas) sets the stage for the birth of the gods *(devas)*.

The circumstances leading to the crisis itself are no less irregular. Droṇa, incarnation of the priest of the gods (Bṛhaspati) and mundane representative of the Brāhmaṇic power, is found to be in the service of the demons. Furthermore, he no longer serves as priest but assumes the role of commander in chief of the demon army (on the death of Bhīṣma). This involves a double corruption of dharma. Service on behalf of the demons is substituted for that of the gods, and a Brahmin usurps the functions of the king. As for his son, Aśvatthāman, he embodies the collective venom of Mahādeva (= Śiva), Antaka (death), Kāma (desire), and Krodha (anger) which almost succeeds in foiling the restoration of the dharma symbolized by the resurrection of the dead Parikṣit, the rightful heir to the Pāṇḍava throne. Karṇa too is a strange mixture, being of divine descent (he is illegitimately fathered by Sūrya, the Sun god, on Kuntī, the mother of the Pāṇḍavas) but linked to the demon Naraka. Bhīṣma (Dyaus = "the Heavens") and Vidura (Dharma) are both captives to the demons. It is evident that the demons have usurped the Brāhmaṇic power to their own advantage, a situation that clearly calls for the intervention of the avatar.

However, since intervention by the avatar inevitably involves destruction on a cosmic scale (or at least on the scale of the three worlds known as the *trailokya*), the Mahābhārata war has been dramatized by the epic author as a cosmic sacrifice analogous to the destruction of the worlds at the "end of the *yuga*" *(yugānta)*. The weapons of war are compared to the fire at the end of a *yuga,* and

> this image is among the most frequent of the whole account. The war is thus a crisis, not only terrestrial, but of the *trailokya,* which suggests the juncture of two *yugas*. We can even say more precisely, between the end of a Kaliyuga and the start of a Kṛtayuga. In fact, since the epic is still a myth, it is not enough to say that the conflict is the image of a *yugānta*. Rather, it is the symbolic transformation, the re-employment of this idea at another level. It is this level, where the *yugas* become asuric princes and the cosmic conflagration becomes war, that defines the epic.[5]

This destruction is represented as a gigantic funeral pyre in which the old order of the world, Pāṇḍavas and Kauravas alike, must perish to give way to a new order established with the assistance of the divine incarnation Kṛṣṇa from the remnant represented by Parikṣit, the perfect monarch embodying the qualities of both Arjuna and Kṛṣṇa.

The question is: what is the significance of this symbolism? In Biardeau's view, it reveals and reflects a sweeping transformation of the ritual values attached to the traditional notion of the Vedic sacrifice. It must be recognized, she says, that the

> victory is not only that of dharma over adharma. The order to be restored is also that taught by Kṛṣṇa to Arjuna at the start of the war in the Bhagavadgītā. Instead of imitating the Brahmin, the *Kṣatriya* should fulfill his royal duties in a spirit of detachment and devotion to Kṛṣṇa, transforming each of his violent actions, beginning with war, into a sacrifice. This is the sense of the year of living incognito prior to the war, corresponding to the period of consecration for the sacrifice: the war being the sacrifice par excellence for the *Kṣatriya* who offers himself as victim with the hope of substituting his enemy for himself.[6]

This leads to the idea that death in battle—the sacrifice of the self *(ātmayajña)* on the battlefield—is the appropriate sacrifice for the *Kṣatriya*. His bow is his sacrificial stake, his bowstring the cord for tying the victims, his shafts are the small ladle, and his sword the large one.

His chariot is the altar and the blood he pours on the battlefield is the clarified butter. His wrath is the fire of the sacrifice and the four steeds yoked to his vehicle are the four sacrificial priests *(hotrī)*. After pouring his own life-breath *(prāṇa)* and that of his foes as libations upon the sacrificial fire of the battlefield, he becomes freed from sin, and secures a place for himself in heaven *(svargaloka)* (cf. XII.24; also XI. Appendix I, nos. 1.33–40; XI.2.11; XI.8,1–4). The initiation theme *(dīkṣā)* of the Pāṇḍavas' forest exile clearly emphasizes the sacrificial character of the war and the yogic preparation necessary for this. This, in turn, leads to the idea that an inner conquest is required to assure victory in the external combat of battle (cf. V.34.52–55; XII.69.4–5).

In this manner, the sacrifice of battle becomes a form of total renunciation *(tyāga* or *saṃnyāsa)* in which one puts one's own life on the line *(ātmayajña)*. Arjuna (that is, the ideal king) can neither abandon his responsibilities nor pursue his own narrow self-interest. Instead, he is called to dedicate his life to the wider goals of human welfare *(lokasaṃgraha)*, undistracted by family ties, and without attachment to the results of his actions. The sacrifice he performs becomes an act of Yoga, marked by one-pointed concentration *(ekāgra)* on the task at hand. In this manner the notion of sacrifice is internalized to become a new ideal of human conduct, a new path to salvation.

This epic symbolism is authenticated, in Biardeau's view, by close Purāṇic parallels to the cosmogonic myths of the epic, whatever chronology of textual development is adhered to (the Purāṇas were written down at a later period than the epics). The epics and Purāṇas both project the old ritualistic and Upaniṣadic ideals into a cosmic panorama of space and time. As will be developed further in chapter 3, what began as the mystical adventure of an individual aspirant in the Upaniṣads develops into a collective spiritual march through a hierarchy of worlds constituted by the creator-god Brahmā, the perpetually transmigrating cosmic person whose life span frames the birth and death of the Universe as a whole. As the mythical personification of the sacrificial power of the Brahmin priest (known as the *brāhman*), he symbolizes the orthodox this-worldly religion *(pravṛttidharma)* with its Veda and sacrificial system. In contrast, the Upaniṣadic alternative of turning away from the world and its values *(nivṛttidharma)* is projected onto the divine figure of the *puruṣottama* (Supreme Person), another mythical transformation with antecedents going back to the Praśnopaniśad and to the Puruṣasūkta hymn of Ṛgveda X.90. This epic/Purāṇic symbolism constitutes a sort of cosmic backdrop to the human events used to dramatize what amounts to a complete transposition of traditional Brāhmaṇic religious values into a new system of *bhakti* devotionalism.

Since the task of this book is limited to a single major theme, it uses these more general insights of others as a point of departure to proceed inductively by exploring the different contexts in which the two fundamental sources of human motivation and activity are illustrated or discussed. Chapter 3 profits largely from Biardeau's comparative analysis of epic and Purāṇic cosmogony to illustrate the cosmological setting, where *Daiva* is a function of cosmic Time (with a capital *T*). This overriding vision of things is the primordial factor driving the responses of individual protagonists to the critical situations faced by them, and that they are inevitably forced to explain to themselves.

3

Cosmic Destiny

Although the merits of human initiative *(puruṣakāra)* are frequently extolled throughout the epic, it is clearly the mood of *daiva* that sets the tone of the work as a whole. The birth of the protagonists is accompanied by celestial pronouncements about their characters and careers, followed by various prophesies by sages and seers, and several on the Kaurava side, including Duryodhana, are actually possessed by demons. We might well expect them to be preoccupied at critical points in their lives by the weight of *daiva*—almost continually haunted by it in the case of Dhṛtarāṣṭra. We sense the frustration and despair of individuals who find themselves caught in a vast web of causality over which they have no control. Kṛṣṇa himself refers briefly to this influence when he reminds Arjuna in the Bhagavadgītā that the Lord (Īśvara) "causes all beings to move like a machine by the power of illusion" *(māyā)* (VI.40/BG 18.61). What is the source of these ideas? And how does the way of thinking of these epic characters come about?

The most general answer to these questions is suggested when we look beyond the mundane events of the narrative to the cosmic setting in which the human drama takes place. As briefly mentioned in the introduction, the Earth is not the only battleground and human beings are not the only actors in this drama. The fate of the "Three Worlds" is at stake,[1] and, beyond them is the inexorable course of a cosmos governed by the yogic rhythm of the Supreme Divinity (*puruṣottama*). We must therefore examine Dhṛtarāṣṭra's "law of the course of time" in order to illustrate the relation of "Time" itself *(kāla)* to the creative Life of the Divinity, and to the decline of the sociocosmic moral order. This moral decline appears to be more a function of "Time" than of human conduct, as we shall see.

The Mythological Background

Insofar as it is linked to the Divinity and to the "worlds" of epic cosmology, macrocosmic *Daiva* (distinguished henceforth by a capital *D*) is "Time" itself (here also capitalized), an inexorable cyclic process of creation, manifestation, and destruction of the cosmos. In the Purāṇic material studied by Madeleine Biardeau, this occurs at two levels of the Divinity and unfolds according to a twofold cyclic arrangement of time. The Divinity in His highest form as *puruṣottama, paramātman,* etc., is in perpetual absorption *(samādhi)*. However this Divinity also operates at a less exalted level at which He acts in the manner of a Master Yogi who periodically emerges from His yogic absorption to manifest, maintain, and eventually to destroy the worlds.[2] To do this He becomes functionally divided into the three forms *(trimūrti)* of Brahmā (creative function), Viṣṇu (preservative function), and Śiva (destructive function). The most extensive of the temporal cycles in which these events occur is known as a *mahākalpa*. This is the period lasting from one "primary" Creation to the complete absorption of the cosmos that occurs at the end of one "life of Brahmā." It is, of course, the Divinity in the form of Śiva who finally acts to destroy the Universe.[3] Brahmā in his various forms is thus a sort of eternally transmigrating "cosmic person" whose "life" is synonymous with the existence of the Cosmos itself. By contrast, the *kalpa* is the secondary cycle of creation/destruction of the Cosmos that begins at the dawn of each new "day" of Brahmā and ends with the corresponding withdrawal of the world system that accompanies the onset of "night." Since the life of Brahmā is taken to last for a period of 100 divine years of 360 days each, the number of *kalpa* in a *mahākalpa* is 36,000.

From a psychological perspective, these epic and Purāṇic cosmogonies are but macrocosmic projections of the traditional Hindu yogic processes of absorption and return to empirical consciousness—albeit in reverse order. Indeed, Biardeau argues that the various cosmogonic stages may be traced to a section of the Kaṭhopaniṣad, with the addition of *ahaṃkāra* (as cosmic ego), taken from other Upaniṣadic (Vedāntic) sources. Significantly, the Yoga outlined in the Purāṇas is described as emergence and absorption *(prabhavāpyayau)*. Looked at in this manner, the kaleidoscopic effects we call "life" and "world" are regarded as the mind or thought-stuff of the Divinity, who contemplates His manifestation for a while before withdrawing it once again for a period of latency, symbolized as a cosmic "night."[4]

The philosophical import of this conception is that the Universe is a figment of Mind or illusion *(māyā)*, established in accordance with the desires *(kāma)* and actions *(karma)* of its living inhabitants *(jīvas)*. The emergence awakens the latent tendency of creatures to act *(pravṛtti)*; the absorption inaugurates the movement back to the primal state of quiescence *(nivṛtti)*. The very purpose of the ritual activities associated with the Vedic sacrifice is to ensure that the "Three Worlds," the centerpiece of this system as far as human activity is concerned, functions in an orderly fashion for the benefit of all (cf. III.101.1–5; XII.329.7; also VI.26/BG.3.10–11). In effect: "It has been declared [in the scriptures] that this [the Universe], having the character of a cause, is the work of ignorance. That [ignorance] which produces the totality of effects is itself connected to causes. As a result, this great wheel [of existence] revolves without beginning or end" (XII.204.6–7). *Pravṛtti,* the tendency to act that keeps the "Three Worlds" in being, is prescribed for the vast majority who wish to improve their lot in the form of rebirth in higher worlds and states of existence. As we shall see further in chapter 6, this path is invariably associated with the creative activity of Brahmā, the alternative path of *nivṛtti* with the Supreme Divinity in His state of yogic absorption (XII.210.3–6). Humans in the Mahābhārata have the option of following one or the other of these two paths, in accordance with the functional requirements of their caste status. However, only by way of the renunciation of the *fruits* of action, the revolutionary new *bhakti* form of *pravṛtti,* can a warrior-king such as Arjuna attain to absolute freedom *(mokṣa)* from this wheel of existence.

The Epic Accounts

Epic accounts of this world process are more difficult to follow than those of the Purāṇas since they are less structured or complete and tend to emphasize a particular aspect or detail of the fundamental myth. Furthermore, the time-scales and levels at which creation and destruction take place are not always clearly delineated. Finally, the epic author has a habit of substituting a *yuga* symbolism for that of the *kalpa* (a matter that Biardeau has studied in great detail). In spite of these anomalies, the three accounts that follow are sufficiently uniform and coherent for us to capture the significance of *Daiva* in the imagination of the epic author and his characters.[5]

A complete picture of the primary cycle of creation and destruction of the Cosmos is offered by the sage Yājñavalkya (XII.298–306). The creative process unfolds in the Purāṇic manner, according to certain principles enumerated in the proto-Sāṃkhya system of philosophy; and Brahmā himself emerges from a golden embryo. (In a similar account [I.1.27] he is depicted as emerging from a large egg.) The durations of time deviate somewhat from the standard versions of the Purāṇas but the juxtaposition of the temporal cycles is in agreement with the Purāṇic scheme.

During the destructive phase, the Supreme Divinity (in the form of Brahmā) urges Mahārudra (a form of Śiva) to destroy the "Three Worlds" by fire. Mahārudra thereupon assumes the destructive form of the Sun (Sūrya) divided into a twelve-part fire. Fire is followed by flood, and the creative process is then taken in reverse, each element being swallowed up by the following element according to its degree of subtlety. Water is absorbed by fire, fire by wind (in eight forms), wind by space, and space by mind *(manas)*. Mind is swallowed up in its turn, and what remains is the immutable, that is, the "Supreme Person" *(puruṣottama)*, in a state of total yogic absorption *(nirvikalpa-samādhi)*.

A brief account of the secondary cycle of existence is given at verse 7 of chapter 9 of the Bhagavadgītā: "All beings, O son of Kuntī, return to Me at the end of the *kalpa*, whereupon I send them forth once again at the beginning of the [subsequent] *kalpa*" (VI.32/BG.9.7). The same process is described at verse 17 of chapter 8, but with the substitution of "one thousand *yugas*" for what should, technically, be a *mahāyuga* (= a *kalpa*). This substitution of temporal symbols is common throughout the Mahābhārata. Biardeau believes this to be the result of the fact that the epic is a double myth involving dimensions that are both cosmic (the avatar intervenes at times of cosmic crisis), as well as royal (the *yugas* are often associated with the actions of the king).

According to a third account by the sage Mārkaṇḍeya, at the end of a thousand *mahāyugas* (that is, a *kalpa*), the Supreme Divinity as Nārāyaṇa takes the form of "most terrifying Time," destroys the Universe, and then goes to sleep for the same period of time—until he awakens as Brahmā. Then: "when the grandfather of all the worlds has woken up, O best of the twiceborn, I, having become one, shall send forth [the universe], from this body of mine" (III.187.46). The Universe is the body of God.

Time itself is structured rather differently for humans, ancestors, and gods according to daily, monthly, and annual periods. These are explained by the poet Vyāsa, to his son Śuka (XII.224–5). He begins at the human level by enumerating the divisions of the day, and explains that a month of human time is equal to a day and a night of the ancestors *(pitṛ)*, that is, to the light and dark fortnights of the lunar cycle. Extending this logic, the human year is made equal to a twenty-four-hour "day of the gods," based on the two equinoctial periods when the sun moves north and south, respectively.

Moving now to the effects of these temporal periods, he explains the dependence of social conditions on the succession of four *yugas* over a period of 12,000 "years of the gods" or 12,000 × 360 human years. During the "Golden Age" or *kṛtayuga,* the subject of morality, together with truth, were so much part of the Vedic curriculum that nothing was accomplished in a manner not in accord with the dharma. However, this dharma progressively declined by a quarter in each of the *tretā-, dvāpara-,* and *kaliyugas. Adharma* progressively took hold as a result of theft, falsehood *(anṛta),* and illusion *(māyā).*[6]

Finally proceeding to the cosmic level of time he explains: "They say that a day of Brahmā extends for a thousand *yugas* (that is, a *mahāyuga*), and his Nights for a similar period" (XII.224.31). According to such reckoning, the interval between a secondary creation and the subsequent dissolution extends over a period of 4.32 billion human years. However, remembering that there are 36,000 *kalpas* in a "life" of Brahmā, the interval between a *primary* creation and the onset of the succeeding dissolution (not dealt with here by Vyāsa) extends the life of the Universe as a whole to 155,520 billion human years, a period well in excess of that currently entertained by modern science.

These details are not provided for their "cosmic" effects, but to highlight the overriding influence of "Time" itself on the moral and social situation. On this point, however, there is a strange divergence of view between the Purāṇic and the epic theories. The Purāṇic view of social decline, outlined once again by the sage Mārkaṇḍeya, is reminiscent of what he says about the end of a *kalpa.* A period of drought is followed by a conflagration of seven suns. There is no flood (as at the end of a *kalpa*) but the rains arrive out of season. And more significantly, instead of the total destruction of the Universe:

> A Brahmin by the name of Kalki Viṣṇuyaśas will arise, impelled by Time, of great energy and courage . . . He will be a king, a turner of the wheel, triumphant by the dharma, and he will bring peace to this turbulent world. (III.188.86, 89, 91)

The gradual decline of the social and spiritual fabric of society is here followed by an abrupt restoration of the dharma. This rather unexpected transition is marked by a "descent" of the Lord to Earth (*ava* √*tṛ* = "to descend"), here in the form of Kalki who will restore the social and moral order "that the self-existent lord has ordained." This is expected to be accomplished on the occasion of a gigantic horse sacrifice (III.189.1–2).

Two things are worthy of note here. In the first place, even God Himself is apparently impelled by Time *(kālapracodita)*. The moral order may be "ordained" by the Lord but here it is "Time" itself that determines when he should act.[7] Secondly, the appearance of the avatar—a third level of Divinity, is associated with the *yuga* cycle—a third cycle of Time. This "lower" level of the Divinity is, of course, very much closer to the human world and its concerns. We can easily imagine how these periodic catastrophes and interventions by the avatar might foster the sense of a divine play (*līlā*—here in the sense of a childrens' game) experienced in the form of a *Daiva* opposed to human effort.

By contrast, the intervention of Kṛṣṇa in the actual story of the Mahābhārata takes place, not at the conclusion of the *kaliyuga* as in this case, but at the close of the *dvāparayuga*. In Biardeau's explanation of this anomaly, introducing Kṛṣṇa at this juncture serves to heighten the cosmic symbolism of a war that involves not only the Earth and its terrestrial kings, but also the gods and the demons, symbolizing the cosmic struggle of good and evil. It is only from the ashes of this violent conflagration involving the "Three Worlds" as a whole, that a new and more perfect dharma can arise. She points out that the Machiavellian Śakuni and the ambitious Duryodhana are portrayed as incarnations of Dvāpara and Kali, personifications of the respective *yugas* in the form of demons. Furthermore, the *yugas* themselves carry the names of the throws of the Indian dice, clearly implying the intervention of a power beyond the collective will of human beings.[8] This *yuga* symbolism is an important key to understanding the epic since, in Biardeau's view "It is [the symbolism of] the 'end of the *yuga*' that creates the unity of the symbols employed by the authors and the characters of the epic. This unity is that of a socio-cosmic crisis in which the regions governed by the dharma are implicated."[9]

Epic expressions used to convey this dominance of "Time" are both colorful and instructive. The whole universe is borne along by the mighty river of Time whose currents are difficult to cross (XII.227.13ff.). Like the flow of rivers, the days and nights are continuously carrying away the lives of human beings, who are but froth on the surface of water (XII.309.6). The ceaseless succession of the lighted and dark fortnights is wasting all mortal creatures without respite, and the rising and setting sun is continuously cooking the joys and sorrows of everyone (XII.318.5–7). In the words of Vyāsa to his son Śuka: "This profusion of Time without end is the source and destroyer of that [that is, the creatures] . . . It is Time that makes them come and go, that is their originator, their support, their Lord and controller, the destroyer of all beings . . . Time is creation, constancy and the Veda. Time is the agent, the action, and the result of action" (XII.230.19–21). And Saṃjaya assures Dhṛtarāṣṭra that "Time ripens all beings; Time rots them; and Time again softens the time that destroys all beings. Time unfolds all beings in the world, pure and impure; Time shrinks them and expands them again; Time, unwavering and impartial, moves in all things" (I.1.188–9). Many other similar passages could be cited.

This sense of temporal inevitability is reinforced by the belief that each cycle of cosmic existence is the same as all others. People, things, and events do not change: "Whatever creatures have come into being and passed away, they will be in the future; whatever are living now, they are all the creatures of Time. . . ." (I.1.190). Everything lost in the dissolution is acquired anew at the dawn of the new creation. The Vedas are recovered by the same Brahmā, the ancilliary texts by the same Bṛhaspati, the political treatises by the same Śuka, the art of music by the same Nārada, the martial arts by the same Bharadvāja, etc. (XII.203.17–19). And this occurs over and over again across an eternity of time: "Thousands and hundreds of *mahākalpa* and creations and absorptions have already passed away, O King of Kings" (XII.326.104). The Earth has seen it all before, and will see it all again. This conveys the feeling of a single script written in advance and played repeatedly according to the periodicities of "Time." In sum, it suggests that *Daiva* is a function of "Time"; that "Time" and *Daiva* are one and the same.[10]

Additional confirmation for this view is provided by the events leading to the birth of the protagonists and to the conflict between the two sets of cousins. In one sense, there is no beginning to this story of conflict and war, for the wheel of time has no real beginning, as we have just seen. However, we may begin with the story of Rāma Jāmadagnya (I.58.5ff.), the avatar whose passage brought the Earth to new destructive heights at the junction of the *tretā-* and the *dvāparayugas*. After the world is rid of the warrior class twenty-one times over, there is a brief Golden Age featuring the rise of a new brood of warriors, who reign over the Earth in strict accord with the dharma: "All the castes devoted themselves to their own tasks, O king, and thus, tiger among men, the dharma was in no way diminished in that age. . . . And the Golden Age continuing in this way, the whole earth quickly became filled with many creatures" (I.58.22 and 24).

However, this idyll does not last long. Soon, the demonic hordes, who had been defeated by the gods, are born once again among the men and kings of the Earth. Bloated with power and strength, they roam the world killing and looting and, worst of all, tyrannizing the Brahmins. Feeling overwhelmed, the goddess Earth takes refuge with Brahmā the creator and "grandfather of the worlds," who agrees to help her by ordering the gods "to throw off the burden of Earth, you must each be born with a part of yourselves on her to hinder them" (I.58.46). With Indra in the lead, these gods then ask Nārāyaṇa-Vaikuṇṭha (that is, Viṣṇu) to join them: "And so the sky-dwellers descended, one after the other from heaven to this earth, for the destruction of the enemies of the gods and the well-being of all the worlds; thereupon they were born in the lineages of Brahmin sages and in the families of royal sages, as they saw fit, O tiger among kings" (I.59.3–4). Once again the point in the *yuga*-cycle arrives for the restoration of dharma on Earth.

From this perspective of cyclic time, the epic drama is but an episode in the recurrent bid of the demons for the destruction of the gods and for the sovereignty of the "Three Worlds." As Vyāsa explains, first to the grieving Dhṛtarāṣṭra (XI.8.12–44) and later to Gāndhārī when the epic action is all but complete—the "eternal secret of the gods" is that the course of things is decided by them *ab æterno*:

> O virtuous [Gāndhārī], the work of the deities could not but be accomplished. It was for this purpose that they all descended to the surface of the Earth as portions of gods. Various heavenly creatures such as *gandharvas* and *àpsaras, piśācas* and *guḥyarākṣasas,* divine sages charged with spiritual powers, deities and demons, and Brahmin sages without blemish, they all went to their deaths on the battlefield of Kurukṣetra. . . . Thus, O thou of great wisdom, the deities came in human form, and returned to heaven when they had accomplished their purposes, O splendid one. (XV.39.5–7 and 16)

In the concluding chapter of the epic (XVIII.6—not included in the Critical Edition), Vaiśaṃpāyana also adds that "The deities of Heaven, O ruler of the Earth, came to this world for sport. Having achieved their task, they ascended once more to Heaven."[11] The sphere of the action is the Earth, but the script is written in Brahmaloka, the highest of the seven worlds in the cosmic hierarchy.[12]

This higher influence on human life is also suggested in the way in which the gods and the demons come and go to shape events. Before she leaves him, the goddess Gangā informs King Śaṃtanu that it was to accomplish a purpose of the gods that she had been with him (I.92.49). The five Pāṇḍavas are born from the gods for the continuance of the dynasty (I.107.2). Vyāsa, the brāhmaṇic representative of Nārāyaṇa in the epic, engineers the birth of the hundred sons of Dhṛtarāṣṭra—including the evil Duryodhana—through a boon to Gāndhārī.[13] Using special powers, Nārada, Mārkaṇḍeya, and Lomaśa also circulate freely within the "Three Worlds."

Since the major protagonists themselves are, for the most part, human embodiments of higher powers, they tend to reflect the qualities and characteristics of their celestial forebears. In one sense, the five Pāṇḍavas alone have all that it takes to secure the final victory. Indeed, this is the human task to which they are called, the very purpose of their sojourn on Earth. In another sense, just as the gods need the help of the Supreme Divinity (here Viṣṇu-Nārāyaṇa) to vanquish the demons, it is inconceivable that their heroic enterprise on the Earth could have succeeded without the close association and guidance of His incarnation in the form of Kṛṣṇa. While technically a noncombatant in the great war, it is he who directs the major figures in the drama and pulls all the strings of the play. His cheerful acceptance of the curse of Gāndhārī to die thirty-six years after the end of the war even hints that his human destiny is sacrificed to his own higher purposes as the Supreme Being (XI.25).

Viewed from such a vast cosmic background of creation, preservation, and destruction, all of which is dependent on the machinations of higher beings, it is hardly surprising that the protagonists would tend to view the terrible avalanche of war as the work of universal *Daiva* made manifest in temporal events. From such a perspective, the script for this drama of history and human life was written *ab æterno* and the ensuing events constitute but a single brief scene in a dramatic extravaganza that repeats itself over the successive "days and nights" of Brahmā. All is under the governance of the Great God who, in a variety of intermediate forms—as the triumvirate of Brahmā, Viṣṇu, and Śiva, or as the mythological Nārāyaṇa who sleeps on the cosmic ocean—is also a personification of this *Daiva:* "You must know that desire, anger, joy, fear, and confusion are all forms of mine, and so is what wise men obtain by doing great acts, speaking the truth, making gifts, performing fierce austerities *(tapas),* and harming no one. My moral code is enjoined on all who live in my bodies; they act, not by their own volition *(kāmata),* but with their minds controlled by me" (III.187.20–22). The descent of the gods and the demons, the transfer of their eternal feud to the mundane plane, the brief ascendency of the forces of *adharma,* and the cosmic restoration by Kṛṣṇa, all may be viewed and experienced as the play of this overwhelming cosmic agency.

4

Personal Destiny

As is now apparent, epic Destiny (as *Daiva*, "Time" etc.) can operate on a number of levels. We have so far been dealing with the larger "cosmic" scale (*Daiva* with a capital *D*) which has little relevance in the context of a single life span. We must therefore lower the microscope from these macrocosmic heights to examine the force of Destiny as revealed and experienced within the microcosm of human life (*daiva* with a small *d*).

The contextual use of the word suggests that *daiva* may either further or, more commonly, hinder human purposes in two ways. First, it may enter our personal lives from within, either in the adversarial role of inner conflict, or simply as what we would now call "motivation." This would suggest that character itself is *daiva*. Secondly, these higher influences may confront the individual from without, either in the form of some insurmountable obstacle, or as a force that deflects or halts the course of an action already launched upon the world. The implication in this latter case is that the sphere of human action is relatively limited. These external intrusions of *daiva* are a common source of complaint. Further implications of these expressions of *daiva* will become evident as we trace their path in the objective circumstances of the story.

Problems and Anomalies

The modern reader is soon confronted with certain philosophical and logical difficulties. Firstly, one might wonder about the dignity of human life in general, and about the ultimate value of personal effort and achievement in particular. For, as Nicolai Hartmann has pointed out: "Where Providence and infinite power prevail, how can man retain self-determination?"[1] The validity of the one destroys the efficacy of the other. What part is man's doing against a higher transcendental intrusion of events that affect even the gods and demons themselves? To all appearances they simply play their appointed roles in an inexorable march of events that culminates in an explosive, though momentously regenerative, climax.[2] Hartmann refers to this problem as the "Antinomy of Providence."

Secondly, one is left to wonder what remains of dharma and moral existence generally without a human "freedom to do." Morality requires a "can" (at least for Brahmins and kings). If one were forced to do what was laid down beforehand, no action could be good or bad, and the actor himself would not be a moral being but an automaton. In short, how could the dharma retain its distinctive meaning if *puruṣakāra* were an illusion? On the other hand, if *puruṣakāra* is indeed an effective "freedom" of volitional decision and action, one wonders what secret ingenuity can weave the activities of vast multitudes into a single strand of events at a particular axial point of history. These issues are touched upon in the epic, but only in discussion about the efficacy of the Vedic ritual; they are not recognized for their general import.

A further anomaly is the curious appearance of a *linear* evolutionary sequence within the cyclic succession of the *yugas*. We are referring here to the quasi-Darwinian progression of avatars from primitive to more evolved forms of life. Both epic and Purāṇic accounts agree on a series that evolves from

> the water creature Fish (Matsya), the amphibian Tortoise (Kurma), the land animal Boar (Varaha), the "Missing Link" Man-Lion (Narasimha), the Hunter "Homo Erectus" Rama-with-Axe (Parashu-Rama), the feudal divinity Rama (hero of the Ramayana, which is also an *itihasa,* the earlier avataras being recorded in *puranas* or ancient texts), the sensitively-loving and erotic divinity Krishna (in the *Mahabharata* seen as an adviser and guide, but revealed in his full eighth avatara personality in the *Harivamsha* and the *Bhagavata Purana*), followed by the ascetically compassionate, sex-renouncing Buddha (or, alternatively, in orthodox Hinduism, Kalki, the still-to-come white apocalyptic horse.)[3]

What is surprising about this evolutionary model is that it is actually provoked by the recurrent "falls" of society from the heights of moral perfection to the depths of depravity, that is to say by the cycle itself. Again and again humanity is raised up by an avatar, and again and again it returns to chaos under the rule of evil kings. The rejuvenation of society (and presumably of the individuals of which it is composed) is dependent on the avatar but this only initiates a new period of decline.

History is repeated in endless cycles of essentially similar content. This clockwork repetition—clearly under the control of *Daiva,* is a reflection of the wheel of the *saṃsāra* as it turns at the level of human society. This, in turn, is governed by the "Time" of the Cosmos itself, endlessly recurring in *kalpa* after *kalpa.*

Social Manifestations of *Daiva*

As if to remind us of the ubiquitous role of *Daiva* in this process, this moral entropy is made to recur, as a sort of echo, at different points in the story itself. As we proceed down the generations of the Kurus, for example, we notice that each generation is given a period of glory from which there is an inexorable decline. Thus, the early reign of Śaṃtanu, the great-great-grandfather of the protagonists, is portrayed as an ideal time in which Hāstinapura was ruled without lust or passion, and the four castes all knew their respective places: "The warriors served the Brahmins, the tradespeople were sworn to the warriors, and the lower orders—devoted to both the Brahmins and the warriors, served the tradespeople" (I. 94.9). This constitutes a description—indeed a virtual definition, of a Golden Age. The first hint of a softening of these ideal conditions is the "fall" of Śaṃtanu himself for the fisher princess Satyavatī.[4] This initiates a chain of circumstances that leaves the kingdom without an heir and eventually leads the family and the world to the brink of ruin. However, as Madeleine Biardeau points out: "let us not look for the first in the line of guilt: there is no one. All is combined in such a manner that we can never tell who is responsible: everyone is, because *daiva* alone is in charge and everyone plays his part in the game set up by it."[5]

Whatever Śaṃtanu's part in this may be, it is certainly compounded in the next generation by his son Bhīṣma,[6] incarnation of Dyaus (= the sky) and a man of undoubted wisdom and courage. He also demonstrates great filial piety and self-sacrifice in doing service to his father. However, in renouncing his claim to the throne (his *artha*) and to the joys of married life (his *kāma*) he seriously compromises the future of the dynasty by committing one of the cardinal sins of the Mahābhārata—performing the dharma of another by adopting the renunciation of the Brahmin in place of his caste duty as a warrior prince born to rule and to beget heirs to the throne. As a result, he spends much of his early career securing brides for other members of the family, including his two younger half brothers and his three nephews (Dhṛtarāṣṭra, Pāṇḍu, and Vidura). And he unwittingly lays the groundwork for his own demise, in spite of good intentions, by his disastrous abduction of the princess

Ambā (who is secretly betrothed to a demon-king). Ambā is regarded by Biardeau as "a good symbol of this wounded earth which Bhīṣma can neither wed nor kill" (since Sky and Earth can never meet).[7]

The problems of the dynasty become more obvious however, when his two half brothers (children of Śaṃtanu and Satyavatī) die without issue, the first after his overweening pride gets him into a fight with a *gandharva* (a celestial musician), the second when he succumbs to venereal disease as a result of an amorous nature. He is portrayed as "deluded by a net of lust" (I.110.2), not untypical for the rulers of the day. This leaves the kingdom not only without an effective ruler (though now under the de facto control of Bhīṣma) but with no succession in sight. Hungry for offspring, Satyavatī is forced to call on her illegitimate Brahmin son Vyāsa to beget heirs on the two surviving queens. These unfortunate ladies have little choice but to submit—ungraciously as it turns out—to the dynastic plans of their mother-in-law.

Prospects for the first child do not look good when Queen Ambikā, the first who is called to this task, is unable to look at the matted orange locks and fiery eyes of the sage. "Prompted by divine injunction" (*vidhi* = *daiva* once again) Vyāsa has to inform the impatient Satyavatī that her daughter-in-law's lack of virtue has condemned the would-be heir to be born blind, effectively disqualifying him from carrying out the royal sacrifices and other functions normally expected of a king (I.100.10). His blindness suggests an incapacity with respect to the dharma, and Biardeau adds that "he can be even less of a warrior, a royal function just as essential as the sacrifice."[8] He will nevertheless be a great royal sage with the life-force of a troop of elephants, wise, highly fortunate, of great spirit and intelligence, and father to a hundred sons.[9]

Ambālikā, the second of the surviving queens, also fails in her duties by paling at the ugliness of the man, and is told that her son (Pāṇḍu = "pale") will come into the world with a sickly pallor. The final attempt also miscarries as a result of the substitution of a slave-girl by Ambikā, who is appalled at the thought of a second night with the wild-eyed sage. However, the girl is rewarded for her good services by the birth of Vidura, the partial incarnation of Dharma. He is thus the only one of the three brothers who is an incarnation of a god.[10] The problem with this form of Dharma-in-the-flesh—apart from the fact that he is of mixed blood and can therefore have no claim to the throne, is that his sagacious advice is never heeded.

While the future already looks somewhat unpromising, the actual childhood of these children is represented as an interregnum (under the regency of Bhīṣma) of perfect pastoral and social harmony (I.102.1–14). We are explicitly told this time that the Golden Age prevails in all sections of the country, and that the wheel of the dharma rolls through the land (I.102.5). Pride, anger, and greed have lost their hold and we are given typical descriptions of plentiful harvests, trees dripping with juicy fruit, and bustling cities where a devout and cheerful citizenry help one another in mutual affection. These good times are captured in the adage that "Of all mothers of heroes [the best are] the daughters of Kaśi [that is, Ambikā and Ambālikā], of all countries the Jungle of the Kurus, of those who know the dharma in its entirety, Bhīṣma [is superior], of all cities, it is the City of the Elephant" (I.102.12).

As the story moves to the third generation from the reign of Śaṃtanu, the aging Bhīṣma voices a certain satisfaction at having established the "threads of the line" as he puts it (I.103.3). He has made Pāṇḍu king, and proceeds to secure brides (and the alliances that come with them) for all three brothers. These include Gāndhārī for Dhṛtarāṣṭra; Pṛthā and Mādrī for Pāṇḍu; and the mixed-caste daughter of King Devaka for Vidura. The choice of Pṛthā (clearly a symbol of the Earth—from *pṛthivī* = "earth") is of great importance for the subsequent course of events, since she is the sister of Vasudeva, the father of Kṛṣṇa. Indeed, it is almost as if her choice of Pāṇḍu from among the thousands of princes assembled at her bridal choice is the work of *Daiva*.

This time the early years of the new ruler are not painted in the same ideal imagery of a Golden Age (they are probably too close for that), but they do follow the characteristic rise to a peak—in this case a peak of material splendor from which there is a sudden and characteristic decline. After returning with the spoils of his successful military campaigns, Pāṇḍu spreads delight among his subjects by distributing largesse in abundance. He enjoys the gratitude of parents and friends by showering them with all the good things they desire. But then, deciding that he has won a well-earned rest, he abandons his administrative duties and takes to the forest to enjoy the hunt in the company of his two wives. It is here that the five Pāṇḍavas are born, spending their childhood on the holy mount Hīmavat (I.115.27). Dhṛtarāṣṭra ensures that he is well supplied with whatever he might want of pleasure *(kāma)* and enjoyment *(bhoga)*—all the while establishing himself and his sons ever more firmly in the seat of power. The stage is being set for the breach to occur between the two sides of the family.[11]

To complete the record of these echoes of *Daiva* down the generations of the Mahābhārata, we follow the rise and fall of the Pāṇḍavas themselves—the fourth generation from our point of departure, after their return to Hāstinapura on the death of Pāṇḍu, another royal victim of a wanton "desire." His funeral concludes on a somber note with Vyāsa advising his mother (Satyavatī) to withdraw to the forest to avoid having to witness the destruction of the dynasty. He offers some prophetic words: "The times of happiness are over and a dreadful period lies ahead. Things are deteriorating by the day, and the earth is losing her youth. [I see] a period of great confusion *(māyā)*, abounding in many vices. It will be a dreadful time when all the acts and practices of the dharma will be violated" (I.119.6–7). Satyavatī leaves with her two daughters-in-law after persuading Ambikā: "Ambikā, we have heard that the imprudent conduct of your son [that is, Dhṛtarāṣṭra] will destroy the Bhāratas together with their followers and their grandsons" (I.119.9).

Satyavatī is referring here to the tragic pattern of inertia of the blind king, arising out of his secret desire to secure the royal succession for his eldest son Duryodhana. In contrast to the five sons of Pāṇḍu who are descended from a portion of the gods (I.109.3) this Duryodhana is Kalipuruṣa—the demon Kali in human form (I. 61.80; XI.8.27). Later (III.240.6), we are told that the demons obtained him from Śiva long ago in recognition of their austerities *(tapas)*. It has been suggested that, in the aggregate, Duryodhana and his ninety-nine brothers symbolize "the brood of ego-centric desires and passions like lust, greed, hatred, anger, envy, pride, vanity, and so on, to which the empirical ego is firmly attached and to which it clings desperately."[12]

Duryodhana grows up with a passionate envy and hatred of his cousins, particularly of the powerful Bhīma who often torments him and his brothers when they are at play. The failure of his various schemes of revenge: to drown Bhīma, put snakes in his bed, and poison his food, serves only to intensify his bitterness and animosity (I.119.30ff.). When it becomes clear that Yudhiṣṭhira, as rightful heir, is also the preferred choice of the population to be king, he can contain himself no longer. He urges his father to destroy "the dreadful thorn in my heart" by removing the Pāṇḍavas to the provincial town of Vāraṇāvaṭa on the pretext of a festival, and plots to kill them (I.130.20; I.131.1–10).

This is the first of many occasions when Dhṛtarāṣṭra allows himself to be swayed by the ambitions of his willful son. In the words of the Brahmins, "Completely blinded by inertia, the evil-minded king Dhṛtarāṣṭra sees the problem but does not see the dharma" (I.133.7). When Dhṛtarāṣṭra learns that the Pāṇḍavas have survived the lacquer-house fire engineered by his son's clique, and that they are now married to Draupadī (the daughter of the king of the Pāñcālas), he is in a quandary. He wants the kingdom for his son but is wary of the power of the Pāṇḍavas, particularly when allied with Drupada. He takes the side of Duryodhana and his other sons but gets conflicting counsel from Karṇa (who advocates a preemptive strike) and Bhīṣma, Droṇa, and Vidura (who advocate conciliation). This time, however, he follows the path of prudence, forms an alliance with Drupada, and agrees to partition the kingdom among the two sets of cousins (I.199.25).

Almost immediately, the fortunes of the Pāṇḍavas begin to change. They agree to settle for a tract of largely uninhabited wilderness (Khāṇḍavaprastha) where they build a radiant city, which, true to its name—Indraprastha (the city of Indra), is like "the unshakeable world of heaven" (I.119.27). Prospects improve further with Arjuna's abduction of Subhadrā (sister of Kṛṣṇa), thus cementing this alliance, the birth of their son Abhimanyu on Arjuna's return to Indraprastha after a year of self-imposed exile, the burning of the Khāṇḍava forest at the behest of Agni, and the subsequent construction of a magnificent Assembly Hall by the demon Maya. With his star clearly on the ascendant, Yudhiṣṭhira has no difficulty endorsing Nārada's suggestion that he legitimize his sovereignty by performing the *rājasūya,* the traditional Indian ritual for consecrating the king as a universal monarch.

It looks as if the world is rapidly moving into a new and more prosperous age of social harmony, a new reign of dharma in the form of Yudhiṣṭhira, the king of Dharma incarnate—in short a Golden Age (though this term is not used). The signs are all there (I.214.1–14; II.30.1–9, etc.). With the help of his brothers, he conquers the four quarters of the world. The elements all work in his favor: crime, pestilence, and disease are banished from the land; all the citizenry are bent upon their own tasks, and not a false word is heard about him. But then suddenly—at the height of his power and glory, when the accumulated income of his treasury cannot be spent in "hundreds of years" (II.30.8), he loses this vast fortune and prosperity to Duryodhana in a dice game, together with the kingdom and his whole family, including himself. With this symbolic collapse of the dharma, the pattern of history has repeated itself for the fourth time in as many generations. It will repeat itself again—this time at the scale of the whole Earth, when the rise of the *adharma* of Duryodhana is terminated by the almost total destruction of the known world, to make way for a new age of dharma under the ægis (or the *Daiva*?) of Parikṣit. When Yudhiṣṭhira has recovered the kingdom "free of thorns" and the funeral rites of the dead heroes are over, life again returns to conditions reminiscent of a Golden Age (XIV.15,1ff. and XIV.51.6). These scenes of pastoral and social harmony are climaxed by the discourse of the Anugītā (XIV.16–50) and the events leading up to the Aśvamedha sacrifice of Yudhiṣṭhira (XIV. 84–91).

Beyond these echoes of the cosmic play of *Daiva,* the *rājasūya* and the dicing are of great symbolic significance in themselves for understanding this process of *Daiva/daiva*. The central role of the *rājasūya* episode has already been noted by a number of scholars. Heino Gehrts has argued that the epic as a whole, including the characters and the distribution of the heroes, is governed by the structural elements of this ritual. J. A. B van Buitenen holds that the Sabhāparvan (Book II) constitutes a dramatization of the *rājasūya* ceremony, including the dicing episode that forms an integral part of the ritual process. Krishna Chaitanya also focuses on the dice contest, suggesting that it is

> perhaps the most crucial episode in the whole epic. Animosities simmering over the decades come to a boil here in appalling wrongs. These in turn trigger chain reactions of sombre causalities that become critical thirteen years later in the terrible implosion of Kurukshetra. Guilt may originate in the self-betrayal of individuals like Duryodhana. But the social group is an interactive field where responsibility necessarily becomes shared; and the reaction when it matures at last is also a social phenomenon and a mass effect, which cannot make nice distinctions, in its aspect as nemesis, between those who endorsed the guilt actively like Dussasana, and those who virtually endorsed it by apathetic tolerance like the vassals in the assembly. The great tragedy is that this mass effect is too gross to have the fine discrimination to spare even sensitive types like Vikarna. He deeply sympathized with Draupadi, but he certainly could not be expected to break away from his family on this issue. And nemesis engulfs him too, along with the others.[13]

However, once again we will turn to Biardeau for the most penetrating analysis of this episode and its symbolism. For her, the *rājasūya* of Yudhiṣṭhira is the central link in a chain of sacrificial symbolism that runs through the Mahābhārata as a whole. As one of the "three sacrifices" announced by a celestial voice at the birth of Arjuna (I.114.33), it constitutes the moment at which the avatar transfers his functions to Yudhiṣṭhira and to his brothers. The myth is revealed in its dual nature as a royal myth in addition to a myth modeled after a traditional avataric myth. This functional shift is also important for understanding what she sees as the double symbolism at work throughout the story, reflecting the different perspectives that may be taken.

From the more comprehensive cosmic standpoint, one may detect behind the events of the ritual: "the enthronement of the king of the dead, who will reign throughout this period for the re-establishment of the equilibrium that has been endangered or to realize the decrees of *daiva*, according to the point of view one may adopt."[14] In effect, a somber prediction by Vyāsa,[15] followed by his announcement of a dream in which Yudhiṣṭhira would see an inauspicious form of Rudra turned toward the direction of Yama, suggest a symbolic link between Yudhiṣṭhira and the god of the dead. From the

> point of view of the avatar, the *rājasūya* is like the coronation of Yama by Rudra, and the work of his reign is relentlessly pursued under the auspices of Rudra-Śiva, thanks to the takeover by Duryodhana.
>
> At the level of the royal myth, the banishment of the "king of Dharma" *(dharmarāja)* leaves *adharma* sovereign and prepares the war for the restoration of the dharma.[16]

Aided and abetted by Śakuni/Dvāpara, the *rājasūya* dicing episode thus has the paradoxical effect of inaugurating the reign of Duryodhana/Kali, which it is the task of the avatar—through the person of the legitimate king, to overthrow. In this respect, the *rājasūya* is the starting point for the events leading to the war: "with all its good and evil consequences, in short, to war and to the salvation of the world that this will make possible."[17]

The most striking finding of Biardeau about the *rājasūya,* however, is the inner connection with the dicing that follows. Significantly, the one thing that Yudhiṣṭhira and the Pāṇḍavas do not lose is their common wife Draupadī, the incarnation of Śrī symbolizing the prosperity of the Earth and the realm (II.72.28). Of course, Yudhiṣṭhira actually loses twice after being saved on the first occasion by the obstinate challenge of Draupadī regarding the dharmic legitimacy of the wager.[18] There is no doubt that Draupadī is

> the real stake, not only of the dice, but of the entire drama. Yudhiṣṭhira has submitted to the two games of dice in a fatalistic spirit, without any illusion as to the outcome. In the end, he is forced in this manner, together with his brothers and their common wife, to live in exile in the forest for a period of twelve years, following which the six of them must live for a year without being recognized by anyone.[19]

Significantly, the Pāṇḍavas leave for the forest as *dīkṣitāḥ* according to a variant reading of II.68.1, that is to say, as initiates who must undergo the necessary ritual preparation for a sacrifice, suggesting the sacrifice of the war to come.[20] What is particularly striking about these events, also noted by Biardeau, is that they are in direct contrast to the descriptions of the actual ritual in the Brāhmaṇas, an integral part of which is a ceremony in which the king is required to win a game of dice for which a cow (and now Draupadī) is the stake.[21] One wonders why the author of the Sabhāparvan would choose to separate the dice episode from the *rājasūya* episode and to transform the outcome into a *loss* of the power and possessions of the rightful king.

It is evident that this loss of kingdom and subsequent exile is directly related to the situation with which the epic opens—the eternal conflict of the gods and the demons. This is confirmed by Duḥśāsana when he gleefully exults as the Pāṇḍavas are leaving: "The reign of the great-spirited king, the son of Dhṛtarāṣṭra, has begun. The sons of Pāṇḍu have been defeated, and have fallen into extreme misfortune. Today the gods have gathered here by their smooth aerial pathways. But we [that is, the demons] are their elders, more cunning and more numerous than they" (II.68.3–4).[22] In the absence of the avatar, who is away battling the demon-king Śālva (III.15–23), the first round in this cosmic war is won by a "play" on the part of the demons, and this is followed by the expulsion of the gods from their lawful place in heaven and their exile in the nether regions (symbolized here by the forest). The natural order of the world is suddenly turned on its head, and we have a break in the course of time, symbolized by the passage from a *dvāpara*- to a *kaliyuga*.[23]

The significance of these momentous events is heightened by the evident associations with *Daiva*, for which the game of dice is the ideal tangible and etymological symbol:

> Whatever it be, from the time the decision is taken by Dhṛtarāṣṭra to allow the game to proceed, one is convinced that the dice game puts the destiny of men in the hands of *daiva*, that mysterious cosmic agency which decides the harmonious or chaotic march of events as a whole, and which we translate, for want of a better word, by Destiny. But *daiva*, related to *deva* (god), and to the radical *div*- (the sky) (nominative: *dyaus*, the name of the god incarnated by Bhīṣma on the earth), is also related to the radical *div*- (to gamble) (the game: *devana* or *dyūta*, the player: *devitar* . . .). We know that Śiva plays dice with his wife. In short, we must never ignore the ambiguity of the dice game which places mankind under the ægis of a divine power that is pitiless and apparently blind. At the same time we note that Kṛṣṇa is the son of Devakī (the player—the divine?), that Yudhiṣṭhira enjoys a second wife in his gynæceum by the name of Devikā (the bad player?) who, strictly speaking, plays no role in the epic but may characterize that of her husband, and, finally, that Vidura is married to a daughter of mixed blood of king Devaka. *Daiva* is thus not so much the equivalent of the Graeco-Latin *fatum* as the global expression for all that concerns the welfare of the gods (and of the earth), the great manipulator of which is Kṛṣṇa together with his counterpart Śiva.[24]

In spite of dire warnings by Vidura, who pictures the dice scheme as "the gate of Kali" and the "face of doom," Dhṛtarāṣṭra is foolishly drawn into this net of intrigue by Duryodhana's threat of suicide and by his own love for his son. In any case, he tells his brother: "Whether good or bad, beneficial or otherwise, the friendly game of dice will go on, for it has clearly been 'divinely appointed' *(diṣṭa)*. I believe that this has occurred as a result of 'supreme Destiny' *(daivaṃ paraṃ)*" (II.45.54 and 57). Here we have an example of *Daiva* in the objective conditions of the world. When Vidura raises the possibility of a split or a breach in the family, he can only reply: "A quarrel in this matter will not trouble me, *kṣattṛ* (addressing Vidura as "son of a slave-girl"); provided that *Daiva* will not be so opposed. This entire cosmos does not run by itself but is obedient to the will of Dhātṛ ("the Bestower")" (II.51.25).

But when Dhṛtarāṣṭra has finally got what he secretly wanted all along, his worries begin to mount, and we catch him in a rare moment of introspection:

> The gods take away the reason of the man to whom they bestow defeat. He sees things reversed. When his mind is confused and destruction is upon him, the wrong course looks like wisdom and cannot be dislodged from his heart. When his end is near, wrong has the appearance of right, and right takes the form of wrong. Rising up before a man, they lull him into complacency. "Time" *(kāla)* does not raise the rod of justice and come down on his head; the power of "Time" is just this perverse view of things. (II.72.8–11)

This is an example of *daiva* (or "Time") sowing confusion from within, specifically in the *buddhi,* the function of the mind used to discriminate what is right (*artha,* here equivalent to *dharma* in the sense of the appropriate course of action) from what is wrong *(anartha = adharma)*.

Yudhiṣṭhira also finds himself in the net of *daiva,* for he has filial obligations to Dhṛtarāṣṭra and has foolishly taken a vow that he would never refuse a challenge (II.52.15–16; II.53.13). Thus he too falls prey to inner conflict and confusion: "It is said that *daiva* obscures our reason as glare blinds the eye. As if bound by nooses, Man is controlled by Dhātṛ" (II.52.18). And when he is recalled for the second game of dice, he resigns himself once again to his fate: "It is by order of the Dhātṛ that creatures obtain success or failure. There is no escape from either of these two if we must play again" (II.67.3).

Prophecies and Pronouncements

Additional confirmation for the existence of a divine plan for the world is given by the roles that define the lives of the major characters themselves. The course of life of individuals appears to be charted in much the same manner as the path of the Sun about the great mount Meru, not in accordance with their own desires and purposes but by divine decree (III.102.2–4). This information is often given in the form of oracular statements. We are told, for example, that the portion of Kali that is Duryodhana has been born for the destruction of the world (XI.8.27), and that his friend Karṇa was ordained in a former time for the purpose of provoking a general war (XII.2.4–5). Ghaṭotkaca, the good demon-son of Bhīma ("good" in the sense that he fights on the side of the Pāṇḍavas) is created by Indra in order to neutralize the javelin he gave to Karṇa (I.143.38). He is finally sacrificed in place of Arjuna on the thirteenth day of the war (VII.154.58). Dhṛṣṭadyumna, the son of King Drupada of Pañcāla, is born for the destruction of Droṇa (I.155.40) and the function of his twin sister Draupadī (Kṛṣṇā = the "dark lady") is to lead the warrior caste to their destruction (I.155.44).

These oracular pronouncements are supplemented by the prophecies and predictions of sages with spiritual vision or advance warning of what is fated to happen. Vyāsa's predictions about his own sons as well as his somber warning at the death of Pāṇḍu have already been mentioned. He has long seen in his mind the perfidy of the Kauravas (I.144.7) and is able to comfort Uttarā with information concerning her son Parikṣit (XIV.61.10) as well as Gāndhārī by enumerating the divine histories and purposes of all the main characters of the story (XV.39.5–16). Mārkaṇḍeya—from the report of his cosmic journey through the body of the child Kṛṣṇa (III.186.90ff), and Nārada, are also important mercurial figures who bring their divine knowledge to bear on the meanings of the lives of the major actors. Not only is Nārada given a preview of the present cosmic cycle (to be described shortly), but he is able to shed considerable light on the role of Karṇa (XII.2–5) and on the post-war period (XV.27.15).

Disembodied voices heard at the birth of the Pāṇḍavas also comment on the roles they are called upon to play; for example, Yudhiṣṭhira will be the greatest of the upholders of the dharma . . . glorious, and full of energy *(tejas)* and good conduct (I.114.6). And a wise Brahmin added that he would rise again after meeting great misfortune (V.132.9). Bhīma will be the greatest of all the men of strength (I.114.10), while the twins will surpass their peers in beauty, truth, and virtue (I.115.18).

The most revealing of these visionary statements is that which accompanies the birth of Arjuna (I.114.29–35; V.88.65; V.135.2–5). The seven verses (I.114.29–35) make it quite clear that it is Arjuna—the equal of Rāma Jāmadagnya (the previous avatar) and the peer of Viṣṇu in strength—to whom the future destiny of the world has been entrusted, not Yudhiṣṭhira, the incarnation of the god Dharma. Arjuna is, of course, the son of Indra, king of the gods (I.114.22). These associations with Rāma and Viṣṇu suggest that his task is no ordinary one.

With the help of his brothers, says the voice, he will offer up three sacrifices *(trimedhā),* which according to the consensus of subsequent tradition, include the *rājasūya,* the "sacrifice of the war," and the *aśvamedha* that follows. Like Rāma, he is destined to vanquish the kings and recover the prosperity *(śrī)* of the realm. In effect, he is given the part of the avatar, since Kṛṣṇa takes no active part in the fighting. These associations also prepare us for the truth about his inner relationship to Kṛṣṇa—he was the sage Nara who dwelt with Nārāyaṇa at Badarī in a previous age (I.210.5; I.219.15; III.37.29; III.45.19, etc.). His association with Kṛṣṇa Vāsudeva in his present embodiment is also foretold (V.135.4).

This divine mission is later confirmed by Yama, the king of the dead and world guardian of the south, just before Arjuna is to visit his father in "heaven" (III.42.17–23). He is told he is the ancient seer Nara who, at the command *(niyoga)* of Brahmā, has now become a mortal to pacify the demons and the Nivātakavacas (a race of demons). Together with Viṣṇu, he will lighten the burden of the Earth. These statements certainly have the ring of the avatar about them. In this respect, victory over the Nivātakavacas in "heaven" is among a number of tests he must undergo prior to his main mission. Arjuna has already shown his command of men and gods (in the form of Indra himself at Khāṇḍava), and he must now show that he is a worthy opponent for the more numerous forces of *adharma.* Purging the heavens of these troublemakers will show he is fully capable of mastering all of the powers of the three worlds.[25]

With all this advance knowledge about the assigned roles of the protagonists (presumably engineered by *Daiva*), we might wonder how any of them can have any confidence in his or her capacity to influence what has all the appearance of an inexorable current of "Time." How could Duryodhana, for example, imagine for one minute that he could prevail against the combined forces of the gods, particularly after witnessing the Cosmic Form of the avatar himself during Kṛṣṇa's personal attempt to mediate a settlement (V.129.1–16)? This cavalier "blindness" with respect to the forces arrayed against them is particularly characteristic of the Kauravas. It is only after the horrendous carnage of war has virtually annihilated his side of the family that Dhṛtarāṣṭra himself is made aware of "the eternal secret of the gods" (XI.8.34), something that Yudhiṣṭhira had known since the warning by the sage Nārada at his *rājasūya* to the effect that "The Pāṇḍavas and the Kauravas will mutually destroy each other. Therefore, O son of Kuntī, do what has to be done" (XI.8.33). The blind king, too, has been an instrument for the unfolding of events that have been ordained from all eternity. What place is there for grief under such circumstances? Vyāsa's counseling eventually has its effect, since, after Dhṛtarāṣṭra is finally granted the vision of his dead sons on the banks of the Ganges, he is able to say that the purpose of his life has been fulfilled (XV.44.20).

But the real secret is revealed a few days later when Yudhiṣṭhira finally learns (from Bhīṣma) that Nārada had been privileged with this information by Kṛṣṇa himself—though not in this birth but in the preceding Golden Age. Not content with his meeting with Nara and Nārāyaṇa, the two forms of the Lord residing at Badarī, Nārada decides to go to the White Island *(śvetadvīpa)*, a mysterious land of the blessed in the ocean of milk beyond Mount Meru. Here he hopes to see the Supreme Deity in his primeval nature (XII.322.2). Other sages have tried and failed in this enterprise, but due to his extreme devotion *(bhakti)*, the Lord is moved to appear before him in his Universal Form (XII. 326.1ff.). Not even Brahmā himself has seen this form, he is told. But more than this, Nārada is offered a synopsis of the course of the three worlds over the forthcoming cosmic cycle down to the birth of Kalkin, the avatar who will reestablish the dharma in the subsequent Golden Age. The linear succession of avatars (through the evolutionary forms of the boar, the man-lion, Rāma, etc.) will eventually pass to Kṛṣṇa.

After recounting his early deeds, Nārāyaṇa proceeds to delineate his own role, together with that of Arjuna, in the events of the Mahābhārata itself:

> Jarāsaṃdha will become king at Girivraja, a proud and powerful demon who will quarrel with all the kings of the earth. His death will be engineered in accordance with my plans (lit. "by the movement of my *buddhi*"). I shall then kill Śiśupala at the *(rājasūya)* sacrifice of the son of Dharma (that is, Yudhiṣṭhira), to which all the kings of the world will bring tribute. The son of Vāsava (that is, Arjuna) will be my only assistant. I shall then re-establish Yudhiṣṭhira and his brothers in their own kingdom. This world will know me as the great Nara and Nārāyaṇa when, putting forth effort *(udyukta)*, I will destroy the warriors for the sake of the world. After the burden of the earth has been lifted as I see fit, I shall wipe out (lit. "undertake the re-absorption or *pralaya* of") all the leading members of the Sātvata (Kṛṣṇa's people) as well as the great city of Dvārakā, by the destruction of my venerable kinsfold. (XII.326.89; 846*; 90; 848*;91–92)

All individual events appear to depend upon the contemporary stage of development of the whole, effectively eliminating the possibility of free action. The use of the term *pralaya* suggests that, from the perspective of the Supreme Divinity, this history is part of the larger wheel of Time involving the periodic creation and destruction of the world. However, and perhaps more importantly, this passage is revealing for the light it sheds on the ultimate source of *Daiva*. For there can no longer be any doubt that this compelling power from on high derives from no ordinary (that is, Vedic) god, but from the new Supreme God of *bhakti* devotion, the primeval Nārāyaṇa Himself (XIII.App.I.No.16.203). Kṛṣṇa Himself is "eternal Time with bloodshot eyes and club in hand." There is no longer any doubt: Nārāyaṇa, Time *(kāla)*, and *Daiva* are one and the same.

Kṛṣṇa as "Master of Yoga"

In order to understand how this arbiter of *Daiva* is able to accomplish the "purposes of the gods" in this world, we must shift our perspective from that of Kṛṣṇa as the source and substance of the world, the "Primeval God" or *ādideva,* to that of the multiplicity of the things and beings in the world. From the perspective of the world (that is, of the *saṃsāra),* including that of Kṛṣṇa as one of the beings in the world, the secret of his success, as we will analyze in some detail in chapter 5, is "Yoga" or *upāya,* the skillful means that enable him to turn the course of events to his advantage. Kṛṣṇa is the master of Yoga *(yogeśvara),* and in the Gītā itself Yoga is defined by him as "skill in action" (VI.24/BG.2.50). Much of this skill is psychological, a knowledge of the mind *(vittajña),* which enables him to provoke quite uncharacteristic modes of behavior, much of which is repugnant to the accepted norms of the dharma (VIII.49.2).

Deaths Engineered by Kṛṣṇa

Kṛṣṇa uses these skills to good effect in engineering the deaths of a number of the combatants. One of the early examples is the death of Ghaṭotkaca on the Pāṇḍava side, who is killed by Karṇa with a magic javelin that could be used only once, and that had always been intended for Arjuna. The other Kaurava leaders had urged Karṇa night after night to employ his magic spear against Arjuna or Kṛṣṇa. However, in some mysterious way, Kṛṣṇa had always managed to stupefy *(√muh)* Karṇa into forgetting about his javelin as soon as he entered the field of battle (VII.157.37).

As the Pāṇḍavas turn in horror and dismay from the sight of Ghaṭotkaca's huge body lying on a full company of Kaurava troops, they are shocked to see Kṛṣṇa dancing about in transports of joy and delight "like a tree shaken by a tempest" (VII.155.3). This lightness of heart is attributed to the success of Kṛṣṇa's long-held plan to use this demon-son of Bhīma to divest Karṇa of the one asset that remained to him for the destruction of Arjuna (he had already been divested of his natural armor and golden earrings). Furthermore, the otherwise invincible Karṇa is now vulnerable to attack when the opportunity comes to Arjuna at the time appointed for his chariot-wheel to sink into the earth (in fulfillment of the curse of a Brahmin sage). He is now like an ordinary man (implying that he is no longer like a god). As Kṛṣṇa explains: "I have also slain [that is, through Karṇa] Hiḍimbā's son by skillful means *(upāya)*. If Karṇa had not slain him with his javelin in a great battle, I myself would have had to slay Ghaṭotkaca, the son of Bhīma" (VII.156.24–25). Kṛṣṇa then assures Arjuna that, when the time comes, he will teach him the Yoga by which Arjuna will be able to slay Karṇa himself. According to Biardeau: "In the killing of Ghaṭotkaca by Karṇa we find the central motif of the avataric myths: the invincible gift of Indra, father of Arjuna, to the asuric warrior Karṇa, has been neutralized by the intervention of Kṛṣṇa. Henceforth, the non-combatant status of Kṛṣṇa may be doubted."[26]

Kṛṣṇa subsequently goes on to list a number of other episodes in which he has had a hand, some of which we hear for the first time. Jarāsaṃdha, the king of Magadha who had visions of world dominion through the sacrifice of a hundred kings incarcerated at Girivraja, was killed by Bhīma shortly before the *rājasūya* of Yudhiṣṭhira. Kṛṣṇa now reveals that this was only possible because he had arranged for the neutralization of a mace carried by Jarāsaṃdha that was capable of slaying all creatures. Furthermore, he hints that he was also behind the decision of Droṇa to ask for the thumb of Ekalavya, a rival of the young Arjuna from the Niṣāda tribe. Without this claim for payment on the part of his guru, Ekalavya would apparently have been able to defeat the assembled multitudes of gods and demons combined. Kṛṣṇa subsequently dispatches Śiśupala, the king of the Chedi, to the abode of Yama. He explains: "I was born to slay him and the other enemies of the gods, with your assistance, tiger among men, out of a desire for the good of the worlds. Hiḍimbā and Baka and Kirmīra have all been killed by Bhīmasena" (VII.156.22–23). That he should list three more "enemies of the gods" at this point could be a hint that he might have assisted Bhīma in some way with their deaths as well. Other heroes on the Kaurava side whose deaths are later ascribed to the dubious machinations of Kṛṣṇa include, in order of their demise, Bhūriśravas (by Sātyaki), Jayadratha (at the hands of Arjuna), Droṇa (by Dhṛṣṭyadumna), Karṇa (killed by Arjuna), and Duryodhana (by Bhīma).

The first example in this line of warriors is the death of Bhūriśravas, a famous elephant-warrior, on the fourteenth day of the war. He is leader of the Bāhlika tribe allied to the Kauravas. Just as he is about to decapitate Sātyaki, a staunch ally of Yudhiṣṭhira, Kṛṣṇa urges Arjuna to shoot off the upstretched arm that holds the sword, an ungallant act according to the rules of single combat (VII.117.62).[27] This enables Sātyaki to reverse the situation by decapitating Bhūriśravas as he withdraws from combat. According to Biardeau, Bhūriśravas is "the somic victim and the substitute for Duryodhana, the reigning king of the lunar dynasty (*soma* = moon and squeezing)"—the somic victim, that is to say, of an abortive horse sacrifice of Duryodhana, for which Jayadratha is the horse.[28]

The Jayadratha incident that follows is also related to Duryodhana by the fact that he is married to Duryodhana's sister Duḥśālā. It is also a good example of how tightly woven is the web of causality in the Mahābhārata. Jayadratha had been a thorn in the side of the Pāṇḍavas ever since his failed abduction of Draupadī during their forest exile (III.248). The extreme austerities *(tapas)* he performed as a result of this humiliation netted him a boon from Śiva that he would be able to keep all the brothers at bay in battle except Arjuna, a boon that created the necessary conditions for the tragic death of Arjuna's young son Abhimanyu (finally clubbed to death by the son of Duḥśāsana). This traumatizes Arjuna to the point of making a rather foolish vow to kill Jayadratha before the Sun goes down the following evening, failing which he would commit suicide.

The text is silent on whether this headstrong act was prompted by *Daiva* but the conclusion could well be drawn. However, the immediate effect is to make Jayadratha the great stake of the battle, and the Kauravas make Herculean efforts to ensure that the Sindhu king is kept far to the rear of the main body of troops. Matters become desperate when Jayadratha is still alive, and well-protected by six mighty and heroic car-warriors of the Kaurava army, as the Sun is about to sink behind a mountain. So critical is the situation that Kṛṣṇa decides on drastic action: "I will resort to skillful means *(upāya)* and (create) a covering of darkness over the sun" (VII.121.1009*.6). Then, profiting from the immediate joy and relief of the opposing side, he orders Arjuna to "Cut off the head of the evil-minded king of the Sindhu, Dhanaṃjaya. The sun wishes to go to the great mountain of Asta" (VII.121.16).

The act itself is a highly perilous enterprise, and is another example of destiny being known from birth by a hidden voice (VII.121.18). For, before retiring to the woods to perform *tapas,* Jayadratha's father Vṛddhakṣatra had uttered a curse to the effect that the head of the man who would cause his son's head to fall on the ground would break into a hundred pieces. Suitably warned by Kṛṣṇa, however, Arjuna is able to charge his magic arrows with *mantras,* snatch away the head like a hawk snatching away a smaller bird, and by repeated shots, direct the airborne head to the lap of Vṛddhakṣatra who just happens to be praying in the nearby woods. As the father rises from his prayers, the head falls to the ground and his own head splinters into a hundred pieces. When light returns, the Kauravas realize to their cost that the darkness *(tamas)* had been an illusion *(māyā)* created by Vāsudeva (VII.121. 1025*.3). Biardeau views this death of Jayadratha as an important turning point of the war. It announces the end of caste disorder, symbolized here by Vṛddhakṣatra (a warrior affecting the life of a Brahmin) and by Droṇa (a Brahmin affecting the life of a warrior). Droṇa himself is the next major figure to be killed.

Droṇa's appetite for battle is first undermined by the hosts of Heaven who inform him in the midst of the fighting that his time has come and that he should lay aside his weapons for them to escort him to Brahmaloka. His taste for life itself is then destroyed when Kṛṣṇa counsels Yudhiṣṭhira—the "son" of Dharma no less, to lie about the death of Droṇa's son Aśvatthāman, charging that under the conditions of the moment "falsehood is superior to truth" (VII.164.98). Bhīma has just killed an elephant by the same name. When Yudhiṣṭhira confirms the fact that "Aśvatthāman is dead"—adding under his breath the word "elephant," Droṇa completely loses heart and is beheaded by his own student Dhṛṣṭadyumna, when in a state of Yoga (VII.165.35).[29] In Biardeau's opinion Droṇa's death symbolizes not only the end of caste disorder, but also the epic teaching regarding the "sacrifice of battle" as being the proper sacrifice of a warrior—who thereby becomes the sacrificial victim, priest, and patron of the sacrifice all in one. Furthermore, Droṇa's assumption of a yogic trance and the fact that he is, in any case, a warrior-Brahmin, also suggest that, in order to be effective, this sacrifice should be a yogic act, undertaken without self-seeking, and for the welfare of the worlds.[30]

This dramatic event is immediately followed by a terrible onslaught against Bhīma by the real Aśvatthāman, who is understandably furious at this deception. He unleashes the Nārāyaṇa, a magic weapon symbolizing the universal Brāhmaṇic force against which the warrior strength of Bhīma is powerless. The *yuga* symbolism is particularly appropriate when one knows the role of Aśvatthāman, the incarnation of Mahādeva (= Śiva), Antaka (death), Kāma (desire), and Krodha (anger), who is given the task of completely annihilating the remnants of the Pāṇḍava forces at the end of the war: "As the *yuga*-fire, which consumes the entire universe with its mobile and immobile creatures when the hour of dissolution comes, shall at last enter the mouth of the creator, even so the weapon of Droṇa's son began to engulf the body of Bhīmasena" (VII.171.6). Once again, however, it is Kṛṣṇa and Arjuna—this time as

Nārāyaṇa and Nara, the One Being in the form of these two friends, who come to the rescue. Diving into the field of energy investing the body of Bhīma, they resort to the power of *māyā* (VII.171.11) and manage to neutralize the power of the Nārāyaṇa by forcing Bhīma to make a symbolic "sacrifice" of his own weapons (by the act of laying them aside).

Daiva and Karṇa

The life and death of Karṇa is one of the best-documented examples of the machinations of "the gods" (that is, of *Daiva*) in the epic. His life as a whole, we are told, had been planned before his birth in order to pave the way for the warrior caste to get to heaven: "How, my Lord, the warriors, cleansed by weapons, should attain to regions of bliss. For this, a child was conceived in a maiden's womb, capable of provoking a general war. Endowed with great energy *(tejas),* he became the son of a lower caste *sūta*" (XII.2.4–5). As Biardeau points out: "Being the son of Sūrya is not a curse per se, quite the contrary since the regular course of the sun is necessary for the well-being of the world. But to be born out of wedlock and abandoned by his mother takes the son of Sūrya out of the ordinary. He then becomes the replica of the dreadful sun, which rises at the end of a cosmic period to destroy the world by fire."[31] He is thus a sort of anti-Arjuna to the extent that his relationship to Duryodhana appears symmetrical with that of Arjuna to Yudhiṣṭhira. This is suggested in Nārada's own brief summary of his trajectory through this world:

> As a result of a Brahmin's curse, as also of the curse of the great Rāma (Jamadagni), of the boon granted to Kuntī and the illusion *(māyā)* practised on him by Śatakratu (= Indra), of his being counted by Bhīṣma in a disrespectful manner as only half a chariot-fighter, of the destruction of his energy caused by Śalya, of the behaviour of Vāsudeva, and of the celestial weapons provided to Arjuna by Rudra and Indra and Yama and Varuṇa and Kubera and Droṇa and the great-souled Kṛpa, the wielder of the Gāṇḍīva succeeded in slaying Vikartana's son Karṇa, who shone like the Sun. Such was (the lot of) your brother, cursed and shunned by many. (XII.5.11–15)

We may also note that his impending death had first been announced by Yama (the "king" of the dead) just prior to Arjuna's sojourn in Heaven (III.42.1ff.).

Karṇa himself obviously had more than an inkling about his role in provoking the war of the Mahābhārata. Significantly, he sees the coming war as the great abortive sacrifice of Duryodhana in which he ends up as the victim with his army playing the part of the wife (V.139.29–49). He tells Kṛṣṇa: "When you see me cut down by the left-handed archer, it will be the re-piling of the fire of his sacrifice. When the Pāṇḍavas drink the blood of Duḥśāsana, bellowing his roar, it will be the soma draught. When the two Pāñcālyas fell Droṇa and Bhīṣma, that will be the conclusion of the sacrifice, O Janārdana. When the mighty Bhīmasena kills Duryodhana, then the great sacrifice of the Dhārtarāṣṭra will end" (V.139.46–49). And he admits his own part in the destruction that looms ahead (V.141.2). He also dreams of Yudhiṣṭhira and his brothers ascending to a thousand-pillared palace, while Kṛṣṇa drapes the blood-fouled earth with entrails (V.141.27–29).

The envy arising from the unfortunate circumstances of his birth drives him to supplement his royal status (improperly conferred by Duryodhana) with the brāhmaṇical powers that would ensure his triumph over Arjuna. When these powers are forever denied him as a result of the two curses, his doom is sealed.[32] Still, the final confrontation of the two on the afternoon of the seventeenth day of the war is dramatized as a duel of giants performed before the celestial hosts of the three worlds (VIII.63.30ff.). As might be expected, the gods (notably Indra) are on the side of Arjuna and the demons (plus the god Sūrya as the renegade sun) are on the side of Karṇa. Differences and disputes arise on all sides, but Brahmā must clearly throw his support to Arjuna in the interests of the gods. The outcome is never really in doubt since, as Kṛṣṇa points out to his protégé, a victory for Karṇa would be the final end of the whole Universe (VIII.63.77).

As the two chariots approach each other, the warriors are compared to Indra and Vṛtra, and the battle itself, involving untold multitudes of men and animals, is compared to the battle in former days between the gods and the demons (VIII.64.1013*; 65.7). The tension builds to a fever pitch, and the hour of Karṇa's death draws near: "At that time, when the hour of Karṇa's death had come, O king, Kāla (that is, "Time" personified), approaching invisibly, alluding to the curse, and desirous of informing Karṇa that his death was near, told him "the earth is devouring your wheel." Indeed, when the time of his death had come, the great Brahmā-weapon that the Bhārgava had given him escaped his memory" (VIII. 66.1122*; 1123*). Karṇa pleads for time, but Kṛṣṇa has no compunction about urging a reluctant Arjuna to take this opportunity to finish him off. As Arjuna inspires his magic arrow with *mantras* into a mighty force ("resembling Nārāyaṇa's discus"), the entire universe of mobile and immobile creatures begins to shake. He finally strikes off his enemy's head "like Indra striking off the head of

Vṛtra" (VIII.67.24) and a light is seen leaving the lifeless corpse to pass into the sun.

The symbolic necessity of his life and death becomes even more apparent, according to Biardeau, when we discover the parallel between his death at the hands of Arjuna-Kṛṣṇa and the cosmic process associated with the end of the world:

> At the same time as he promotes the destruction of the war, Arjuna's task is also to limit it and to prepare the fecundity of the "remnant." As grandfather of Parīksit and close associate of the avatar, this is effectively the part he plays, but this part necessarily includes the death of Karṇa: it is Nārāyaṇa's task to preside over the "humid" and fecund period of the *pralaya* after putting an end to the conflagration with the help of the clouds brought by Vāyu. At the epic level it is the responsibility of the king, Indra's son, to put limits on the fires of war. This is the meaning of the death of Karṇa: in symbolic terms it promises the death and the end of the reign—the *cakra,* of Duryodhana, and through this the end of the war, the disappearance of the evil karma, fomenter of *adharma,* just as the death of Jayadratha announced the death of Droṇa and the end of the disorder of the *varṇa*. We are thus able to understand the final scene when Arjuna kills Karṇa by profiting from the instance when the wheel—*cakra,* of the hero's chariot sinks into the earth and he tries in vain to free it.[33]

Karṇa is thus the tragic antihero of the Mahābhārata who exhibits a strange mixture of pride, arrogance, and malignity, yet also great generosity to Brahmins and loyalty to his friend Duryodhana. This loyalty is carried to the point of refusing a suggestion by Kṛṣṇa to change the course of history by exposing his true identity to Yudhiṣṭhira (V.138.6ff.). Caught between his duty to Duryodhana and the realization that his cause is hopeless, he opts for the tragic path of loyalty to the one who has befriended him. As Krishna Chaitanya puts it, in Karṇa

> we have a splendid portrait of a man who triumphed over the tragic to relish its austere yet resplendent beauty. Karṇa sees the war that is imminent as a tremendous ritual sacrifice where the lives of courageous men will be offered and burnt up in the fire to the ritual music of the war-drums, trumpets and conches. He describes what he sees in his mind and so vivid is the vision that he says that it causes horripilation in him—an important detail because this psychosomatic reaction is repeatedly mentioned in later texts on poetics and dramaturgy as a feature in aesthetic experience and relish. Karṇa knows that he will be burned up in this flaming sacrificial fire. But no regret lingers; instead, there is a surging euphoria, because his death will be a heroic lay that will be sung by men as long as the great earth with its mountains and

rivers will last. The exaltation here is not one of unbalanced hypertrophy of emotions. The finest perceptions of Karṇa occur at this moment so near to his death, a death he longs to meet as if it were a beloved. He realizes that the only chance for a finer world to be born is this tremendous holocaust; he recognizes that Yudhiṣṭhira will be a better man for the reconstruction than himself or Duryodhana; he asks Kṛṣṇa not to disclose his real identity as the son of Kuntī since Yudhiṣṭhira would not be able to take up the role for which he is the fittest person.[34]

Daiva and Duryodhana

The concluding rite of the great sacrifice of the Dhārtarāṣṭra in this war, as Karṇa had also been only too aware, is the death of Duryodhana at the hands of Bhīma. Here, too, the work of Kṛṣṇa is much in evidence although, as we shall see shortly, his fate had already been sealed by a conclave of gods (that is, by *Daiva*) long before he was born. Duryodhana has been located hidden in a lake called Dvaipāyana (suggesting the deluge of the dissolution, that is, *pralaya*) the waters of which he had solidified by the power of his *māyā* (IX.29.7). Kṛṣṇa immediately urges Yudhiṣṭhira: "With your own powers of illusion *(māyā),* O Bhārata, destroy the illusion of this master of illusion (*māyāvin* = Duryodhana). A master of illusion should be slain with illusion. This is the truth, O Yudhiṣṭhira. With acts *(kriyā)* and means *(upāya)* and applying your power of illusion *(māyā)* to these waters, slay, O best of the Bhārata, this Suyodhana who is evil incarnate" (IX.30.6–7). He then goes on to illustrate how the gods themselves prevailed over the demons by means of "acts and means," providing a list of various episodes in the lives of the gods (IX.30.8–14). Then, when Yudhiṣṭhira—"out of compassion," gives Duryodhana the choice of arms in single combat with any one of the Pāṇḍavas, Kṛṣṇa is furious: "You have once again initiated a dangerous game of chance similar to the one in former days between yourself and Śakuni, O lord of the people" (IX.32.7). In fact, the situation constitutes a reversal of the original dice game since, as Biardeau has noted: "In the light of the fixed game of dice of the beginning, we now have a duel with the mace—thus a veritable confrontation of warriors, but modelled as closely as possible on the dice game because everything must be resolved at a stroke—though this time it is Yudhiṣṭhira who has a substitute to fight in his place and to cheat, something he cannot do himself."[35] Nevertheless, Kṛṣṇa is understandably worried since he knows that none of the brothers is a match for Duryodhana with the mace, not even the powerful Bhīma who boldly offers a challenge.

Before the battle can begin, however, Balarāma arrives from a long pilgrimage and suggests that they all return to Kurukṣetra. For Kurukṣetra: "That spot in the world of the gods *(devaloka),* is known as the northern sacrificial altar of Prajāpati. Thus, he who dies in battle on that eternal and most auspicious of all the places in the three worlds is sure to reach Heaven" (IX.54.5–6). This means that Duryodhana is assured of a heavenly reward in spite of his boundless greed and will to power. But from the perspective of *Daiva* this is only right since Duryodhana has faithfully accomplished the "lightening of the burden of the Earth" the goddess of the Earth had been seeking at a celestial conclave of gods before his birth. As they announce to her: "He who goes by the name of Duryodhana is the one who will accomplish your [that is, the godess Earth's] purpose. Once he is king, your business will be accomplished" (XI.8.24). And, as the learned Sāmba indicates in absolving the Kauravas of all responsibility for the crimes against humanity they have committed: "The destruction that has overtaken the Kuru dynasty was not brought about by Duryodhana. It was not brought about by you (that is, Dhṛtarāṣṭra). Nor was it brought about by Karṇa or the son of Subala (that is, Śakuni). We know full well that it was brought about by *Daiva* and that there was no avoiding it. There is no way that *Daiva* can be resisted by human exertion *(puruṣakāra)*" (XV.16.1–2). He concludes that since everything is due to destiny, Duryodhana should be allowed to sport blissfully in Heaven (XV.16.9).

For the final act of the sacrifice of the Dhārtarāṣṭras to be concluded, however, it is imperative that Duryodhana be killed (VII.77. 18).[36] It is the task of Kṛṣṇa, the master controller of *Daiva,* to give the necessary push in the right direction, and, once again, he does this by urging the Pāṇḍavas to resort to what amounts to unfair means. The term he uses is *anyāyena*—that is, by a method that is "not according to rule," as opposed to *dharmena,* that is to say, "according to the dharma" (IX.57.17). Arjuna is therefore encouraged to give Bhīma a sign that the time has come to fulfill his vow and to break the thighs of his adversary with a low blow of the mace.

The resulting sense of shame and dishonor in the Pāṇḍava camp (in the face of the angry denunciations of Balarāma and others) prompts a vigorous response from Kṛṣṇa that not only offers an interesting lesson in epic morality but also throws light on his own role in the fighting. In his view, such a stratagem is justified by the fact that the Pāṇḍavas had lost the kingdom by unfair means in the first place and also by the need for Bhīma to fulfill his vow. But beyond this is the bitter truth that the Machiavellian forces of evil *(adharma)* are far too powerful to be dislodged in an equal contest by the gentle forces of the good (dharma).

Such a task calls for the kind of extraordinary means that the gods themselves are wont to employ against the demons. Kṛṣṇa then goes on to admit—in a statement that leaves no doubt about his involvement in the war, that he himself is responsible for their demise:

> It would have been impossible to kill the king (that is, Duryodhana) according to the dharma or any of these great chariot-warriors and archers with Bhīṣma at their head. It is I who killed them on the battlefield with the use of various stratagems *(upāya)* that include my *māyā* and my Yoga, for I desired your welfare. Indeed, had I never acted in this deceitful manner *(jihma)* during the battle, how could you have gained your victory, your kingship and your riches? It was my *upāya* that sealed the fate of these kings who could not be vanquished in any other manner by the Pāṇḍavas. . . . Do not worry about the fact that your enemy has been killed. I had to kill your more numerous enemies by means of these dubious stratagems *(mithyopāya)*. This is the path followed in former times by the gods in order to slay the demons. It is the path followed by men of goodwill, and the whole world follows their example. (IX.372*; IX.60.57; 61–62).

Needless to say such justification is hardly acceptable to Aśvatthāman for whom Duryodhana was brought down "by a most infamous act" (IX.64.33).

Kṛṣṇa as *Daiva*

We introduce these lines not for the moral issue, interesting though this may be, but for what they reveal of the central and indispensable role of Kṛṣṇa in the destruction of the Kauravas and of their great war machine. Evidence for this has been growing throughout the war. However, we must return to an event that took place just before the outbreak of hostilities if we want to understand the true nature of his relationship to *Daiva* and to the conflict as a whole (V.129.1–15). After a last-ditch appeal to Duryodhana had failed, Kṛṣṇa offers dramatic proof of his divine power in the form of a theophany reminiscent of the subsequent manifestation of his Universal Form for the benefit of Arjuna in chapter 11 of the Bhagavadgītā. At first sight, this extraordinary display before the entire Kaurava court might appear to symbolize the traditional opposition between the party of the gods and the party of the demons (now led by Duryodhana). However, as Biardeau has noted: "a closer look reveals Rudra among the divinities present—Rudra who appears in Aśvatthāman and even in Kṛpa in the form of the Rudra; as well as

Brahmā—whose presence is assured in the Duryodhana camp in the form of Droṇa, incarnation of Bhṛaspati, and the Sun—the true father of Karṇa."[37] The truth is that Kṛṣṇa is not committed to either side, only to the course already laid out by *Daiva*. We find additional support for this "noncommital" view in the fact that Kṛṣṇa leaves the assembly hand in hand with both Sātyaki (who will fight on the side of the Pāṇḍavas) and Kṛtavarman (who has already offered his services to Duryodhana).[38] And he already has one foot in the Kaurava camp in the form of his Nārāyaṇa "army of the gopis" bequeathed to Duryodhana—following his own recruitment by Arjuna as a noncombatant member of the Pāṇḍava forces (V.7.15).

Although the triumvirate of Brahmā, Viṣṇu, and Śiva (or Rudra) is explicitly mentioned on only one occasion in the epic (in Appendix 27 following III.256.30 of the Critical Edition), the three gods are assimilated to each other on numerous occasions, notably in the Nārāyaṇīya-parvan section of the Śāntiparvan where Kṛṣṇa makes the claim that "I am the soul of all the worlds, O son of Pāṇḍu. And Rudra is my very soul; therefore, O foremost one, I revere Him . . . He who knows Rudra knows Me; he who follows Him follows Me also. Rudra is Nārāyaṇa. Both are One Being in two forms" (XII.328.21; 23; 24. Cf. also III.187.5–6; XII.330.64). And Kṛṣṇa goes on to explain how "Under my protection you have won a great victory in battle. Know, O son of Kuntī, that He whom you saw going before you in battle was none other than Rudra, that god of gods known as Kapardin. They say He is "Time," born of my wrath. Those foes you [think you] have slain were, in fact, first slain by Him" (XII.330.67–70). This only confirms what Arjuna already knew from previous conversations with Kṛṣṇa (VI.33/BG.11.33) and with Vyāsa (VII.173.2ff.) respectively—that he had been the instrument of the Supreme Divinity during the battle, revealed in the "terrible" form of Viṣṇu or in the form of a mysterious figure, lance in hand, who destroys all his foes ahead of him (which turns out to be Śiva). This finally prompts Janamejaya to remark that "With Vāsudeva as his ally my ancestor Dhanaṃjaya accomplished nothing extraordinary in achieving that great victory at Kurukṣetra" (XII.331.9).

In effect, what the Supreme Divinity in the form of Kṛṣṇa reveals by these happenings is not so much His opposition to the party of the demons (or His partiality for that of the gods) but His omnipresence on the battlefield—His encompassment of *both* sides in this conflict. As the avatar, Kṛṣṇa necessarily takes the side of the dharma. However, this preference merely reflects the conditions obtaining at a particular point in the sociocosmic cycle of the *yugas* when the divine assistance of the avatar is called for. In His true nature *sub specie aeternitatis*, He embodies a *Daiva* that transcends the destiny of the three worlds with their petty jealousies of gods and demons.

Kṛṣṇa (and the *Daiva* He controls) thus emerges as the driving force behind the conflict as a whole, and whatever partiality is shown for the Pāṇḍavas is an expression of a greater fatality of which they are only dimly aware (cf. also VI.29/B.G.7.6; XII.337.905*; XII.337.68–68, etc.). His vital role is later acknowledged in a profusion of devotional *(bhakti)* sentiment as Kṛṣṇa prepares to return to Dvāraka after the funeral rites of the slain heroes have been concluded. After worshiping him as the Lord of the Universe who creates, maintains, and destroys the cosmos of mobile and immobile creatures for His "playful sport," Arjuna continues:

> The destruction of the Kaurava, the son of Dhṛtarāṣṭra in battle, that you [that is, Kṛṣṇa] have undertaken out of friendship for us, is a great accomplishment. For that host which was vanquished by me in battle was [in fact] destroyed by you. It was thanks to your actions (karma) that victory is mine. It was the power of your mind *(buddhi)* that showed the way *(upāya)* for effecting the destruction of Duryodhana in battle, as also of Karṇa and the evil Sindhu king [that is, Jayadratha] and of Bhūriśravas. (XIV.51.17–20 and 45)

And Yudhiṣṭhira adds: "It is through your grace *(prasāda)*, O Mādhava, that the whole earth, great hero, has been subjugated by us, and our enemies have all been slain." Though not an active participant in the fighting, Kṛṣṇa has somehow managed to turn the course of events to their advantage—not, of course, in their personal interests or as a reward for good conduct, but in accordance with the needs of this particular juncture in the continuing "course of Time."

In a later dialogue, the dying Bhīṣma also reminds Yudhiṣṭhira that what he has won is due only to the subtle behind-the-scene maneuverings of Kṛṣṇa/Nārāyaṇa. Using the sacrificial imagery found throughout the Mahābhārata, he reveals that

> Your complete victory, O son of Pṛthā, your matchless achievements, and the dominion you have achieved over the whole earth are all due to the protection of Nārāyaṇa. Because you have the inconceivable Lord Nārāyaṇa in your heart, you have become an Adhvaryu for pouring multitudes of kings as libations on the blazing fire of battle, using Kṛṣṇa as your great sacrificial ladle resembling the all-destroying fire that appears at the end of the *yuga*. Duryodhana, with his sons, brothers and kinsmen was much to be pitied inasmuch as, moved by wrath, he made war with Hari and the wielder of Gāṇḍīva [that is, Arjuna].

> Many sons of Diti [that is, demons], many foremost of Dānava [also demons], of huge bodies and vast strength, have perished in the fire of Kṛṣṇa's discus like insects in a forest conflagration. How incapable, then, must human beings be of battling against that Kṛṣṇa,—human beings who, O tiger among men, are destitute of truth *(sattva),* strength and might. As regards Jaya [that is, Arjuna], he resembles the all-destroying *yuga*-fire in energy. Capable of drawing the bow equally with both hands, he is always in the vanguard of the fight. With his energy *(tejas),* O king, he has slain all the troops of Suyodhana. (XIII. App. I. No. 16. 175–187)

The reference to Kṛṣṇa as Nārāyaṇa, the intermediate form of the Supreme Divinity who contains the worlds within himself at the end of a cosmic period *(kalpa),* suggests, according to Biardeau, a symbolic link between his various tricks and strategems (analyzed further in chapter 5) and his divine powers as master of Yoga *(yogeśvara).*[39] Finally, the deference shown to him is also revealing since "it is in this manner that the teachings of the Bhagavadgītā are put into practice, and we witness heroic warriors renouncing the glory of battle. They fought truly for the dharma and not for themselves."[40]

5

Destiny and Human Initiative

Chapters 5 and 6 explore the interplay between the workings of Destiny *(Daiva)* and the countervailing forces of human initiative *(puruṣakāra)* and effort *(yatna)*. This chapter focuses more on the philosophical aspects of the subject, including the notion of "freedom" in the Mahābhārata, while chapter 6 deals with the practical implications as regards religious practice and spiritual advancement. Chapter 6 also introduces Kṛṣṇa's concept of the human personality as this may be interpreted from his advice to Arjuna in the Bhagavadgītā. This is followed in chapter 7 by a summary and analysis of the more important epic debates about the duties and responsibilities (that is, the dharma) of the warrior *(kṣatriya)*.

It should now be evident that "Destiny" appears in a number of guises depending on the perspective taken. On the one hand, *Daiva* is the eternal rhythm of the Supreme Divinity in his sociocosmic role as regulator of the various classes of things and beings in the Universe. This Supreme Divinity is Kṛṣṇa, we are told: "The blessed Keśava (= Kṛṣṇa) ceaselessly drives the wheel of time, the wheel of the Universe, the wheel of the *yugas* in a ceaseless round by means of his own Yoga. The Lord alone governs time and death, and the mobile and immobile creatures. What I say is the truth" (V.66.12–13). He is a Great Yogi *(mahāyogi)* who keeps the world in motion as if in play *(krīḍanniva)*, and the rise and fall of human societies are also functions of this yogic rythm (V.66.10). From this perspective *Daiva* and *Kāla* (Cosmic Time) are one, although, from our limited vantage point, the mechanics of the process are a mystery. All we can see are the effects in terms of the progressive "fall" of the old society and its values to the greed and ambition of evil kings. This is represented on the higher plane by the ascendency of the demons who banish the gods and their values; on the lower plane by the banishment of Yudhiṣṭhira (as "King Dharma") to the forest wilderness (that is, to the outer peripheries of the human world).[1]

On the other hand, a significant shift occurs when *Daiva* is viewed from the level of the avatar, that is to say, from the perspective of the divinity engaged in the affairs of the world. According to Saṃjaya (V.66.8–11), Kṛṣṇa could reduce the world to ashes with his *manas* (presumably by erasing all thought of the world from His Consciousness). But the "Time" is not ripe for destruction on a truly cosmic scale but for a new beginning for the wayward earth. Kṛṣṇa can only outwit the demons at this juncture, probably because their total destruction would destroy the necessary balance of good and evil on which the existence of the world cycle depends. Not omnipotence but a strange mixture of trickery and deceit is called for here, albeit in the service of the good (dharma).

Tricks and Stratagems

Kṛṣṇa is supposedly a noncombatant in the war, yet, as we saw in chapter 4, he has a habit of influencing events in a number of subtle or indirect ways. The various terms for his different abilities include *upāya* (skillful means), *moha* (delusion), and *māyā* (illusion), all of which convey a sense of subterfuge, ruse, or mental trickery. To begin with, he clearly has a shrewd sense of human psychology—a knowledge of mind *(vittajña)* that allows him to play upon the natural propensity of human beings to misrepresent the true facts of existence (V.66.15). Ignorance *(avidyā)* at this level involves confusion about the roles they are called upon to play in life. This is primarily the mistaken belief that the script they are following has been written by their own desires and inclinations. In truth, however, the strings are in the hands of the Supreme Puppet-master (V.39.1; V.156.15). As he explains the matter to Arjuna: "The Lord abides in the heart of all beings, Arjuna. He makes all beings turn by his *māyā* [as if] mounted on a machine" (VI.40.61/BG.18.61). Living beings do not act by virtue of their own power but at the behest of the Lord (XIV.3.1–2); they have no volition *(kāmata)* of their own but function "with their minds controlled by me" (III.187.22). This skill in action (the *karmasu kauśalam* of BG.2.50) is often referred to as his Yoga of delusion *(māyāyoga),* which is why he is sometimes called the master magician *(māyāvin)*. In the final analysis, Kṛṣṇa himself is also a product of this *māyā*.

Kṛṣṇa also demonstrates a more "magical" ability to create real perceptual distortions of some kind (also described as *māyā*). The darkening of the sun to lull Jayadratha into a false sense of security is so convincing that Kṛṣṇa must warn Arjuna beforehand to "make sure you don't imagine that the sun is really going down" (VII.Apendix I, No.16.10). This facility is also evident in his creation of thousands of separate forms of Arjuna himself on the battlefield, which creates panic among the Kaurava troops (VII.18.11–13), and in the transmutation of the destructive force of Bhagadatta's *vaiṣnava* weapon into a victory garland that appears on Kṛṣṇa's chest (VII.28.17–18). An invocational formula may have been employed in this latter case (mantras being the preferred method for charging, deflecting, or defusing a weapon in the epic).

The moral implications of these questionable interventions of the divine are not lost to the protagonists themselves. In the Bhagadatta case, for example, doubts are raised as to whether the violation of Kṛṣṇa's prior commitment of nonparticipation is justified by the need to save Arjuna's life. The criterion commonly given is the situational conditions of "place and time" (XII.79.31; XII.297.16). As Bhīṣma explains to Yudhiṣṭhira: "Dharma becomes *adharma,* and *adharma* becomes dharma according to the conditions place and time *(deśakāla).* Such is the power of place and time [that is, in judging the morality of human acts]. Even by doing acts of cruelty friends have reached the highest heaven. Even by doing sinful acts good people have achieved the highest state" (XII.79.31–32). He nevertheless has to admit that "the course of the dharma is subtle."

Truth is, by definition, the very absence of trickery and deception, and a "Truth command" is an even more potent force for the "welfare of the world." It is surprising therefore, that Kṛṣṇa resorts to this power of "Truth" only once, to resuscitate Parikṣit, the only surviving heir to the throne of Hastinapura, who was killed in the womb of his mother by Aśvatthāman. The reanimation of the dead king is shown to take place by an exchange of energies; as the energy of the *brahmāstra* weapon that killed him is withdrawn it is replaced by the life-energy *(tejas)* of the infant-king, which illuminates the room as it returns to his body (XIV.68.18–24 and XIV.69.1). The potency of this "Truth Command" is demonstrated by the permanence of Parikṣit's revival (he lives to ascend the throne).

Finally, Kṛṣṇa also admits to the advantages of his human estate. In addition to his legendary psychological acumen (the *vittajña* just mentioned), he also profits from the fact that his divine nature and power are hidden from the ignorant masses by his very appearance as a normal reasoning and acting human being. He explains: "When, O descendant of Bhṛgu, I live in the order of the gods, then I quite naturally act in every respect like a god. When, O descendant of Bhṛgu, I live in the order of the *gandharvas,* I act in every respect like a *gandharva,* O Bhārgava. When I live in the order of the *nāgas,* or in that of the *yakṣas* or the *rākṣasas,* or in the order of humanity, I must act accordingly" (XIV.53.16–19). This enables him to give the impression of a "powerless peasant," and to use the Pāṇḍavas as a cover *(satraṃ)* for his avataric mission (V.66.14–15). He can thus work tirelessly in this manner behind-the-scenes, though with no purpose of his own in the normal egocentric sense (VI.25.22/BG.3.22).

Daiva in Human Expression

These interventions of Kṛṣṇa are, of course, hardly typical of the various manifestations of *Daiva.* More common in personal life is the sudden change of fortune or the agonizing choice that immobilizes or defeats one's purposes. This is most clearly apparent in the case of the blind king Dhṛtarāṣṭra. As the war progresses, the mounting Kaurava losses appear to him as a superior fortune opposed to reason and human volition. Four types of battle situation have been noted by Georges Dumézil:

> Whenever a great warrior of his army falls or fails, he sees such misfortune as proof of the overriding power of an opposing destiny: otherwise, how could such a man be vanquished? 2. In contemplating total defeat, a massive retreat of his army, the proof is of a similar nature: were it not for destiny, how could such troops, well-armed, well trained and commanded as they are, give way? 3. In judging a "train of blows" where his side is merely checked, this is proof once again: without destiny, why would success and failure not be evenly divided? 4. When, in seeking to explain this inequality in the effects, he is forced to concede an inequality at the level of cause, in other words that in all areas the Pāṇḍavas are superior to his army, this is again proof: natural law is flawed from within, with respect to the very resources and relations of protagonists who should be equal (in terms of their birth, education, technical know-how), and are not.[2]

Dumézil sees the blind king as the incarnation of the Vedic god Bhaga, the traditional distributor of the "shares" allotted to each man and woman at birth.[3] As such, he is an ambiguous figure, associated, on the one hand, with unjust chance *(haṭha)*[4]—the "blind Bhaga" of classical mythology, and, on the other, with love and marriage and general good fortune (*phālguna,* the spring marriage month is *bhagadaivata,* that is, bestower of conjugal felicity). Dumézil traces this ambiguity to the division of the king's life into a disastrous earlier period culminating in the death of Duryodhana, and in his postwar reconciliation with the Pāṇḍavas and with his own past.[5]

One is in no doubt about his troubles through most of the story, however, owing to the endless litany of complaints against cosmic justice as he becomes more and more convinced that he is the victim of an opposing *daiva*. Of course Saṃjaya, Vidura, and other critics all agree in tracing his difficulties to a weakness of resolve, a failure to take action where action is due. Although supposedly endowed with "the eyesight of insight" he is quite unable to exercise it. As he laments: "It is fate *(diṣṭa)* that is superior in my view, and man's efforts *(pauruṣa)* are of little value. While I fully realize that the evils of war will bring destruction, I cannot restrain my deceitful son who cheated at gambling nor act in my own interest. My mind *(buddhi)* does indeed see that it is wrong, O bard, but on encountering Duryodhana, it goes into a spin" (V.156. 4–6).

Duryodhana is clearly the very opposite of his father. Driven by hatred of the Pāṇḍavas and by an unbridled will to power, he knows exactly what he wants and spares no effort to see his ruthless ambitions fulfilled. His references to *daiva* in the days of Pāṇḍava ascendency (for example, I.192.10; II.43.30; II.44.1) are clear expressions of despondency and frustration at the growing fortunes of his cousins, who have not only thumbed their noses at all his evil schemes, but married the Pāñcāla princess, gained half the kingdom, and made themselves masters of the world to boot. However Śakuni reassures him by telling him not to worry about the "good luck" of the Pāṇḍavas but to trust in Śakuni's own superior knowledge of the dice.

Yudhiṣṭhira too, looking back upon the game, believes it to be the product of an uncompromising *daiva* that cannot be avoided, even at the prospect of losing all. His predicament is rooted in what he experiences as the moral conflict between his filial obligations, and the duty he had imposed on himself by an ill-conceived vow.[6]

These differences in response to individual circumstance suggest that the problems of epic characters in relation to their fellows, and to the society and world around them, are the product of complications and contradictions inherent in their own being. Although not acknowledged in so many words, there is often a sense that *daiva* is a function of character. Bhīṣma, for example, tells Yudhiṣṭhira: "When I consider that the propensities for action *(pravṛtti)* proceeding from nothing but [one's own] nature are all determined by [one's own] nature, I am not tormented by anything" (XII.172.11). According to a statement by Vyāsa (III.9.10), this character is fixed at birth, a view supported by the absence of any notable example of one who becomes enlightened during the course of the epic *(jīvanmukta)*.[7]

Puruṣakāra

Given the countless occasions for frustration or impotence before the weight of circumstance, it may seem remarkable how much credit is given in the epic to our human ability to pursue not only our own ends but the means to achieve them, fair or foul as it pleases us. This potential "freedom" not only provides the necessary conditions for moral and spiritual growth, but it constitutes a radical break from the instinctual determinism of the lower orders of life. We alone of all creatures are made to answer for what we do: "Dharma and *adharma* apply only to human beings, O king. They do not exist in this world among creatures other than man" (XII.283.28). Human life is thus regarded as a privilege to be cherished. It is also an opportunity that should not be wasted, for a human birth is "exceedingly difficult to obtain, even that of an outcast *(caṇḍāla)*. For the foremost of births, O lord of the earth, is that by attaining which the soul *(ātman)* can be rescued by pure acts" (XII.286. 31–32).

It is nevertheless important not to confuse the differences between the various epic "freedoms" and our modern Western notions; in particular we must distinguish between *mokṣa* as the culmination or end-state of moral and spiritual growth, and the "freedom of doing" and deciding that serves as a means for achieving such a state. The former is a "freedom of being" analogous to Rollo May's "essential freedom." Whereas "freedom of doing" is the power to decide and to accomplish what has been decided, the former "refers to the context out of which the urge to act emerges. It refers to the deeper level of one's attitude and is the fount out of which "freedom of doing" is born."[8] Modern talk of freedom and "free will" focuses almost exclusively on "freedom of doing" although the terms are not always well-defined.[9] *Puruṣakāra* is clearly a "freedom of doing" but here too we must be careful not to conclude that it is the same as "free will." For the epic author, and indeed for Indian tradition generally, it is only the self-realized transcendental "self" or *ātman* that is *really* free, not the so-called will of the empirical self *(jīva)*. The empirical self or "ego" can, at best, identify with particular motives, cast its lot with them, and, to that extent, "will" them. But this so-called will is only the mental construct of an entity whose true freedom is effectively blocked by its identification with the various dispositions and impulses that collectively constitute what is subjectively experienced as I *(ahaṃkāra)* and objectively described as a person *(pu-*

ruṣa). The great problem of human life is precisely the bondage *(√bandh)* of this so-called will, a fact that may explain why, as R. N. Dandekar has noted: "the theoretical question as to whether the human will is free or not does not seem to have particularly bothered a Hindu."[10] This may also explain why epic Sanskrit has no specific term(s) to express the "free will" of an embodied self.

This state of bondage is not the result of a moral "fall" but of an epistemological lapse into ignorance *(avidyā)*. It also involves a "self-forgetting" in the sense that the ego is mistaken for the real "self" or *ātman*. This process is outlined by one of the Brahmins accompanying the Pāṇḍavas in the Kāmyaka forest (the name of which is associated with *kāma* = "desire"):

> When the six senses *(indriyas)* are focused on their respective objects *(viṣayas)*, the mind *(manas)*, prompted by habitual modes of thinking (*pūrvasaṃkalpa* = "the thought processes of the past"), is set in motion. With the mind provoked in this manner by the various objects of the senses, desire *(autsukya)* is born and action *(pravṛtti)* is initiated. Then, being pierced by desire *(kāma)* amplified by the force of habit, with the arrows of the sense objects, he falls into the fires of greed *(lobha)* as a moth falls from its attraction to the light. Caught up in fun and feasting he finally sinks into the jaws of the great delusion *(mahāmoha)*, and forgets who he really is. In this way, he falls into the *saṃsāra*, spinning about in womb after womb, [his mind] afflicted by ignorance *(avidyā)*, inherited tendencies *(karma)* and want *(tṛṣṇā)*. He cycles through the forms of existence from Brahmā to a blade of grass, born again and again in water, on land, or in the air. (III.2.63–68; see also VI.24.62–63/BG.2.62–63)

This state of the ignorant is contrasted to the condition of the wise who "delight in freedom," clearly referring to an end-state of freedom in contrast to the means or "doing" of human initiative *(puruṣakāra)* or self-effort *(yatna)*. "Freedom of doing" must somehow always remain constrained or "bound" in the Indian context. Furthermore, the epic terminology is not usually employed to describe a spiritual striving but a worldly one. In other words it is the "freedom" to enjoy—rather than to abandon, the fruits of one's actions. This is born out by the etymology of the word *puruṣakāra,* which suggests the ability to accomplish (√*kṛ* = "to make") something human *(puruṣa)*, that is to say, to realize the object of one's desires *(kāma)*. It is the drive to overcome the resistances of the world, to counter the *daiva* that thwarts the realization of human purposes. It is also the courage to push ahead in the face of adversity.

The Mahābhārata has no lack of terms to characterize the interplay of divine and human agencies. Words that may safely be rendered as "destiny" include (in approximate order of popularity): *daiva, diṣṭa, iśvaranirdiṣṭa, vidhi, bhavitavyaṃ,* and *vidhātvihitaṃ*. Terms that convey the sense of chance or "luck" include *haṭha, yadṛcchā, bhāgadheya, bhāgya,* and *saṃgati*. And among the numerous terms expressing a sense of human self-determination and initiative we may note (again in order of popularity): *puruṣakāra, pauruṣa, yatna, puruṣārtha, prayatna, puruṣaprayatna, mānuṣya, utthāna, utsāha, vyāyāma, īha, tejas, svaceṣṭita, svakarmatā, dākṣya,* and *vyavasāya*. Some combination of destiny, chance, and human initiative are deemed to be operative in the success or failure of any human enterprise. Draupadī, for example, talks of them as the three determinants *(traidha)* or three doors *(tridvāra)*. They are reviewed by her as follows:

> There are those who hold that everything is done by chance *(haṭha)*, those who hold that it is fate *(diṣṭa)*, and those who hold that everything springs from human effort *(puruṣaprayatna)*. These are called the three determinants *(traidha)*. But there are others who think that this is not enough to account for what happens. But we cannot really determine whether it is chance or fate that brought it about; for we only see the causal connection of events, springing either from chance or fate. Some comes from destiny, some from chance, some from one's own doing *(svakarmatā)*; and it is thus that a man gets the fruit; there is no other causal factor; so profess capable men, wise in first principles. (III.33.30–32)

Kṛṣṇa elaborates further on the vicissitudes of action in response to Bhīma as follows:

> However well intended and conducted and however effectively carried out, human action (karma) may be opposed by fate *(daiva)*. On the other hand, some activity (karma), or something left undone by *daiva*, may be salvaged by human effort *(pauruṣa)*—like cold and heat, as well as rain, hunger and thirst, Bhārata. And again, an action personally undertaken by a man with the right understanding may not be impeded by fate *(diṣṭa)*. These are known as the [three] marks of action. Action is the only way of creating an effect in the world, O Pāṇḍava, and the smart man will carry on fearlessly, whatever the result may be. One who has come to realize this will perform action without being discouraged by failure or overjoyed with success. (V.75.8–12)[11]

The successful realization of human purposes in the world is subject to the interplay of the various causalities of self and other, here designated as human effort and fate. Chance as a third ingredient is not mentioned, presumably because it would complicate matters and contribute nothing to the main purpose of his discourse—which is to prompt a change of attitude on the part of Bhīma.

Kṛṣṇa is thus in substantial agreement with Draupadī that human beings have certain powers of their own for realizing the objects of their desires in the world. Their respective triads both recognize that *puruṣa-kāra* is impeded or assisted by a complex web of causality already operating in the external world. Tampering with this intricate fabric can affect the world and ourselves in an unforeseen manner. When the attempt to realize our desires fails, as is often the case, Kṛṣṇa's advice is to accept the situation with equanimity. Of course this calls for a change in attitude rather than circumstances, which is considered to be more a function of knowledge *(jñāna)* than of raw effort *(puruṣakāra)*.

In contrast to this position is the frequent claim that the very notion of an agent *(kartṛ)* is an erroneous one, implying the denial of *puruṣa-kāra*. This is typical of the happy few who enjoy the true freedom of release from the conditions of the world *(mokṣa)*. A couple of illustrations will suffice. Questioned by Yudhiṣṭhira as to whether or not the agent is the doer of an action, Bhīṣma quotes the "good" demon Prahlāda, advising Indra as follows: "Whoever believes himself to be the author of acts good or bad suffers from an erroneous understanding, indeed is the very epitome of ignorance in my opinion. If, O Śakra [= Indra], the person were really the agent, then all those acts undertaken for his own benefit would certainly be crowned with success, and none of them would ever come to grief" (XII.215.17–18). He then goes on to argue that it is not the agent *(kartṛ)* but one's own nature that is responsible for the fruits of action:

> I will instruct you in full on the subject of action (karma). Now listen! Just as a crow eating some food causes it to be known [to other crows] by the sound it makes, all our acts are an expression of our own nature. He who does not know the highest state of nature but only her superficial forms becomes stupefied in consequence of his ignorance [lit. his "childlike perplexity"]. But he who is capable of understanding that everything here is really the result of his own nature is never at a loss. In consequence of one's certain conviction in this respect how could one ever be affected by pride or arrogance? (XII.215.24–27)

From this perspective, there is no agent since all the effects that we know as the world, including the effects of human action, flow from the inner nature of things (including what we label as character in human beings). The word own-nature *(svabhāva)* is a generic term that describes the inherent tendency for any being or thing to express its own inner being. Just as it is the nature of the sun to shine, so it is the nature of a particular human being to express his desires and purposes in action. There is no agent with a liberty of indifference between acting in one way rather than in another.

This emphasis on the inner life may also be observed in another discussion of the three elements (including the element of chance). Of particular interest here is the link between past and present action that is established through the substitution of *pūrvakarma* (previous acts), for the more common term *puruṣakāra* (human initiative). After voicing the belief that "A man is not the agent of his good and evil deeds: he is helplessly manipulated like a wooden puppet *(yantra)*" (V.156.14), Saṃjaya adds: "Some people are fated *(nirdiṣṭa)* by the Lord, others by chance *(yadṛcchā)*, others by previous acts *(pūrvakarma)*. It is this triad *(traidha)* that is being torn apart" (V.156.15). The "fate of previous acts" appears to refer to those habitual patterns of behavior we would call "character."

Morality (Dharma) and Moral Conflict

Of course, in order to act one must first decide, and here a helpful distinction may be made between practical, prudential, and moral choice. The epic has little to say about the numerous practical decisions that crop up in daily life involving no conflict between what the agent wants to do and what he or she believes ought to be done. It has somewhat more to say about prudential choice where a conflict has arisen between immediate satisfaction and one's own long-range interests. We have seen how Vidura repeatedly warns Dhṛtarāṣṭra about the potential disasters inherent in his constant appeasement of Duryodhana's ambitious scheming. A situation such as this might be interpreted by saying that the resolve *(puruṣakāra)* of the blind king has been undermined by the volitional resistances *(daiva)* that plague him.

Most common as a topic of discussion is the question of moral choice, where both short- and long-range self-interest conflict with the demands of a scriptural ordinance or a categorical imperative. These ordinances and imperatives involve the moral teleology of a value, directing us to actualize an "ought-to-be." But an "ought" is merely a claim, not a compulsion like the determination of a natural law. However this very indeterminateness has the effect of forcing upon us a "freedom" and a responsibility for choosing whether to pursue or abandon the value to be actualized or the direction to be followed.[12] The capacity to choose between a life governed by the moral order of the world (or dharma) and one of unbridled self-indulgence is among the most important of the powers recognized in the epic (VI.39/BG.16.10). Unfortunately, only a few are able to exercise it. The majority of epic humanity evidently show little promise of moral or spiritual development: "Dependent on other forces" like lumps of clay (XII.277.19), they are as worthless as the pith of the banana-plant (XII.287.16). Even men of wisdom engaged in spiritual practices are like blind men who have finally succeeded in moving about their own home (XII.287.18).

We reserve more detailed discussion of these moral issues for chapter 9. Suffice it to say that the necessary conditions for moral choice are seen to be twofold; the intellectual capacity *(jñāna)* to discriminate "right" from "wrong" courses of action, and the volitional strength (or *puruṣakāra*) to opt for the appropriate alternative. The Kantian maxim that an "ought" must imply a "can" is implicitly acknowledged by the assignment of moral responsibility and accountability—in the form of the fruits *(phala)* of the action, to the one who acts. It would be the greatest hoax, says Yudhiṣṭhira, if acts were fruitless (III.32.26). The connection between act and fruit is the guarantor of the entire structure of Vedic morality, the whole edifice of the dharma with its duties and rewards. He is, nevertheless, forced to admit that "The distribution of the fruits of acts, both good and bad, their origin *(prabhava)* and disappearance *(apyaya)*, are mysteries of the gods, my angry wife. Nobody knows them, these creatures are in the dark about them, they are guarded by the gods, for the *māyā* of the gods is a dark secret" (III. 32.33–34). Note the use of the same term as that used in the mythology to describe the creation and disappearance of the cosmos (cf. *prabhavāpyayau*, p. 16).

The Four "Goals of Life"

The dying Bhīṣma discourses at length on the subject of dharma (focusing more particularly on the *rājadharma* of the king). Dharma in general, which in the Indian context is taken to mean the meticulous accomplishment of religious and social obligations, is considered one of four legitimate goals of human striving and fulfillment *(puruṣarthas)*. The three others are sensual and æsthetic pleasure (*kāma*, lit. "desire"), material and psychological security and well-being *(artha)*, and the commitment to self-realization and essential freedom *(mokṣa)*. However, the most radical choice that presents itself is between the secular and the spiritual paths, between a decision to follow the pleasures and prospects of this world *(saṃsāra)*, or to seek spiritual happiness by severing all ties to the world.

The following debate on this matter, which takes place at the conclusion of the Rājadharma section of the Śāntiparvan (XII.161.1–48), is particularly instructive for what it reveals about the moral dispositions and attitudes of the Pāṇḍavas. The brothers are returning home from their first visit to Bhīṣma who lies dying on the field of Kurukṣetra, when Yudhiṣṭhira suddenly asks the question: "The course of the world depends upon dharma, *artha* and *kāma*. Which among them is the most important, which the second, and which the least in importance" (XII. 161.2)? Not surprisingly, Vidura argues for the supremacy of dharma. By this he does not mean the socialized rules of caste or stage of life *(varṇāśramadharma)* but the inner values and attitudes essential to a meaningful life of spiritual accomplishment. He emphasizes a mix of orthodox and devotional *(bhakti)* values such as scriptural study, austerity *(tapas)*, renunciation *(tyāga)*, faith, the performance of sacrifices, forbearance, purity of heart, compassion *(dayā)*, truth *(satya)*, and self-restraint. He is the mouthpiece of tradition in concluding that "It is said, O king, that dharma is the best in point of merit, that *artha* is the second, and that *kāma* is said by the wise to be the least significant" (XII.161.8).

By contrast, Arjuna is a man of action rather than of reflection, and it is only natural that he would support the goal of *artha*. The world is a field of action *(karmabhūmi)*, and it is *artha* that constitutes the sum and substance of all acts. Without a social order based on material security *(artha)*, there would be no dharma or *kāma*. Nakula and Sahadeva also agree that *artha* must be pursued in a firm and vigorous manner, but they add the important caveat that it must be based on dharma. They thus adopt the middle position that "The first to be practiced should be dharma followed by *artha* based on [the principles of] dharma. Pleasure *(kāma)* comes only at the end, for it is dependent on the successful accomplishment of the other two" (XII.161.26).

At this point we are jolted out of our orthodox comfort by what looks like a defense of sensual pleasure *(kāma)* by Bhīma who is, of course, the embodiment of the impetuous passions of the wind (Bhīma = Vāyu). This turns out to be a false alarm, however, when we realize that he has shifted the focus of debate from the notion of *kāma* as a *goal* of life (that is, a *puruṣārtha*) to the more penetrating and vital truth that "Without desire (*kāma* in the sense of motivation), one would have no desire for worldly prosperity *(artha)*. Without desire, one would have no wish for dharma. One destitute of desire has no wish for anything. It is for this reason that *kāma* is superior" (XII.161.28). He points out that the very sages engaged in austere penance *(tapas)* in the forest are prompted in their activities by *kāma*, not to speak of more ordinary folk engaged in the mundane tasks of life. Everyone in this world is driven by desire and "The man or woman beyond the reach of desire is not, was, and never will be seen in this world. This, O king, is a fact. Both dharma and *artha* are thus based on desire" (XII.161.33). It is the very source *(yoni* = lit. the "womb") without which the various activities of the world would no longer be seen. From these very valid premises he draws the conclusion that "Dharma, worldly prosperity *(artha)* and pleasure *(kāma)* should receive equal attention. The one who attends to only one of them is an inferior person. He is said to be mediocre who devotes himself to two of them. But superior is the one who attends to all three" (XII.161.38). His conclusion makes use of the fact that the term *kāma* is used in the general sense of "desire" and in the more specialized sense of a goal of human activity.

This passage is important in providing the foil for the response of Yudhiṣṭhira in what follows. He has long been caught between the need to protect the legitimate rights of the family and a sincere conviction that war is an unmitigated evil. This conflict is the source of his constant inclination to abandon the kingdom in favor of a life of renunciation in the forest—which has been denied him under the dharma of a warrior-prince *(kṣatriyadharma)*. It is thus easy to understand why he would wish to break the bondage of desire. In his opinion: "The man who is not attached to good or evil deeds; the one who is not attached to *artha* or dharma or *kāma,* who is free of all faults, who looks equally at gold and a clod of earth, he is liberated from all worldly ambitions that are productive of pleasure and pain" (XII.161.42). Interestingly enough, Yudhiṣṭhira uses the very buddhist-sounding term *nirvāṇaparā*—supreme extinction (of all desires), to describe this state of being (verse 44). For him, the state of emancipation *(mokṣa)* is the best of all possible worlds. And, as far as he is concerned, this conclusion has all the force of a divine decree:

> This [view] is the best. We cannot do as we please. I act as I am bound to act. All creatures are governed by divine decree *(vidhi)*. All of you should realize that this divine decree is the greatest influence [that is, in our lives]. What is unobtainable can never be had by means of acts. You must realize that everything happens as it is meant to happen. Even one who is devoid of efforts to achieve the three goals of life, still achieves his ends. Therefore this is kept secret for the benefit of the world. (XII.161.45–6)[13]

Yudhiṣṭhira's negation of action is more a reflection of a natural passivity, a dangerous weakness in a warrior, than a mark of spiritual accomplishment. It will take some heated discussion with family and friends to set him straight, as we shall see in chapter 7.

6

Action and Contemplation

It is apparent that Bhīma and Yudhiṣṭhira represent contrasting poles of the epic spectrum of values. On the one hand, there is the man firmly anchored in the affairs of this world, for whom fulfillment consists in the satisfaction of his desires; on the other, a troubled soul committed to escape from what he regards as an impossible burden. Madeleine Biardeau goes even further in depicting these two personalities as "the two extreme values that command the cyclical 'history' of the universe. Creation occurs to allow individuals to crave for *mokṣa,* and to ensure the continuity of that process, the world of *kāma* should be kept constantly recurring through alternating cosmic days and nights (the cosmic nights being equated to the yogic sleep of the Puruṣottama at the highest level, or of Nārāyaṇa between two *kalpas)*."[1] As an advocate of the world of *kāma,* Bhīma would be a natural ally and sponsor of a desire-driven freedom of doing *(puruṣakāra),* while the more reflective Yudhiṣṭhira might be more conscious of the unfreedom inherent in the very nature of human desire.

In the present chapter we shift our attention from the goals of life *(puruṣarthas)* to the means, in terms of religious practice, by which these goals may be achieved. For what has so far been contrasted in the language of ends (that is, the *puruṣarthas*) finds its practical counterpart in another important distinction that runs through the epic between the *pravṛttidharma,* based on the injunctions and social rules contained in the ritual sections of the Vedic corpus and the Dharmaśāstras, and the *nivṛttidharma* advocated in the Upaniṣads. The former is prescribed for the vast majority of epic humanity bent on the attainment of the worldly satisfactions related to the first three ends of life *(puruṣārthas)*. These satisfactions lead to bondage, and are temporary since they are all conditioned by "Time." The *nivṛttidharma* on the other hand—involving the abandonment of all ritual and social obligations *(saṃnyāsa),* is proposed for those opting for the most radical of the solutions to life, namely the fourth *puruṣārtha* of liberation *(mokṣa)* from the eternal round of birth and death *(saṃsāra).* The rationale behind these two philosophies of life is expressed, as usual, in mythological story form. However, the concepts are radically transformed by Kṛṣṇa in the Bhagavadgītā. In particular, his novel psychology will offer a picture of the epic "person," the stage, as it were, on which this play of *Daiva* and *puruṣakāra* takes place.

The conflicting injunctions of the Veda on the merits of action were clearly a source of considerable confusion and misunderstanding in epic times. As Vyāsa himself must concede, they constitute something of an enigma *(gahvara)* for most people (XII.233.4). And his disciples, including his own son Śuka, find it necessary to ask why the Lord would sanction two dharmas leading to such radically different states of existence (XII.327).

The Mythological Background

As might be suspected, the reason lies ultimately in the yogic nature of the cosmic process whereby the Supreme Divinity emerges from His *mahāsamādhi* to create a new world system at the beginning of each *kalpa.* The *pravṛttidharma* is thus the human counterpart of the active phase *(pra√vṛt* = "to go forth") of the Supreme Divinity in the form of Brahmā (the creator) and Viṣṇu (the preserver). The sacrificial system on which it is based is a form of generalized reciprocity designed to keep the three worlds with their various orders of being in a state of good order and prosperity. The *nivṛttidharma,* on the other hand, corresponds to the destructive phase of the *pralaya* during which the Supreme Divinity returns to a state of quiescence. *Kāma* (desire), the human equivalent of the outgoing cosmic energies, is reabsorbed by the withdrawal of *saṃynāsa.*

The *bhakti*-inspired Nārāyaṇīya section of Śāntiparvan (XII.327) legitimizes these two religious paths in the mythological history of two groups of celestial sages *(suraṣaya),* seven of whom,—the so-called preceptors of the Veda *(vedācārya),* are associated with the *pravṛttidharma,* while the remaining seven—the preceptors of the scriptures on liberation *(mokṣaśāstrācārya),* probably referring to the Upaniṣads, are associated with the *nivṛttidharma.* First among created beings (they are all mind-born sons of Brahmā), the seven *vedācārya* are immediately faced with the issue: how should the entire system of worlds be upheld and kept in operation (XII.327.37)? Since Brahmā himself had no answer to offer, they all decide to seek the guidance of Nārāyaṇa in His unmanifest form as Mahāpuruṣa (that is, the Supreme form of the *bhakti* divinity). But they first have to get His attention (He is, after all, engaged in perpetual *samādhi).* This they do by performing *tapas* for a thousand celestial years, "for the well-being of the worlds," on the northern shores of the Ocean of Milk.

Their devotion has the desired effect. The Lord assigns each a cosmic function and orders a sacrificial system in which each level of being agrees to offer a share of the sacrificial offerings to the level above in exchange for a share in the general well-being that results. Brahmā is established as the *guru* and grandsire *(pitāmaha)* of all the worlds (XII.327.46). The gods receive their respective marks of authority in exchange for the dedication of their sacrificial offerings to Nārāyaṇa. Owing to their propensity for action *(pravṛtti),* these gods are granted the possibility of temporary enjoyments only. These enjoyments include a share in the sacrificial offerings associated with the sacrifices performed by human beings. Significantly, Nārāyaṇa also promises that "I will accord a share *(bhāga)* to whoever gives Me a share of these great sacrifices, (as stated) in the Vedasūtras" (XII.327.55).

In this manner, the deities become the custodians of the world system, and they are supported in this work by the sacrificial activities of humanity. Each level of being supports the other and enjoys the (temporary) fruits that the higher level is able to bestow (XII.327.56–58). Everyone eventually gets back the equivalent of what he or she gives up in the sacrifice—a parallel to the renunciation *(saṃnyāsa)* involved in the *nivṛttidharma,* and a perfect model for a karmic theory of retribution in which one reaps what one sows. On the other hand, such an arrangement does not appear to offer much scope for creatures to choose their own way of life, at least in a single life. Creatures are created for different purposes, some for the active path of *pravṛtti* associated with return *(āvṛtti),* and some for the path of *nivṛtti*—leading to a permanent state of beatitude: "Different creatures have been created for different types of work. But whether [on the path of] *pravṛtti* or [on that of] *nivṛtti* they have no control over what happens" (XII.327.68). The gods themselves are granted control over the acts *(karma)* of creatures as well as over their path and span of life. In the last analysis, it is the Lord Himself who reserves the *nivṛttidharma* for those whose dharma is the indestructible path, that is, the path that yields fruits that are indestructible. At the same time He creates the *pravṛttidharma* to give variety to the world.

In practice, as Vyāsa explains to his son Śuka in an earlier passage (XII.233), the two dharmas were established to cater to the great diversity of need and aspiration among human beings, most of whom are caught in a predicament they are unable to understand, let alone resolve. He replies to his son's questioning as follows:

> These are the two paths upon which the Vedas are based; the dharma characteristic of *pravṛtti,* and the dharma based on *nivṛtti* that have been so well expounded [that is, in the Vedas]. Through [ritual] acts a living creature is bound [that is, to a life of unfreedom]. By means of knowledge *(vidyā),* however, he is liberated. For this reason, clear-sighted yogis never perform [ritual] acts *(karma).* The result of acts is rebirth after death with a body composed of sixteen elements. Through knowledge, however, one is always reborn into that which is eternal, immutable and imperishable. There is, however, a class of persons of the very lowest intelligence whose needs are satisfied through acts. In consequence of this they are trapped in a ceaseless dance of [different] bodies. (XII.233.6–9)

The path of *nivṛtti* is here associated with knowledge *(vidyā),* and leads to a state of existence and experience very different from the path of action:

> The results that flow from acts consist of pleasure and pain, of existence and non-existence. By knowledge, however, one attains to a state of being from where there is no occasion for grief; from where there is no chance of death or rebirth; from where there is no possibility of growing up or growing old; the highest state of that Brahman which is unmanifest, deathless, secure, unrestricted, above the reach of pain, of the quality of nectar, inalienable; where no one is bound by the pairs of opposites *(dvandva)* or troubled by mental agitations. Persons in this state look at everything with an equal eye (here *samāsarvatra)* and revel in friendship and goodwill to all beings. (XII.233.11–14)

While he is not explicit about the role of human initiative *(puruṣa-kāra)* in choosing one path over the other, Vyāsa does suggest that it is somehow linked to what constitutes the source of action itself: "They say that it is the *guṇas* of the conscious individuality *(jīva)* that acts and causes all [bodies] to act. [But] those acquainted with the field of reality *(kṣetravid)* recognize that beyond [the conscious individual] is He who keeps the seven worlds in motion *(pra√vṛt)*" (XII.233.20).

Kṛṣṇa's Transformation of Vedic Values

We compare this response, given to a Brahmin (Śuka), with Kṛṣṇa's response to a similar question by Arjuna, a warrior with caste duties that preclude the traditional Vedic *saṃnyāsa* according to epic tradition.

Vyāsa's commentary on the respective merits of action *(karma)* and knowledge *(vidyā)* is in response to his son's perplexity over the conflicting Vedic injunctions to act *(kuru karma)* and to abandon action *(tyaja karma)* respectively (XII.233.1). Arjuna too is puzzled by the fact that "On the one hand you praise the renunciation *(saṃnyāsa)* of actions, Kṛṣṇa. And then again also Yoga. Please make it clear to me which of these two is the most beneficial" (VI.27/BG5.1)? Kṛṣṇa had introduced the idea of a twofold dharma as early as the second chapter of the Bhagavadgītā (VI.22/BG2.39) by drawing a distinction between the Sāṃkhya and the Yoga systems of philosophy. In the introduction to his commentary on chapter 3 of the Bhagavadgītā, Śaṃkara specifically relates these two paths to the *nivṛttidharma* and the *pravṛttidharma,* respectively. However, in contrast to Vyāsa (and much to the discomfiture of Śaṃkara), Kṛṣṇa specifically comes out in favor of the Yoga of action—*karmayoga,* over *karmasaṃnyāsa:* "Both the abandonment of action and *karmayoga* lead to the highest bliss; but of the two, *karmayoga* is favoured over *karmasaṃnyāsa*" (VI.27/BG.5.2). This change of emphasis has to do with the reversal of Upaniṣadic values brought about by the *bhakti* attempt to extend the prospect of salvation to all (including women). As we have already seen in the case of sacrifice *(yajña),* this involved extending and adapting many of the traditional Vedic notions. As Krishna Chaitanya puts it:

> The concepts of all the systems are closely studied; but because of their insufficincies *[sic],* they are radically transformed, deepened in meaning, integrated into a unitary system of great stability, a world-view to which the most advanced modern thinking in a multiplicity of fields becomes a foot-note. Vyasa's Purusha and Prakrti are not the Purusha and Prakrti of Samkhya; his Karma is not the Karma of the Mimamsakas; his Yoga is not the Yoga of Patanjali. His treatment of the four ends of human existence (purushartha) is radically new.[2]

This is evident in the case of karma. The action advocated by Kṛṣṇa is no longer undertaken for the satisfaction of personal desires but "for the welfare of the world" and for "the benefit of all beings" (VI.25/BG.3.25; VI.27/BG.5.25). Kṛṣṇa has nothing but scorn for the person dominated by attachment to pleasure and power (VI.24/BG.2.43–44). In contrast to the traditional ritual goals of progeny, prosperity, heaven, etc., the practice of *karmayoga* is extended to any action undertaken in a spirit of nonattachment to the results (VI.24/BG.2.47–48). What must be sponsored in the sacrifice *(yajña)* is not personal gain, but the ecological cooperation of the gods *(devas)* responsible for the administration and good order of the cycle of life (VI.25/BG.3.16). What is taken from the natural environment must be returned. Only a thief enjoys the gifts of the gods (that is, the bounties of nature) without offering anything in return (VI.25/BG.3.12), and the person concerned only with his own sense pleasures lives in vain (VI.25/BG.3.16).

This preliminary extension of the Vedic notion of karma as *yajña* is broadened considerably in BG chapter 4 to include the entire gamut of religious practices (VI.26/BG.4.24–33). Kṛṣṇa thus rejects all notion of a physical abandonment of action, pointing out that action is part and parcel of embodied life (VI.25/BG.3.8) and vital to the very existence of the world (VI.25/BG.3.24). However, while all ritual and caste obligations constitute a duty (VI.40/BG.18.9), the actions themselves must be surrendered to the Lord (VI.25/BG.3.30; VI.34/BG.12.6; VI.40/BG.18.57). Performed in this spirit, Kṛṣṇa says, the various activities of life simply melt away (VI.26/BG.4.23).

In this manner, Kṛṣṇa is able to transform action itself into a new form of nonaction (renunciation *in* action) analogous to the traditional *karmasaṃnyāsa* (renunciation *of* action) of the Upaniṣadic *nivṛtti-dharma*—reserved for the traditional Brahmin *saṃnyāsin* in the epic or for the warrior at the very end of his active life (exemplified by Dhṛtarāṣṭra in Book XV or by the Pāṇḍava brothers themselves in Book XVII). According to M. Hiriyanna:

> The negative way of *nivṛtti* still continues to be more or less the same as it was originally, but the positive one of *pravṛtti* has become profoundly tarnsformed *[sic]* by the incorporation in it of the essence of the other. . . . What particularly marks the later conception of *pravṛtti* as distinguished from the earlier, is the *total* exclusion of self-interest from it. It does not aim at merely subordinating the interests of the individual to those of the community, or of any other greater whole to which he may be regarded as belonging, but their entire abnegation.[3]

Furthermore, all of the activities of life performed in this spirit (dictated by one's caste and stage of life) may now become a legitimate spiritual practice *(sādhana)*. Indeed, they are transformed into a form of worship of the Lord: "Whatever you do, whatever you eat, whatever you offer, whatever you give, whatever *tapas* you perform, O son of Kuntī, do this as an offering to Me" (VI.31/BG.9.27). In all he wills and does, Arjuna must henceforth be totally subservient to the Lord.

This higher form of *karmayoga*—dubbed by later commentators as *bhaktiyoga* —is characterized by Kṛṣṇa as the "greatest of all secrets" and "My supreme word" (VI.40/BG.18.64; cf. also VI.31/BG.9.1). The true *saṃnyāsin* is no longer confined to the Brahmin who ritually abandons his caste obligations for a life of mendicancy (VI.28/BG.6.1), but is open to anyone who is a *karmaphalatyāgi* (VI.40/BG.18.11), that is, "one who abandons the fruits of action" (or "one who abandons both action and its fruit" according to certain commentators). The way of salvation is opened to all, including women, tradespeople *(Vaiśyas),* and even to the lower-caste *Śūdras* (VI.31/BG.9.32). All classes can reach perfection by performing their own line of work (VI.40/BG.18.45–46). Even the greatest of all sinners can cross over all sin with this raft of wisdom (VI.26/BG.4.36). Indeed for one with such an attitude: "all actions in their entirety, O Pārtha, culminate in wisdom" (VI.26/BG.4.33).

In this manner, even the acts of the warrior in the most violent war, including the sacrifice of his own life in battle, are promoted to a legitimate way of salvation *(mokṣa).* Conduct that would otherwise lead to bondage and grief (as Arjuna had earlier feared), is transformed into a means of liberation from bondage. The author is no longer soiled by such behavior since his actions are consumed by the "fire of wisdom" (VI. 26/BG.4.19). Biardeau comments:

> We are far from a sanctification of violence pure and simple, even if the result is the same. In effect, it is not enough that violence be a sacrifice for it to be justified and fully salvific for its author. It must also be completely detached. The king is the representative of the supreme divinity, thus a form of *avatāra* on earth, who must watch out for all that threatens the *dharma.* His violence is exclusively in the service of the *dharma,* that is to say of the only order capable of safeguarding the integrity of the three worlds and their place at the center of the universe. On this condition, which implies perfect devotion to the Lord of *bhakti,* his violent acts do not soil him, since he seeks no fruit for himself. Here we leave the orthodox world of the *Manu-smṛti* which is still the world of *kāma,* of egocentric desire. One sacrifices because one desires a certain personal good, albeit only heaven after death. It is this link between the act—*karman*—and the fruit reaped by its author that must be broken.[4]

The Human Complex of Body and Spirit

This transformation of social values is only the surface reflection of what is happening to Arjuna on the more important psychological plane. For, as will become increasingly clear as we proceed, the epic view of the human personality is a key factor in understanding this interplay of destiny and human initiative in the Mahābhārata. Since our Western psychological terminology is based on an entirely different view of the human being, we have, in the interests of greater clarity, appended more than our usual complement of Sanskrit vocabulary to the descriptions of this chapter.

Arjuna's despondency and confused babbling over his dharma point directly to the source of the problem, his identification with that part of himself that derives from the material element of his personality *(prakṛti* in the form of his present incarnation as the body, senses, and mind of Arjuna). This leads him to regard his duty as a warrior *(kṣatriyadharma),* performed in the interests of kingdom and power, as an unmitigated disaster for all concerned. Kṛṣṇa is particularly disturbed by Arjuna's brief flirtation with the idea of abandoning his responsibilities by enjoying the life of a beggar (VI.24/BG.2.5). He knows that Arjuna cannot exchange the battlefield of life for a mendicant existence: "Better the performance of one's own dharma, though deficient, than the dharma of another well-performed," Kṛṣṇa warns him on two occasions (VI.25/BG.3.35; VI.40/BG.18.47). But he understands too, that Arjuna will "get up and fight" only when he realizes the real psychological truth about himself as a human being.

What this real truth is has been a subject of continuing debate down the centuries in both India and in the West. We favor the "qualified nondualist" or Viśiṣṭādvaitic reading of Rāmānuja, since we find that, by and large, his interpretation better reflects the form and content—and certainly the spirit, of the text than, for example, the strictly "nondualist" (Advaitic) views of Śaṃkara.[5] Arjuna's predicament is directly related to his state of embodiment, since embodiment necessarily involves "a fall into the flowing stream of the *guṇas*" (RBG.13.4). As a result, says Rāmānuja, his natural omniscience (that is, as a spiritual entity or *ātman*) becomes veiled by a kind of trick of the mind *(dehātmābhimāna),* and he begins to relate to the things and beings around him with false notions of I *(ahaṃkāra)* and mine *(mamatā*—RBG.3.16).[6] In short, he identifies with that part of himself that derives from the material element of the personality *(prakṛti)* in the form of his body, his senses, and his mind. This identification is reflected in language when one says (identifying with the body), "I am hungry"; or (identifying with the senses) "I am blind"; or (identifying with the mind) "I am happy, sad, angry," etc. (RBG.13.1). The embodied "person" (that is, considered as a composite of spirit and matter—*puruṣa* and *prakṛti)* thus becomes subject to desire, hatred, fear, anger, and other false feelings that prompt him to engage in egocentric activities *(kāmyakarma)* resulting in pleasure and pain and in the formation of unconscious drives or "archetypes" in the mind *(vāsanas* or *saṃskāras).*

These habitual patterns *(pada* = lit. "footsteps") from the past prompt further activity leading to similar situations in the future, perpetuating a vicious cycle of birth and death (cf. RBG.5.15; 7.20; 13.21; 15.7, etc.). In this manner, desire-prompted activity becomes the motive force that drives the entire wheel of life *(saṃsāra),* and constitutes the main cause of the blatant inequalities of embodied existence (RBG.4.14).

The most unfortunate effect of this veiling of the natural light of the *ātman* is that it estranges the resultant personality from its own vital source and makes it impossible, without outside assistance, to escape this abject state of delusion *(moha).* It also veils the fact that the Universe itself is the Body of the Supreme Divinity (dramatically demonstrated in chapter 11 of the Bhagavadgītā), who is also the inner Self of all sentient and insentient things and beings. Although, in fact, inseparable from the Lord Himself, "He" is not part of "his" self-understanding. Arjuna can thus have no experience, or even conception, of the unsurpassable bliss of communion with Him. What Arjuna needs is, first, the basic facts about his own real nature (introduced at VI.24/BG.2.12–30) and then some direction or path that would lead him to the experience of Brahman, the supreme goal of human existence. This is the main topic of the Bhagavadgītā. In the meantime, however, he has no inkling that his own warrior duties—now seen as a recipe for disaster, can serve as a legitimate *sādhana* that provides a far better means of escape from his abject condition than the mendicant life, provided he is able to reverse his attention and attachment from the habitual extrovertedness of his mind through the senses to their objects (that is, the *prakṛti*), to the *ātman* itself.

Kṛṣṇa's Yoga of Transformation

The situation he has brought upon himself through karma can thus be undone through other forms of karma *(karmayoga* and *bhaktiyoga)* based on self-knowledge *(ātmajñāna).* God Himself can be attained only through the higher form of karma known as *bhaktiyoga* (introduced by Kṛṣṇa at VI.29.47/BG.6.47 according to Rāmānuja). Arjuna must first wake up to the vanity of the world and change the direction of his life by abandoning all goals but that of liberation *(mokṣa).* Kṛṣṇa mocks the *vedavādaratha* (VI.24/BG.2.42), that is, the person who delights in the Vedic formulas for securing worldly fruits *(bhogaiśvārya).* He exhorts Arjuna, *nistraiguṇyo bhavārjuna* (VI.24/BG.2.45), that is, be free of the realm of *prakṛti* and its *guṇas,* free of the play of opposites *(dvandva),* free of the desire to have and to hold *(yogakṣema).* Seek the *ātman* alone in all you do! Arjuna must be introduced to a way of transforming himself from an *indriyārāma* (a person attached to the objects of the senses—including his kinsmen in the opposing ranks) (VI.25/BG.3.16) to an *ātmarati,* (one who revels in the *ātman*) (VI.25/BG.3.17). This way passes through the destruction of *ahaṃkāra* and all sense of possession *(mamatā)* that goes with it, by progressively shedding the illusory identity with the body-mind-intellect complex, and with the senses and their objects. These modifications *(vikāra)* of the *prakṛti* are owned by God alone (that is, as His Body), not by any egocentric self.

Having made this initial change of focus, the actual practice of *karma-yoga* can begin in earnest. For once Arjuna has accepted *mokṣa* alone as the goal of life, the worldly ties to action (such as war in his case) will tend to weaken by themselves. He will be less inclined to fret about who wins and who loses, who lives and who dies. The very shift of goals will initiate and facilitate the readjustment of attitude with respect to the conduct and outcome of the war. However, since desire in any form is a form of bondage (even the desire for *mokṣa*), Kṛṣṇa adds the significant warning that "to work alone is your right, never to its fruits" (VI.24/BG.2.47). Arjuna has no choice but to play his preordained role on the stage of life. However, he can play it in one of two ways. He can identify completely with the role he has been given and panic about the outcome. This is a recipe for bondage. Or, he can play it as "he" is in reality—the *ātman,* free of involvement with the role. This is the way of knowledge and freedom from bondage.

He cannot immediately follow this advice completely since he has only an intellectual understanding of his true nature at this stage (provided by Kṛṣṇa at VI.24/BG.2.12–30). However, the very attempt to do so is a *sādhana,* a means of weakening the unconscious drives of the mind *(vāsanas),* and hence of removing the causes of his present state of ignorance *(avidyā)* about himself. However, Kṛṣṇa (according to Rāmānuja) has little faith in the ability of the human species to pull itself up by its own bootstraps (or *puruṣakāra*) and, in the final analysis, the sublimation of these energies into knowledge is the work of the Lord Himself. Rāmānuja comments that "one who strives to conquer the senses with the weight of his own exertions *(svayatna)* and without fixing his mind on Me in this manner, becomes lost" (RBG.2.61). What happens is that "pleased by sacrifices and other such works, the Supreme Self (*Paramapuruṣa,* that is, the "Supreme Divinity") bestows on him the undisturbed vision of the self *(ātmāvalokana),* after eradicating the traces *(vāsanas)* of the actions [of the person] which have accumulated from time immemorial" (RBG.3.9).

The second line of VI.24/BG.2.47: "Be not the cause of action or its fruit; neither be attached to inaction" is of great significance, both for Rāmānuja and for our main topic. The second part of the line is simply another warning to Arjuna against taking the escapist route of false abandonment of action—the rājasic form of abandonment later criticized by Kṛṣṇa (VI.40/BG.18.24). However, the first segment leads directly to our main issue since it deals with the ambiguous status of the agent *(kartṛ)* in a world *(saṃsāra)* of mistaken identity *(abhimāna)*. For if the spiritual nature *(ātman)* is confused into identifying with the body *(śarīra)*, senses *(indriyas)*, and mind *(manas)* that is, with the material element of personality *(prakṛti)*, who then is the actor *(kartṛ)*, and who reaps the fruit of "his" or "her" acts? The warning "Be not the cause of action and its fruit" is, in fact, the first hint of the truth of the matter, which Kṛṣṇa progressively reveals in the following chapters of the Gītā, where He points to *prakṛti* (nature) or to *svabhāva* (character) as the source of all desire to act in the *saṃsāra* (cf. VI.25/BG.3.5; 3.27–28; 3.33: VI.27/BG.5.14: VI.35/BG.13.30: VI.36/BG.14.19).

The first significant statement for our purpose appears where He says: "All actions without exception are performed by the material qualities of nature *(guṇas)*. Deluded by the sense of I *(ahaṃkāra)*, the *ātman* thinks: 'I am the doer' *(kartṛ)*" (VI.25/BG.3.27). Commenting on this verse, Rāmānuja defines *ahaṃkāra* as "the mistaken notion of 'I' in regard to the *prakṛti* which is not the thing denoted by 'I'" (RBG 3.27). The actor is thus not the *ātman* but the qualities *(guṇas)* that make up what we would regard as the personality of the individual, derived from the material element of the human composite (that is, the *prakṛti*). So powerful is this belief in one's own personality that even the man of knowledge *(jñānavan)* is forced to follow the dictates of the *vāsanas* and confront his two enemies of love and hatred *(rāgadveṣau)*. As Kṛṣṇa points out: "living creatures follow their nature *(prakṛti)*. What use is there to fight it" (VI.25/BG.3.33)? And these inner drives have nothing to do with the Lord Himself, since "The Lord of the world is responsible neither for agency *(kartṛtva)*, nor the work performed *(karma)* of [the people of] the world, nor for the link between work and its results *(phala)*. It is the nature *(svabhāva*, that is, of a person) that is responsible" (VI.27/BG.5.14). Rāmānuja explains that

> Agency *(kartṛtva)* and the other factors [that is, work performed (karma) and the results *(phala)*] have nothing to do with the intrinsic nature of the *ātman (ātmasvarūpa)* but are the result of unconscious drives *(vāsanas)* arising from the mistaken identity *(abhimāna)* of the *ātman*, on account of the entanglement *(saṃsarga)* with *prakṛti* in the form of gods, men, etc., born of a karmic inheritance *(pūrvapūrva-karma)* stretching back to beginningless time. (RBG.5.14–15)

In effect, the various embodiments of the *ātman* act out their natures *(svabhāva)* as a direct result of this accumulation of inherited tendencies *(vāsanas)* leading to further activities (karma) in a perpetual cycle of error. In the words of Rāmānuja:

> Knowledge is veiled *(āvṛta)*, that is to say, contracted *(saṃkucita)* by the accumulation of previous karma opposed to knowledge, contracted in this manner in order that the aspirant *(sādhaka)* might reap the experience of his own fruits *(svaphalānubhāva)*. As a result of this karma, which forms a veil over knowledge *(jñānāvaraṇarūpa)*, union with the bodies of gods, etc. and delusion *(moha)* in the form of the false identification *(abhimāna)* of the *ātman* with these bodies is produced. In this manner, there arise the *vāsanas* of the false identities of the *ātman*, and the *vāsanas* in favour of karma suitable for them. From these *vāsanas* arise the mistaken identity *(abhimāna)* of the *ātman* with that which is contrary to it [viz., the body], and the initiation of activity. (RBG.5.15)

And thus the cycle is perpetuated.

However, since these agents ultimately belong to the transcendent Lord who owns them as His Body, the ultimate seat and source of all action must be in Him alone (as the Inner Self and Controller of all beings). Kṛṣṇa therefore makes the further suggestion that Arjuna free himself of all anxiety over the battle by surrendering all actions to Him with a mind [identified with] the *ātman* (VI.25/BG.3.30). In effect, the technique *(sādhana)* proposed by Kṛṣṇa is an attempt to reverse the focus of the mind through abandonment of the three most important causes of bondage, the sense of agency involved in the action *(kartṛtva)*, the action itself (karma), and its results *(phala)*.

The rationale for this is briefly summarized by Rāmānuja in his commentary on Kṛṣṇa's remarks at VI.40/BG.18.4. The first part of this three-part advice is designed to eradicate the sense of doership (I do) in the action by attributing the source of all activity to the *guṇas* or to their ruler who is the Lord Himself. Thus: "abandonment *(tyāga)* of the sense of agency *(karttvaviṣaya)* is abandonment [of our own idea] of ourselves as an agent by attributing all agency to the Lord." The second part of the teaching is designed to eliminate the sense of ownership *(mamatā)* in something that can only belong to the Lord. Thus: "abandonment of the activity itself *(karmaviṣaya)* is the complete abandonment of the sense of possession *(mamatā)* with respect to the action, thus abandonment [of the idea] that this action belongs to me and is the means *(sādhanatā)* for the realization of my own ends *(phala)*." Finally, abandonment of the ends *(phala)* should involve the notion that "Abandonment of the results [is the idea that] the fruits *(phala)* that result from action such as heaven and so forth should not be mine." The results clearly belong to the Lord who resides in the heart of all beings (VI.40/BG.18.61).

In this manner, the practices and techniques proposed by Kṛṣṇa together constitute a sophisticated program of "deconditioning" designed to introduce Arjuna to his real self, that is to say, to his *ātman* that exists in an inseparable relation *(apṛthaksiddhi)* to the Lord Himself. As he progressively detaches himself from his identification with the material constituents of his nature (that is, with the *prakṛti* and its *guṇas*), he will begin to act in the world in the knowledge that it is not "he" that is really acting, that "the *guṇas* act among the *guṇas*" (VI.25/BG.3.28). These *guṇas* will certainly compel him to act in the world (VI.40/BG.18.59–60). But with a being that has, to a large extent, been purified *(ātmaśuddha)* of the *vāsanas,* he will henceforth express the quality of *sattva* in his actions and fight without attachment, in total submission to the avatar (VI.40/BG.18.23).

In place of the traditional practices that constitute the *pravṛttidharma*—the desire-prompted rites and activities *(kāmyakarma)* that keep the world in being (albeit at the cost of entrapment in the cycle of the *saṃsāra),* Kṛṣṇa thus substitutes a new dharma of unattached action *(naiṣkarmya)* leading to liberation *(mokṣa)* from the cycle of rebirth. The principle of abandonment *(saṃnyāsa)* is internalized by detaching it from its traditional associations with caste and stage of life *(varṇāśrāmadharma)* and building it back into the individual psyche as a set of attitudes by which all of the functions of life and society must henceforth be undertaken. The traditional opposition between *pravṛtti* and *nivṛtti* is resolved by linking the goal of liberation *(mokṣa)* to the active principle. In doing this, however, the individual must abandon the sense of autonomy he possesses within the traditional *pravṛttidharma* (that is, that it is "I" who acts). The human being is a unity of *puruṣa* and *prakṛti* (with the Lord Himself in the "heart"), but the driving force behind all action is the *guṇas,* which are modes of the *prakṛti.* Until this is understood Arjuna will be unaware of his true individuality, the *ātman,* and must consequently experience the effects of his conduct and character in the form of pleasure and pain. His real goal is the Supreme Divinity in the "heart" *(hṛdi)* who "permits" the action to take place. Of course Arjuna does not yet know this since his consciousness is still "veiled" from the truth (VI.35/B.G.13.21–23). This compartmentalized anthropology necessarily leads to a denial of all agency in human action together with the action itself and its results. Such conditions hark back to the Upaniṣadic path of *nivṛtti* as exemplified in the discourse of Vyāsa on behalf of his son Śuka.

In light of these considerations, we might expect to observe a tendency for the epic author to extol the merits of human exertion *(puruṣakāra)* in the context of the traditional *pravṛttidharma*—that is to say, activities undertaken in pursuit of the three worldly ends of human existence (dharma, *artha* and *kāma*), and ignore it when the attention shifts to sages and seers who have already transcended the cycle of *saṃsāra*. This is, indeed, what we find. Clearly, if (as at XII.330.16): "the greatest dharma and the highest felicity for anyone to attain is extinction *(nirvāṇa)* [that is, of individual consciousness by dissociating oneself from *prakṛti*]," the notion of human agency or effort, a major part of the problem, will be understated (as at VI.35/B.G.13.28–33).

Some Alternative Views

The most noteworthy examples given by Bhīṣma in the Mokṣadharmaparvan section of Book XII are taken from stories of demons who attain *mokṣa* as a result of reflection on the adversities of the embodied state (defeat at the hands of the gods in their case). These beatified demons (no doubt chosen to highlight the point) all exhibit a stoic resignation before a world that brooks no human (or demonic) tampering with its ineluctable course. But this is a quietism *(nivṛtti)* of detachment rather than one of despair. We have already noted the case of Prahlāda (XII. 215) who traces the source of action to inherent character *(svabhāva)*. But other grounds for human activity are not lacking, including Śāstṛ (the Ordainer) or Dhātṛ (the Bestower), "Time," and chance controlled by a divine overseer (*prabhu*, lit. "the boss"), and Viṣṇu-Nārāyaṇa, the Supreme Lord of *bhakti* devotionalism.

The example of Namuchi (XII.219) is perhaps the most extreme; a demon totally reconciled to his loss of celestial prosperity and powers at the hands of Indra. There is indeed little cause for sorrow and self-pity if

> There is one Ordainer (Śāstṛ or "divine lawmaker") and no second. His control extends to the human being resting in the womb. Controlled by the Ordainer, I continue down the path to which I am confined, like water running down an inclined slope. Though fully cognizant of the merits of both existence [that is, as a *jīva* or "embodied soul"] and non-existence [that is, liberated from this condition] and knowing full well which of the two is to be preferred, I do nothing [to achieve either of these states]. Leading my life according to the dharma resulting in pleasure or otherwise, I go on as I am impelled to do. Whatever one is to achieve will be achieved and whatever destiny (*bhavitavyam* or "that which is to be") awaits one is what one gets. Again and again we are placed in whatever conditions of birth the Bestower (Dhātṛ) so wishes without the slightest choice in the matter. But one is never upset if, having achieved a certain state of being, one is always able to adopt the attitude of, "This is what has to be" *(bhavitavyam)*. People are governed by alternating periods of pleasure and

> pain. There is only sorrow if one thinks, "I am the agent" *(kartṛ)*. (XII.219.8–13)

And he concludes by saying:

> I will suffer the consequences of whatever the Bestower (Dhātṛ) decided before I was born. [Under such conditions] what can death do to me? One achieves the success that is due to one; one goes wherever one has to go; one experiences the joys and sorrows that are one's lot in life. Knowing what it is that creates the false impression of agency, a man is indifferent to pleasure and pain and becomes master of all circumstances. (XII.219.21–23)

The demon Bali (now living as an ass in an empty room after losing the sovereignty of the three worlds) takes a similar position by attributing all change of fortune to the workings of Time *(kāla)* and chance *(yadṛcchā)*, both of which are really only extensions of the Supreme Divinity (XII.216–217; 220). He first warns Indra not to flaunt his newfound prosperity by reminding him that "It is 'Time' *(kāla)* that gives all and takes all. Everything is ordained by 'Time.' Do not brag about your great manliness *(pauruṣa)*, O Indra" (XII.217.25). The new Lord of heaven is mistaken in attributing what has occurred to his own doing, since "What we have now become, O Indra, is not because of anything we have done. Nor is your present fortune, O Indra, due to anything you have done. You have done nothing, O thunderbolt-wielder, by which you are now enjoying this affluence; nor have I done anything by which I am now divested of this affluence. . . . It is 'Time' that maintains everything, and it is also 'Time' that destroys all things" (XII. 217.35–36, 39).

These conditions are subsequently attributed to chance in a passage in which the claim is made that "I am not the agent—*kartṛ* [of acts that appear to be mine]; nor are you the agent of other acts [that appear to be performed by you], O Lord of Śacī. It is chance *(yadṛcchā)*, O Śakra, that governs the worlds" (XII.217.45).

Finally, however, all agency is attributed to a divine overseer who controls the forces of "Time" and of chance: "I am not the agent; nor are you the agent. It is the 'Lord' *(prabhu)* who is always the agent. Thus it is 'Time' *(kāla* being synonymous with *prabhu)* that ripens me like a fruit emerging from a tree" (XII.220.84).

The evident tension between these two paths is well illustrated in the story of Vṛtra, a well-known Brahmin demon who falls foul of Indra's ambitions and is eventually killed by him with the help of Viṣṇu and Śiva (XII.270–273). The account of the spiritual education of Vṛtra (the so-called Vṛtragītā) is first introduced by Bhīṣma to reassure Yudhiṣṭhira (who wishes, as usual, to abandon his duties for a life of *saṃnyāsa)* that there will someday be an end to his tormented life. Since all things in this world come to an end, and even the cycle of rebirth must have an end, he is able to tell the king that "Your efforts, O knower of the dharma, will pull you through in time. But always [bear in mind], O king, that the embodied soul *(dehin = jīva)* is always the author of its merits and demerits [resulting from his activities in the world]. And it is from the darkness *(tamas,* that is, of ignorance) that envelops him that these [merits and demerits] come about" (XII.270.7–8).

This cryptic statement reminds Bhīṣma of how Vṛtra first failed the test of his guru (his knowledge being limited at this point to the immediate consequences of the *pravṛttidharma*), whereupon he is exposed to the wisdom of the sage Sanatkumāra about the extended wanderings of the soul *(jīva)* through the seven world-systems over a period of many *kalpas*. Most noteworthy is what he reveals about the role of action (karma and *pravṛtti*) in this immense spiritual pilgrimage to the abode of Viṣṇu. Whatever the practices undertaken for this purpose (scriptural study, *tapas,* sacrifice, etc.), they are far from useless (as some might claim) since the soul

> attains the infinite reaches of these higher worlds by relying on external practices *(karma)* and acts of mind to purify his (nature) with his own understanding *(buddhi)*. Just as a goldsmith, through repeated effort *(atiprayatna),* is able to purify the [unrefined] metal by [repeated castings of the metal into] the fire, the soul is likewise able, as a result of his noble activities, little by little to purify itself over the course of some hundreds of births. Some, with great efforts *(yatna)* may even succeed in purifying themselves in the course of a single birth. (XII.271.10–12; see also XII.194.11)

Reference to "purification" probably refers to the elimination of mental habits *(vāsanas)* that have accumulated from time immemorial. He is thus driven to conclude that "In this manner, problems *(doṣa)* arising from attachment to the *guṇas* [that is, to the charms of the material element of the world—*prakṛti*] are dispelled by the understanding *(buddhi)* over the course of some hundreds of births by dint of repeated efforts *(yatna)*" (XII.271.16).

Human effort is thus given a role but only insofar as the *ātman* is not yet "cleansed" of the inherited tendencies arising out of its false identification with the *prakṛti*. This emphasis on the cleansing nature of noble [that is, sāttvic] acts is a recurrent feature in the epic, exemplified by Kṛṣṇa's description of "the yogin who, abandoning attachment, performs actions with the body, the mind, the intellect, and even with the senses, for [the sole purpose of] purification of the *ātman*" (VI.27/BG.5.11; see also VI.40/BG.18.5). In such a case the goal is not self-indulgence *(kāma),* worldly success *(artha),* or the practice of dharma for the sake of temporary relief in heaven or in the next life (with the prospect of further entanglement in the *saṃsāra*) but the experience of *mokṣa* in the form of inseparable union with the Lord Himself. Vṛtra is thus told that he "should know that this entire universe is under the control of one divine being. The unity of all the various creatures is implied in this fact, O prince of demons. A living being who sees this [unity] as a result of wisdom *(jñāna)* is imbued with noble qualities *(sattva)*" (XII.271.28–29). This divine being is the infinite Viṣṇu, the author of the universe propelled by the wheel of time: "Listen, O demon, to this complete account [lit. "this all" *(sarvamidaṃ),* a word also used for "universe"] of the supreme greatness of Viṣṇu. Know, O scorcher of foes, that the entire universe is supported by Viṣṇu. It is He who engenders the teeming throng of mobile and immobile creatures, O mighty-armed one; and, in the course of time, it is He who destroys them, and once again brings them into existence" (XII.271.7–8).

This leads to the conclusion that the fruit of all action undertaken in the embodied state ultimately leads to a new self-understanding whereby the *ātman* shifts its vision, from the material embodiment with which it has long been identified, to Nārāyaṇa (= Viṣṇu) Himself. The fruit of all action, as well as the fruit of all renunciation of action is thus conceived as Nārāyaṇa Himself. In this manner He is the fruit of action *(karmaphala)* as well as the fruit of nonaction *(akarmaphala)* (XII.271.24–25).

7

The Path of the Warrior

The foregoing analysis suggests that epic attitudes to human action are dominated by two separate perspectives. From the cosmic vantage point, *puruṣakāra* is the product of a fictional ego-identity *(ahaṃkāra),* whose existence is predetermined by the ignorance *(avidyā)* that invests it with reality: "He is the actor, and He is what has to be accomplished" (*sa kartā sa karyam* Cf. XII.327.89; also XIII.143.12). On the other hand, as active subject in confrontation with an objective world, this fictional ego-identity enjoys some control over itself, as well as over the course of events in the world "out there." *Akaṃkāra* literally means "I do" (from *aham* = "I" and √*kṛ* = "to do"). This raises questions about the reality of *puruṣakāra,* its ultimate source (one's character, the "Lord in the heart," "Time," etc.), and its scope of effectiveness. At the same time, we are told that liberation itself remains dormant in the absence of a pure mind, and that it is only through right action that purity of mind can be achieved. This suggests that action is the key to bringing changes in the inner as well as in the outer world.[1]

Such issues are never raised directly, and certainly do nothing to dampen the epic's enthusiastic support for *puruṣakāra* in its concern over the tendency of kings to abdicate the responsibilities of their office, their *rājadharma.* Yudhiṣṭhira in particular needs the constant reminder that "the dharma consists in the administration of justice, O king, not the shaving of the head" (XII.24.30). The *Kṣatriya* path does not involve the renunciation of the Brahmin *(nivṛtti)* which would be the "dharma of another," but the active path of renunciation-in-action, the *pravṛtti-dharma* advocated by Kṛṣṇa in the Bhagavadgītā. A king who turns away from confrontation (as Arjuna was initially tempted to do) or from his royal duties (as Yudhiṣṭhira is inclined to do throughout) becomes an object of censure. *Puruṣakāra* may be founded upon a mistaken identity, as suggested in chapter 6, but it is strongly endorsed for the warrior-king as the key to both worldly and spiritual achievement.

Debate over *puruṣakāra* arises primarily in connection with family differences over Yudhiṣṭhira's character and policies.[2] As events unfold, his atypical (for a *Kṣatriya*) passivity appears more and more to belie the promise of his name, "firm in combat." We have already had a taste of his hankering after *mokṣa* at the end of chapter 5. Eventually, this "son of Dharma" becomes the storm center of a conflict between two dharmas, between his responsibilities as householder and king (that is to say, his duties according to the traditional *pravṛttidharma*), and his natural preference for the *nivṛttidharma*. This fault line in his character is dramatically revealed in the pressure of the war's aftermath by a sudden shift from the one dharma to the other, as Yudhiṣṭhira makes a final bid to abandon his rule in favor of the life of a forest sage. As Norbert Klaes has pointed out:

> Thus Yudhisthira stood before the dilemma that the renunciation of his kingdom was sinful according to the law and that war, the means of regaining the kingdom, was sinful according to his conscience. . . . The problem was, which dharma ruled in which way: whether the caste-dharma prevailed by the active destruction of the anti-social *adharma* or the ethical dharma by its own moral strength converting *adharma* into dharma and thus guaranteeing the order of society.[3]

This chapter will focus on three occasions when family arguments come to a boil over this pacifist streak. They have all been chosen for what they reveal about epic theories of action and particularly on the importance of *puruṣakāra* in the life of the king. The first instance is sparked by Draupadī during the first year of exile, that is to say long before any inkling of the catastrophe to come. Yudhiṣṭhira has no desire to abandon his rightful claim to the throne at this point, but neither is he prepared to abandon the undertaking to remain for twelve years in the forest. The second occasion is a message from Kuntī, Yudhiṣṭhira's mother, conveyed to Yudhiṣṭhira by Kṛṣṇa after the failure of the latter's last diplomatic mission to the Kauravas prior to the outbreak of hostilities. Her strong call to arms helps galvanize him into marshaling the Pāṇḍava forces (V.149.3). The third occasion is prompted by Yudhiṣṭhira's crisis of conscience after the war is all over. He is so appalled at what has happened that he wishes to abdicate the throne and repair to the forest. His family is understandably appalled, leading to a lengthy debate about the moral and practical consequences of abandoning action. The resolution of this latter conflict—more significant by its insight and intensity, leads directly to the questioning of Bhīṣma concerning the *rājadharma* that Yudhiṣṭhira had wished to abandon. Bhīṣma thereupon continues to extol the merits of *puruṣakāra* by various commonsense arguments in traditional story form, two of which are included in the present chapter.

Draupadī's Impatience

Ironically, the dispute with Draupadī (III.27–33) is sparked by concern over the most appropriate policy to adopt for recovering the worldly life and kingdom he will subsequently wish to abandon. It occurs while the brothers and their common wife are residing at beautiful Lake Dvaitavana, portrayed as an idyllic time of social concord when the Vedic chants of the Brahmins blend in perfect harmony with the "song of the bowstring" (that is, of the *Kṣatriyas*). In short, we once again have a scene like the world of Brahmā himself. This is reminiscent of a Golden Age *(kṛtayuga)* for which Yudhiṣṭhira might be expected to have a natural affinity (III.27.2ff.). In fact, the very contrary is the case, and we find them all mired in grief. One evening, Draupadī turns to Yudhiṣṭhira to inquire how it is possible, under the circumstances, that he has no anger for the Kauravas. A *Kṣatriya* without anger is unheard-of in her experience, but Yudhiṣṭhira is just the opposite (III.28.34): "Why doesn't your anger grow?" she asks repeatedly. A *Kṣatriya* is expected to show his mettle *(tejas)*. This is a time for revenge, not forgiveness, and she seeks to drive the point home with an old discourse on the subject between Prahlāda and Bali Vairocana (III.29).

After listening to Yudhiṣṭhira extolling the merits of patience *(kṣamā)*, and finally concluding that it is the "eternal dharma of those who have mastered themselves" (III.30.50), her own patience runs out. She begins to berate him for the kind of dharma he protects (which certainly smacks of the *nivṛttidharma*), but which—as she points out, has been incapable of protecting *him* (III.31.8). How could the situation arise in which, all of a sudden, he is seized with the spirit of gambling? She suddenly recalls an old legend that leads her to conclude that he is somehow in the power of the Dhātṛ who, she has been told, manipulates all living creatures like wooden dolls. Human beings have no control over themselves or over others, since the Dhātṛ operates from within their bodies and uses them as mere instruments to realize his own good or evil purposes (III.31.24–30). Spreading confusion with his powers of illusion *(māyā)* he plays with their fortunes like a child with its toys (III.31.31–36).

Now this, too, sounds like a pure *nivṛtti* theory which Yudhiṣṭhira would later be inclined to adopt. At this early stage, however, this "son" of Dharma is appalled at what he considers to be heresy *(nāstika)*. He defends his policy of appeasement with a strong appeal to the need for governing standards of morality, in this instance the governing standards of the traditional *pravṛttidharma* of his caste and station of life (he describes himself as *gṛhānāvasata*—"a person established in a household"). He himself obeys this dharma not for its rewards *(phala)* however, but because it is his very nature *(svabhāva)* to do so (III.32.4).[4] Famous seers and teachers greater than the gods have all reached their positions of eminence and power through strict adherence to this dharma. Casting doubt upon it and upon the motives of the Dhātṛ is thus a dangerous course. Without some kind of standard, human beings would each become standards unto themselves and, driven by desire and greed, fall into hell. Nor can there be any doubt about acts bearing fruit, since if the various religious practices laid down by the Veda were without effect, it would be the greatest hoax of all time, and the men of old would have abandoned them (III.32.25–26). As J. Bruce Long has noted:

> Yudhiṣṭhira counters Draupadī's condemnation of God with essentially the same message as that delivered to Job by the voice in the whirlwind: "*Dharma* always bears [appropriate] fruit . . . [and] is never fruitless. . . . The fruition of acts, good as well as bad, their appearance and disappearance, are the mysteries of the gods."[5]

The wizardry of the gods is obscure, but neither the dharma nor the gods should be doubted just because the results are not seen. In the words of Brahmā to his sons: "work has its rewards—this is the eternal dharma" (III.32.37). The dharma (here the *pravṛttidharma*) should under all circumstances be obeyed, and Draupadī should abandon her lack of faith.

Yudhiṣṭhira's vigorous defense of the merits of action seem strangely at odds with his prevailing mood. It nevertheless forces Draupadī to abandon what was, in effect, a *nivṛttidharma* perspective (III.33). She does not, of course, really understand either position (she admits that she is babbling from grief), but what she now says is revealing, if a trifle confusing. She is now willing to admit—repeating what she once overheard from a Brahmin visitor to her father's house, that the survival of all living things is dependent on effort (the word she uses is *utthāna*): "Do your own duty and do not slacken"; for one's task is to increase and to preserve what one has. Without action the whole system of life in the world would collapse. The key to success is motivation (*karmabuddhi* or "thought in the act"), not fate *(diṣṭa)* or chance *(haṭha)*, since "Whatever happens to a man from the combined effects of chance *(ha-*

ṭha), destiny *(daiva)* and character *(svabhāva),* as well as from the work put into it (karma) is the result of his previous conduct *(pūrvakarma)*" (III.33.18).

This sounds like the classical karma theory that one reaps what one sows, except that the Dhātṛ is brought in to apportion the results (III. 33.19).[6] This intervention from above seems at odds with the following two verses, which make it clear that the seed of action germinates in the human mind: "One [first] makes up one's mind *(manas)* on what one wants (the *artha*) and then acts on it. Basing himself on prior deliberation *(buddhipūrva),* the cool-headed man *(dhīra)* is thereby the cause *(kāraṇa,* that is, is responsible) for what follows. While it is not possible to provide an exact accounting of the [chain of] acts involved, social progress is the result of human choice" (III.33.23–24). However it turns out that the Dhātṛ is required to weave these three causes into a single effect, and "If he did not exist, none of the creatures would be wanting in anything whatsoever. A man could perform an act to achieve whatever purpose he had in mind" (III.33.33–34). She also reveals that the means *(upāya)* for achieving the intended result is decided by evaluation *(dhī,* that is, of the alternatives), but we can never know what part of the final outcome is due to our own efforts *(puruṣaprayatna)* since we do not enjoy a complete view of how the chain of causes are linked (III.33.19–31).

Whatever happens, however, the most important thing is to act, since there is glory even in failure, provided that the act was well planned and executed. If the monsoon fails after the peasant has tilled the soil and planted the seed, what fault is it of his? The smart man thus uses his intelligence to evaluate the conditions of place and time *(deśakāla),* applying various means *(upāya)* according to his strength and capacity *(śakti),* and not forgetting an appeal to "good luck" (III.33.44–49). These arguments of Draupadī do apparently have the desired effect on this occasion, since Yudhiṣṭhira is later reported to have agreed to slay Duryodhana and "enjoy the earth" (cf. XII.14.8–11). As Madeleine Biardeau suggests: "Throughout this dialogue, the princess evidently plays the role of *śakti* for the king. This is well within the logic of her personality, the human projection of the Goddess, the active element in the creation but at the same time (within the logic) of philosophy."[7]

Kuntī's Exhortation

Yudhiṣṭhira's compliant approach to the impending crisis later becomes the subject of an impassioned plea by his mother Kuntī shortly before the outbreak of hostilities (V.130–134). This is clearly intended to awaken his latent *puruṣakāra* and energize him to action. She begins by rating him an ignorant fool, the likes of a scholar *(śrotriya)* with nothing but a rote understanding of the Veda (a reproach later repeated by Bhīma). She even calls him a "failure." She feels he must be weaned away from the "single dharma" he is following (presumably *nivṛtti*), and galvanized into a more aggressive stance: "Come now! you should observe the dharma promulgated by God Himself (*svayaṃbhu* or "The Self-existent"). The warrior caste was born from his chest to live by the strength of its arms, to act forever harshly for the protection of the people" (V.130.7). In other words, he should follow the *pravṛttidharma* of the *Kṣatriya* attested by the primal sacrifice described in the *Puruṣa-sūkta* hymn (Ṛkveda X.90). She reminds him of his caste duty *(varṇa-dharma)* that "The Brahmin should live as a mendicant, the *Kṣatriya* should protect, the *Vaiśya* should generate wealth, and the *Śūdra* should serve the rest of them" (V.130.28). And she further buttresses her argument with the significant *pravṛtti* answer: "To the question: 'is it the time that is the cause of the king or the king the cause of the time?' you should have no doubts. It is the king who is the cause of the time. It is the king who initiates the *kṛtayuga* (Golden Age), the *tretāyuga* and the *dvāparayuga,* and it is also the king who is the cause of the fourth age [that is, the *kaliyuga*]" (V.130.15–16). This pronouncement is, of course, the exact opposite of what the *nivṛtti* response to such a question would be, and echoes similar statements made in the Rājadharma section of Book XII (for example, XII.92.6; XII.139.7).

She also exhorts him further with an ancient chronicle called "Victory" to be heard by "one who wishes to triumph" (V.134.17). This is cast in the form of a dialogue between Vidurā and her son Saṃjaya (completely demoralized by defeat at the hands of a Saindhava king). Vidurā provokes him to action in no uncertain terms, telling him to stop wallowing in self-pity and to have some backbone. When a man shows courage he has nothing to be ashamed of, since success or failure is not a matter of concern to the learned (V.131.15). It is superiority over others that is the measure of a man, whether in sacred knowledge, *tapas,* good fortune, or gallantry. But most important for a *Kṣatriya* like her son is her significant warning: "Do not pursue the contemptible existence of a mendicant, vile, dishonorable, wretched, practised by people of dubious reputation" (V.131.23). She continues further with this not-so-subtle snub addressed no doubt at certain Brahmins and their *nivṛtti* ways, by saying that without desirable possessions a man soon becomes a nonentity "like the Ganges flowing into the ocean" (V.133.16). This is, of course, a common image employed in the Upaniṣads (that is, in the *nivṛttidharma*) to symbolize the dissolution of the ego in a man of realization; it is here employed in the pejorative sense of one lacking in ambition. By contrast, a man is called *puruṣa* because he is a match for a city (*pura* in Sanskrit). Instead of lying down like a beaten dog, "the time has come for action," she tells him (V.133.5). To fight and to win is the task of the *Kṣatriya* on this earth, and "to act forever harshly for the protection of the people" (repeating the third line of V.130.7 just quoted) (V.133.11). She admits that the fruits of action provide only temporary relief, but "Those who know that it [that is, the fruits] is impermanent may prosper or they may not. However, those who do nothing never get anywhere. Apathy *(anīhā)* has but one consequence—nothing; exertion *(īhā)* has two. There is either a result, or there is not" (V.133.24–25). The right attitude is always to think, "it will be" *(bhaviṣyati)*. Her admonitions finally lead Saṃjaya to announce that he will rise up, subdue his enemies, and win victory (V.134.14). Once again Yudhiṣṭhira is moved to exercise his *puruṣakāra*.

Yudhiṣṭhira's Grief

As already mentioned, Yudhiṣṭhira's latent desire for *saṃnyāsa* reaches its peak immediately after the war is over and the enormity of the destruction hits home. In contrast to Arjuna whose personal crisis had been resolved before the onset of hostilities, Yudhiṣṭhira becomes paralyzed by grief and a sense of guilt when it is all over. This is due to the fact that the victory he had gained as a king "was a complete defeat for him as a man, since he was disloyal to his own nature."[8] In particular, he must come to terms with the knowledge that it was his own covetousness, and not his caste dharma *(kṣatriyadharma)*, which was responsible for the deaths of thousands of brave warriors, including his elder brother Karṇa. As Krishna Chaitanya notes, his fault had been "personal aggrandizement through the acquisition of a realm that could be regarded as a personal possession, not a trust involving great moral responsibility."[9] This triggers his growing propensity to abandon all worldly responsibilities, and, addressing Arjuna, he muses on what might have been: "If we had led a life of mendicancy in the cities of the Vṛṣṇi and the Andhaka, we would not have come to this sad end by sending our kinsfolk to extinction" (XII.7.3). He directs his anger and remorse squarely against the *Kṣatriya* values, and bursts out: "Fie on *Kṣatriya* practices, fie on might and valor and wrath, all of which have brought us to this calamity" (XII.7.5). Further indictment of the evils of war, and the disclosure that grief is the only legacy of his initial hatred and anger at the enemy, is followed by his announced intention of leaving for the woods: "Therefore, Dhanaṃjaya, disregarding the pairs of opposites, I will go to the woods, O scorcher of foes, and become a *muni* dedicated to the path of knowledge" (XII.7.36). In effect, his natural propensities have led him to abandon the *pravṛttidharma* of the *Kṣatriya* and to adopt the *nivṛttidharma* of the Brahmin. This is tantamount to the "rājasic abandonment" already condemned by Kṛṣṇa (VI.40/BG.18.8), as well as involving "the dharma of another," also condemned by Him (VI.25/BG.3.35; VI.40/BG.18.47). The assembled company of family and friends, plus various important sages who had come to offer consolation and comfort to the king, are understandably appalled.

The subsequent debate between him and his well-wishers is reminiscent of the dialogue between Kṛṣṇa and the despondent Arjuna at Kurukṣetra. It is important in showing the inevitable convergence of ideas between *puruṣakāra* and the various dharmas associated with the warrior king *(pravṛttidharma, kṣatriyadharma,* and *rājadharma),* as well as throwing into sharp relief the differences in character and worldview of the various interlocutors. The discussion has a tendency to drag on in slow motion, but the reader who manages to stay the course will note that Yudhiṣṭhira's interlocutors are forced more and more into philosophical arguments about human action in general, and about the vital necessity for the king (and, by implication, for other human beings) to exercise his initiative *(puruṣakāra)* in the administration of justice *(daṇḍa),* and for his own future self-development and happiness.

First Intervention of Arjuna

The first to speak out (XII.8.5–36) is Arjuna who, as might be expected, makes the point that without material well-being *(artha),* there can be no religious life at all. He begins by asking rather pointedly why, after performing the dharma of his own order well enough to win the entire earth, Yudhiṣṭhira now wishes to throw it all away. Why then did he slay all these kings in the first place? If he abandons the kingdom now to adopt the miserable life of a mendicant, what will people think of him? Making no provision for the morrow may be all right for a recluse, but Yudhiṣṭhira has been born into a race of kings, and the dharma of a king *(rājadharma)* depends entirely on material prosperity. Indeed, practically everything in life—religious duties (dharma), sensual pleasures, heaven, courage, anger, learning, and human dignity, are all grounded in material prosperity *(artha),* the purpose of which is to perform sacrifices. The very gods have acted in this way, slaughtering their own kinsmen (that is, the demons) in the process. He suggests that Yudhiṣṭhira should perform a horse sacrifice as a means of cleansing himself and his subjects (XII.8.5–37).

Needless to say, this line of argument does not sit very well with Yudhiṣṭhira (XII.9.4–36). Rather than the course advocated by Arjuna, he would abandon the pleasures and practices of men and wander the forest, living with the animals on fruits and berries, and performing the strictest *tapas*. Looking to others like a blind and deaf idiot (which the others no doubt think he is already), he plans to live contentedly by deriving happiness from his own soul. Why do this? He says it is all the result of his reflection on the conditions of existence. He sees how human beings are caught in relations of cause and effect by everything they do in life, such as looking after their wives and children and supporting their kinsmen. And when it is all over and they leave this world, the consequences, good and bad, must then be born by them alone. No one else is responsible. This makes him realize that "In this manner, doing what they have to do, the world's creatures all come into this wheel of life *(saṃsāracakra)* that resembles the wheel of a chariot. Coming here, they meet with their fellow-creatures. Whoever abandons the *saṃsāra*—which is worthless and insubstantial, being soon afflicted by birth, death, old age, disease, and pain—is a happy man" (XII.9.32–33). When even the gods and great sages in Heaven itself stand to fall from their positions of power and eminence, what better then, on the strength of this nectar of wisdom, than to opt for what is permanent, eternal, and secure? Needless to say that this is a pure *nivṛtti* argument.

Intervention of Bhīma

It is now Bhīma's turn to brand his elder brother "an ignorant fool of a *śrotriya* (scholar) with nothing but a rote understanding of the Veda" (XII.10.1). He repeats the verbal jab made by his mother Kuntī before the war. Why tell us all this now, after a battle that could otherwise have been avoided? He acts like a person who gets covered in mud from digging a well but refuses to drink the water. Other similar unflattering comparisons are made. However, the main thrust of his argument is that a king should fulfill his responsibilities. He points out that "It has been laid down that *saṃnyāsa* is to be adopted [by kings] only in times of distress, when defeated by foes, or overcome by old age. Therefore, the wise do not approve of renunciation *(tyāga)* in this case. Indeed, those that understand the subtleties of things believe that such [a course of life] involves a violation of the dharma" (XII.10.17–19). And he ends with the significant statement that "Just as success in life is won on the strength of one's own good fortune and not on that of another, you should do your own duty (that is, and not that of another). Success is not achieved by doing nothing" (XII.10.26). And Arjuna enters here with a story to the effect that true *tapas* can be obtained only through a life of domesticity (XII.11.20).

Intervention of Nakula and Sahadeva

The baton is then passed to Nakula who carries this theme a step further (XII.12). One who adopts the next mode of life by abandoning his responsibilities as a householder is an *ātmatyāgi* (that is, one who abandons his own true self). The domestic mode is the foundation of all the other modes of life. When the four modes were once weighed in a balance, he claims, it required the three other modes on one scale to balance it on the other. But more importantly—and here the discussion moves to another level, the true renouncer is not the one who escapes to the woods, but the one who fulfills all his domestic duties in the right spirit: "It is said, great king, that the action undertaken in a spirit of vanity is not productive of fruit; but that those acts that are performed in a spirit of renunciation *(tyāga)* are productive of abundant fruit" (XII.12.15). If Yudhiṣṭhira wishes to renounce his wealth, he should perform sacrifices, such as, the *rājasūya* and the *aśvamedha*. A king is the very embodiment of Kali who does not provide for his subjects. The true yogi is the king who abandons all internal and external attachments, not the one who abandons his worldly responsibilities for a life in the woods.

This argument is, of course, strongly supported by his twin brother, who pronounces what amounts to a sentence of death on the selfishness and greed of the Kauravas: "Let the dharma and happiness of him who has cast off external objects while still inwardly coveting them be that of our foes. On the other hand, let the dharma and happiness of him who has cast off all internal attachments also be that of our friends. Death is a two-letter word, [while] the Eternal Brahmā is a three-letter word. Death is [the two-syllable word] mine *(mama)*; Eternity is [the three-syllable word] not-mine *(namama)*" (XII.13.2–4).

Draupadī, too, puts in a word here (XII.14.8–34). She recalls what he had planned while in forest exile at the Dvaitavana lake and reminds him that friendship toward all creatures, charity, study of the Scriptures, and *tapas* constitute the dharma of the Brahmin, not that of a king. It was not by study, gift-giving, mendicancy, or sacrifice that he has won the earth. She even goes as far as to suggest he is out of his mind and in need of medical treatment.

Second Intervention of Arjuna

Arjuna once again urges the king to look to the natural course of things and take up his duties. Social order is dependent on the threat of punishment *(daṇḍa)* administered by the king. There is no way that one can live without inflicting some injury to others. In fact, the whole universe with its mobile and immobile creatures has been ordained by the gods to be food for living beings. There is no point in getting upset by it; "you must adjust to the role you have been given, O king" (XII.15.23). Even in the woods he would be killing living beings. His task is to protect his subjects by a judicious application of the *daṇḍa,* which constitutes the root of all civilized life. Our acts are dependent on our level of material prosperity *(artha),* but this in itself is dependent on the *daṇḍa* of the king. It is *daṇḍa* alone that prevents matters from degenerating into the law of the jungle. Better by far to injure from righteous motives than not to injure from fear of sin, for there is no act in this world that is wholly meritorious or wholly sinful. There is something of both in every act. In any case (as Arjuna himself recalls [VI. 24/BG.2.19]), we must remember that whoever is slain in this process, is not really slain.

Additional Family Interventions

Bhīma uncharacteristically chimes in at this point with a more profound philosophical observation; that his elder brother now has a battle on his hands even more critical than the battle just fought with Bhīṣma, Droṇa, and his other enemies. This is the battle for his own mind, which, if he does not conquer before he dies, will bring him back to this earth to fight these very foes again (XII.16.20–23). This provides Yudhiṣṭhira with an opportunity for some well-chosen words about Bhīma's notorious appetite for food and for the pleasures of the world (XII.17.6–22). Appetite for worldly things has no bounds. Only those who have renounced all enjoyments and have subdued the demands of their bodies by *tapas* can attain to the highest state of beatitude. He challenges Bhīma to free himself from the great burdens of dharma and *adharma* with which the nature of kingship is invested. Enjoyments in this world are a form of bondage, and have also been called action (karma). The highest state is attained only when one is liberated *(vimukta)* from both enjoyment and action. He recalls the words of King Janaka of Mithilā who reportedly made the claim that "Truly immense is my wealth, yet I have nothing. If the whole of Mithilā were reduced to ashes, nothing of mine would be burned" (XII.17.18). Human beings have a faculty of understanding *(buddhi)* that should be used to rise above the obvious and come to a broader understanding of the whole. The way to Brahmā is to see the one homogeneous essence behind the infinite diversity of things.

The argument on the respective merits of *pravṛtti* and *nivṛtti* continues when Arjuna wryly observes that Yudhiṣṭhira must have forgotten the serious doubts raised by Janaka's wife about whether Janaka did, in fact, truly abandon his attachment to the things of this world (XII. 18.20–34). If it is true as you claim (she challenges Janaka) that the kingdom and a handful of barley are all the same to you, what basis then your desire to abandon the kingdom? And what has become of your duties as householder (as support to your wife and family) and king (as support to the true mendicants who depend on you for their existence)? Only those who are "unattached in the midst of attachments," who are independent of the world, who have broken their bonds, and who look on friend and foe with an equal eye, are truly liberated. And this apparently does not apply to the king in his present life. His place in the scheme of things has been ordained by the very fact of his birth as a *Kṣatriya,* and his prospects for *mokṣa* will depend on the spirit in which he is able to fulfill the role he has been given to play in this life. She therefore exhorts Janaka to keep his senses under control and "win the worlds, O king" (that is, the interim rewards of heaven) by supporting those given to his charge.

Yudhiṣṭhira is not yet prepared to accept any of this (to his mind, misleading) advice, particularly from a younger brother (XII.19.3–21). He responds in a rather patronizing tone by suggesting that Arjuna may well know all there is to know about the art of weaponry and the practices of heroes, but he has little sense for the Scriptures. He proceeds to give Arjuna a short pep talk on religious practice, although "you may have difficulty understanding it." Although most people look for salvation in the wrong places, there is indeed a path, the path of knowledge, which leads there. What purpose, then, in relying so much on material prosperity *(artha),* which leads to all sorts of problems?

Intervention by Sage Devasthāna

With neither side prepared to budge from their original positions, the discussion is showing signs of degenerating into a dialogue of the deaf. One of the assembled sages, Devasthāna, decides that the time has come to resolve the issue once and for all (XII.20.3–14). The parties have only part of the truth they claim for their respective positions. Salvation is no doubt the goal of all existence, but having won the whole earth according to the dharma (that is, the *rājadharma* of kings), "you should not abdicate on impulse, O king." And he lays down an important criterion. A king should pass through all four modes of life that have been laid down by the Veda, one after another. His role is to perform great sacrifices involving large amounts of material wealth *(artha)* in the form of *dakṣiṇā*. He further points out that "those who take their stand in action" (here using the term *karmaniṣṭha*) are to be found in the ranks of the sages themselves.

The truth is that "The Bestower (Dhātṛ) created wealth for sacrifice, and he designated human beings to take care of it. For this reason, the whole of one's wealth should be applied to the performance of sacrifice. Pleasure *(kāma)* will follow soon after" (XII.20.10). For this reason everything should be offered in sacrifice. It is the satisfaction that comes from mastering both desire and aversion that human beings are seeking above all else (XII.21.2–4). However, the ways of achieving this are many and various. Some opt for a life of tranquillity, others for an active life, some conduct sacrifice, others renunciation *(saṃnyāsa),* charity, indulgence, meditation *(dhyāna),* sovereignty, or just prefer to be alone. But one born to rule should vigorously (*prayatnena* = "with effort") practice the dharma laid down by Manu, keeping himself forever in control without preference for what is dear and what is not. The extinction of all desires *(nirvāṇa)* is difficult to achieve and attended by all sorts of obstacles, the implication being that Yudhiṣṭhira is not yet ready for such a path. Yudhiṣṭhira should not grieve for what is past (Arjuna interjects). In any case, death in battle is the highest sacrifice for the *kṣatriya. Tapas* and *tyāga* are the duties of the Brahmin (XII.22.4). Rather than wallow in remorse he should "Be ready for action." Having conquered the earth he should now conquer himself *(vijitātmā)* and perform sacrifices on the model of Indra.

Intervention of Vyāsa and Other Sages

Judging the time is right for him to throw the weight of his considerable authority behind these arguments, Vyāsa now also intervenes in support of the domestic mode of life (XII.23). What Arjuna has just said is true. The forest life has not been ordained for him, and Yudhiṣṭhira should shoulder the burdens of his ancestral kingdom like an ox. He reiterates the leading principles of the *kṣatriyadharma,* which include, significantly, exertion (here *saṃutthāna*) and "discontent with present prosperity," meaning Yudhiṣṭhira has more work to do before he is ready for the contentment *(saṃtoṣa)* that Devasthāna suggests is the goal of life. He emphasizes that the real misery of his forest exile has ended. Stretching before him is a period of happiness in which he can enjoy the material rewards of life (dharma, *artha,* and *kāma*) with his brothers (XII.25.4–33). Only after he has fulfilled his obligations to the mendicants, the ancestors, and the gods, will he be ready to practice other modes of life. In the meantime, he should perform the *sarvamedha* and the *aśvamedha* sacrifices, and see to it that his subjects—particularly the Brahmins, are well taken care of. Human initiative *(puruṣakāra)* is particularly important since "It is not contrary to the dharma, O Yudhiṣṭhira, if an act is performed with vigor *(pauruṣa),* after due deliberation, and with the good counsel of men well-versed in the scriptural ordinances. Human enterprises succeed or fail on account of destiny *(daivata)*. However, if the king acts with initiative *(puruṣakāra)*, he is free of sin *(enas)*" (XII.25.20–21). To make his point, Vyāsa recounts the story of King Hayagrīva who is now sporting in the heavenly world *(devaloka)* after pouring his own life-breaths onto the field of battle in the great sacrifice of war.

But with the lamentations of the wives of the dead heroes still ringing in his ears, Yudhiṣṭhira finds little joy at the prospect of earthly sovereignty, and Vyāsa decides he must raise the level of the discussion (XII.26.5–32). He quotes from what appears to be a traditional adage of some kind (the meter changes from *anuṣṭubh* to *triṣṭubh)*:

> Nothing is achieved by action or thought, nor is anything given to another. The Ordainer (Vidhātṛ) has laid it down that the course of time be the means of acquisition *(yoga)*. Man acquires everything through time. No desirable object can be obtained by intelligent planning or scriptural study if the time is not ripe. There are times when even a fool can enjoy material prosperity *(artha)*. For "Time" is indifferent with respect to results. In difficult times neither technical skills nor *mantras* nor medicinal herbs will give the desired result. In good times, on the other hand, these same acts, if well-prepared, are favoured by "Time" and achieve success. (XII.26.5–7)

This is not, as it appears to be at first sight, a denial of *puruṣakāra* (which he will endorse soon enough). What Vyāsa seems to be saying here is that things happen in this world in cyclic fashion, modeled on what we would now call the "laws of nature." The examples he provides include the cycle of the seasons, the diurnal cycle of day and night, other motions of sun and moon, of the tides, etc. Happiness and sorrow alternate in a similar pattern, and there is thus no point in indulging in grief if things do not turn out the way one expects. Ignorant fools or spiritual masters may enjoy happiness here, but the vast majority of us have to accept these conditions. And, of course, those who are upset at other people's problems will clearly never be happy. Translating the *kṣatriyadharma* into the forms of religious practice, he says: "To be an aspirant for battle is said to be the sacrifice for a king; due attention to the science of punishment *(daṇḍanitī)* in the kingdom is his Yoga; and the *dakṣiṇā* payments in the sacrifice are his "renunciation" of wealth. These should all be known as acts that sanctify him" (XII.26.32).

When Yudhiṣṭhira continues to blame himself for the deaths of so many of his kinsmen, and even threatens to starve himself to death (XII.

27.25), Vyāsa intervenes once again to advise that "all this is destiny" *(diṣṭa),* since "Life-forms entering this world are sure to pass through stages of union and dissolution. Like bubbles in the water, they exist for a time and then they are gone. All things composed of parts are sure to be destroyed and all things that rise are sure to fall. Union ends in dissolution, and life ends in death" (XII.27.28–29). On the other hand: "Idleness, though pleasant in the beginning, ends in sorrow; right effort, though painful in the beginning, ends in happiness. Affluence, prosperity, modesty, fortitude, and success, do not proceed from idleness" (XII. 27.30). In other words, without troubling himself about the grand scheme of things that happen as a result of the very nature of the world, Yudhiṣṭhira should focus instead on making the best of his own responsibilities. Happiness and misery do not depend on what happens in the world, but on the *attitude* taken to the role one is called to play. And in Yudhiṣṭhira's case: "Son of Kuntī, do what the Dhātṛ has ordered for you. Success abides in work alone. You are not capable on your own, O king" (XII.26.32).

Further authority in support of these themes is offered in the Aśmagītā that follows (XII.28). It is useless to grieve for those who are dead and gone. The circumstances in which he finds himself have all occurred as a result of "Time." "Wonderful is the course of 'Time.'" Creatures meet and separate like logs on the ocean or travelers at a wayside inn. We have no lasting companionship with our own bodies, let alone with those of others. Yudhiṣṭhira is therefore once again exhorted, in a phrase reminiscent of Kṛṣṇa's exhortation to Arjuna at VI.26/BG.4.42: "throw off your grief and rise up" to fulfill your dharma as householder and king! But all to no avail.

Similar positions taken by Kṛṣṇa and Nārada also fail to strike a responsive chord in the despondent king (XII.29–31). This wisdom and good advice about the true dharma of kings is all well and good, Yudhiṣṭhira agrees, but his conduct of the war was motivated by more than just a royal duty to ensure that justice be done (XII.32). It is his covetousness and desire for rulership that are the real source of his despondency. He killed not because it was his duty to do so, but "for the sake of sovereignty." Vyāsa thus realizes the need for more radical arguments to deflect his sense of guilt. He therefore goes directly to the heart of the moral issue by seeking to show that this sense of responsibility is misplaced. For who is really responsible for human action and for what happens as a result of it?

This, of course, brings him directly to a discussion of our theme, and we will, therefore, cite the relevant passage in full:

> Is it the Lord who performs the action or is it the man himself? Is everything that happens in the world the result of chance *(haṭha)* or is it to be considered the result of [previous] action, Bhārata? If human beings, O king, are driven to perform good and evil actions by the Lord, then the responsibility for them [*phala* = "for the results"] should belong to the Lord. For if a man cuts down a tree in the forest with an ax, it is certainly not the ax that incurs the sin *(pāpa)* but the one who does the cutting. Alternatively, the ax being only the material cause, the responsibility *(phala)* for the action could be attributed to the man who made the instrument of punishment *(daṇḍaśastra)*. This, however, is hardly credible. If this [untenable position] that one should assume the responsibility *(phala)* of an act undertaken by another be rejected, son of Kuntī, then, on this basis, the responsibility should be assumed by the Lord. If, on the other hand, the human being himself is the perpetrator *(kartṛ)* of all his good and evil acts, then there is no higher [that is, no Supreme Lord], and you may do whatever you find appropriate [that is, without incurring sin]. There is no way, O king, that anyone can avoid destiny *(diṣṭa)*. But, [by the same token] it is not fair to attribute the responsibility (*pāpa* = "sin") to "him who fashioned the means of punishment" *(daṇḍaśastrakṛta* [that is, Yudhiṣṭhira is in the same position as the man who made the ax that cut down the tree]). If, O king, you believe that the world is ruled by chance *(haṭha),* then it is clear there is no such thing as an evil deed, and there never will be. If you need to know what is good and evil in the world, look to the scriptures. There it has been laid down that kings should stand with the *daṇḍa* uplifted in their hands. I think, O Bhārata, that actions continually revolve in this world, and that men receive the fruits of the good and evil deeds [that they do]. (XII.32.11–20)

The implication of these lines is that we are not punished *for* what we do (since we are either not responsible for our actions in the first place, or, if we are, there is no one above that judges us), but we are punished *by* what we do (since we will inevitably experience the causal effects of our past actions as they "continually revolve"—*sam-ā* √*vṛt*— in this world). This karmic argument is, of course, designed to urge Yudhiṣṭhira to perform his scriptural duties, that is, according to the *pravṛttidharma* of kings *(rājadharma)*: for Vyāsa adds, significantly, that even if the acts themselves are reproachable, the king should still adhere to his own dharma (that is, his *rājadharma)* and then perform the necessary expiations *(prāyaścitta)*.

Unfortunately, Vyāsa muddies the waters of this karmic doctrine by bringing in the instrumentality of Time *(kāla)*. In reply to Yudhiṣṭhira's self-incriminating allegation that he is guilty of an infinite sin (XII.33.11), he argues (XII.34.4–12) that it was "Time," not any human being (and certainly not Yudhiṣṭhira) who was responsible for this killing. It is "Time" that distributes the just deserts of the good and bad actions of creatures, working through other creatures. The responsibility, in fact, must be attributed to the dead soldiers themselves, since it was their own past acts which (through the instrumentality of "Time") were the cause of their demise. Yudhiṣṭhira himself is totally blameless, being forced by the faults of others to act in the manner he did. In effect, says Vyāsa, he was forced to it by fate itself *(vidhi)*, adding: "This universe moves by actions controlled by 'Time' in a manner similar to that of an instrument made by a carpenter which is under the control of the person handling it" (XII.33.10).

Although created by the Supreme Carpenter, it is again "Time" that controls the operations of the Universe (presumably because the Divinity in his Supreme State is forever absorbed in *samādhi*). The message, however, is clear; whatever the cause, it has nothing to do with Yudhiṣṭhira (in verse 11 the responsibility is further shifted to "chance" or *yadṛc-chā*). However, if he persists with this insidious entanglement of the heart, he may, if he still so desires, perform an act of expiation such as a horse sacrifice. After a detailed review of the available expiations (XII.34–37), Yudhiṣṭhira is finally persuaded to cast off his grief and anxiety (XII.38.28).

Bhīṣma's Instructions

As Vyāsa had predicted, Yudhiṣṭhira now begins "to enjoy a period of great happiness" (XII.42.12). Following the coronation (XII.41) and the *śrāddha* rites for the dead warriors (XII.42), Kṛṣṇa urges him to seek the guidance of Bhīṣma about the obligations of the traditional *pravṛtti-dharma* (XII.46.22). As a veritable treasure-house of the ancient wisdom of king-craft *(rājadharma)*, this grandsire is the key link in the chain of transmission to the new generation, and Kṛṣṇa does not wish to see this go to waste with his passing. Bhīṣma loses no time in emphasizing the importance of *puruṣakāra* in the life of the king (he tends to use the word *utthāna*). It is, indeed, one of the four major topics in which he divides the *rājadharma*.[10] From the very first question (XII. 56.2), Bhī-ṣma is very specific about its importance, insisting: "Yudhiṣṭhira, you should always be ready to put forth effort *(utthāna)* my son; for without the merit of exertion, destiny *(daiva)* is not a sufficient condition to realize the purposes *(artha)* of kings. While both exertion *(utthāna)* and destiny are causal factors, I believe that exertion *(pauruṣa)* is superior, for destiny is said to be governed by it" (XII.42.14–15).

And a little later he quotes three verses reportedly spoken by Bṛhas-pati, the priest of the gods:

> Bṛhaspati has said that the exertion *(utthāna)* of kings is the very foundation of the duty of kings *(rājadharma)*. Listen to the verses pronounced by him. "It was by exertion that the nectar *(amṛta)* was obtained; it was by exertion that the demons were slain; it was by exertion that Indra won the sovereignty of the heavens and the earth. The man who acts decisively is greater than the man of strong words alone. The great men of words [that is, the Brahmins] worship and revere those who act decisively. For the king who is destitute of exertion *(utthāna)*, even though possessed of intelligence *(buddhi)*, is always overcome by his enemies like a snake bereft of poison." (XII.58.13–16)

Somewhat later (XII.120), Yudhiṣṭhira asks Bhīṣma to summarize the key points to make it easier for him to remember them, and Bhīṣma once again emphasizes the merits of exertion:

> Knowledge, *tapas,* great wealth, and indeed everything else is possible through exertion *(vyavasāya)*. As it occurs in embodied creatures, exertion is governed by Brahmā. For this reason, exertion *(vyavasāya)* is regarded as of utmost importance. Here [that is, in embodied beings] is where reside many intelligent creatures such as Indra, Viṣṇu, Sarasvatī and other beings. No sensible person should thus ever dismiss [the importance of] the body. (XII.120.43–44)

Although the power of exertion still derives from within, there is more than a hint that, in this case, it comes not from the individual himself, but from various spiritual beings that have taken up residence within him.

The Tale of Brahmadatta and Pūjani

To further illustrate the importance of exertion, Bhīṣma recounts a conversation between King Brahmadatta and the bird Pūjani on the subject of trust (XII.137.45–80). Brahmadatta argues for a continuation of their friendship, in spite of the fact that his friend has just put out the eyes of his son in revenge for the unfortunate slaying of Pūjani's son by the young prince. He is prepared to exonerate the bird on the strength that it is really Time *(kāla)* that is responsible for every act: "Who, therefore, injures whom?" he asks. If neither of them is the cause of the other's sorrow, there is no reason why Pūjani should not continue to live at the palace as before.

But Pūjani is too astute to be taken in by this line of reasoning. If "Time" be the cause of all acts, no one would harbor any feelings of animosity toward anyone else. Why, then, he asks, do friends and family seek to avenge one another? Why, indeed, did the gods and the demons slay each other in days of yore? If it is "Time" that is the cause of happiness and misery and birth and death, what need is there of medicines for the sick? More importantly, how could dharma be acquired through human agency? The animosities they bear for each other cannot be washed away in a hundred years. Putting one's trust in the injured party (Brahmadatta in this instance) would be the height of folly and lead to great misery.

While it is common sense to avoid doing certain things (walking with sore feet, opening sore eyes against the wind, etc.), there are many occasions when action is indicated, and Pūjani concludes that

> Destiny *(daiva)* and exertion *(puruṣakāra)* exist in mutual dependence on each other. Persons of good character take acts to be essential, while the impotent pay court to destiny *(daiva)*. Whether it be harsh or mild, a person should act in his own interests *(ātmahita)*. The unfortunate man of inaction *(akarmaśīla)* is always overtaken by all sorts of problems. Therefore, even in dubious affairs, one should exert oneself energetically. Abandoning all else [in the sense of concentrating on the task at hand], people should do what is in their own interests. (XII.137.78–80)

Needless to say, Pūjani follows his own advice about acting in his own interest by leaving the palace never to return.

The Tale of the Jackal and the Vulture

These attitudes are further elaborated in the conversation between a jackal and a vulture. Effort *(prayatna* or *yatna)* must be supplemented by confidence in one's own abilities and steadfastness of purpose. In this story, the parents of a dead child finally obtain the grace of Śaṃkara (= Śiva) to revive their dead son. This is due to the advice of a jackal (with his own interests at heart) who is made to say: "One should always put forth effort *(yatna)* for, when done, [efforts] become successful according to destiny *(daiva)*. Destiny and human exertion *(puruṣakāra)* come into fulfillment through the results of previous actions. Things should be undertaken with confidence. How can there be happiness in despondency? For prosperity *(artha)* can be won only through exertion *(prayatna)*. Why go so heartlessly" (XII.149.46–47)?

The Relative Strengths of Destiny and Exertion

Yudhiṣṭhira finally comes directly to Bhīṣma with the question: "which of the two is the most powerful, destiny or human exertion" (XIII.6.1)? Adding the weight of orthodoxy to his own considerable authority, Bhīṣma responds with a most interesting twist to traditional imagery in the form of an old legend entitled "The relative strengths of destiny and exertion," purporting to be Brahmā's answer to a similar query by the sage Vasiṣṭha. Brahmā here uses the important metaphor of seed in a field to suggest that, while *daiva* (here characterizing current conditions as the effect of the past) is fruitless without human effort *(puruṣakāra)*, it also forces us to confront our circumstances and serves as an important goad to further effort in the direction of inner transformation and change. They are thus seen to depend on each other: "Just as the well-prepared field remains fruitless without the seed, so without individual effort *(puruṣakāra)* destiny *(daiva)* is of no avail. But the field is [also] said to be the effort, while the seed is the destiny [that is, which prompts it]. It is from the union of the field and the seed that the harvest is produced" (XIII.6.7–8). This reversal of the traditional imagery of the field and the seeds has been noted by Krishna Chaitanya whose observations will be taken up in chapter 8. What is important to observe here is that the quality of the fruits, when they come, appears to depend entirely on the quality of the seed in the form of human effort rather than destiny: "The farmer reaps the fruits, good or bad, as he sows the seed in his field" (XIII.6.6).

As already indicated, *puruṣakāra* in the sense of the inner power to act is, of course, also a necessary condition for any theory of individual moral responsibility. Brahmā introduces what looks like the beginnings of such a theory in what follows, claiming that "It is for all the world to see that the doer reaps the fruits of the actions he performs, as well as of those he does not perform; that noble actions lead to good while evil actions lead to sorrow; that actions performed always produce results but have none if not performed" (XIII.6.9).

But he quickly returns to what is his first interest: to demonstrate the value of individual initiative in the pursuit of human needs and ends: "By applying oneself, one is able to acquire beauty, good fortune, and riches of various kinds. Everything is possible through work (karma) but not through destiny *(daiva)* by one without initiative. Heaven, worldly enjoyments, and all the desirable things of the earth can be acquired by well-directed individual exertion" (XIII.6.12–13). Work is the secret of the success of all those who have attained to high status, including such beings as the heavenly bodies and the gods. Different types of activity are prescribed for the various castes—pure living for the Brahmin, prowess for the warrior *(vikrama* is placed ahead of *puruṣakāra* in this case), initiative *(puruṣakāra)* for the *Vaiśya,* and service for the *Śūdra.* Men would become mere idlers if events happened through destiny alone.

And Brahmā now reveals the real purpose of *puruṣakāra,* namely, that it "allows for the development of innumerable virtues." In effect, it strengthens the moral worth and spiritual development of the individual. We recall that this "practice of virtue" is one of the methods sponsored by Kṛṣṇa in the Bhagavadgītā to attain *mokṣa.* But this is not all: the greater the moral worth of the act the more likely it is to achieve its purpose. Due to a constant rivalry between men and gods (who fear our growing powers) *puruṣakāra* and *daiva* are forever at odds in this world. However, the gods are forced to give way before the superior merit of the person who acts. This harks back to the earlier Brahmāṇic belief that the gods are forced to act through the power of the sacrifice. The (rather convoluted) text is as follows:

> Applied [in the right manner], *puruṣakāra* enhances *daiva;* but when not properly applied, *daiva* [alone] leads to nothing whatever. When we see that the positions of even the deities themselves are not eternal, how can destiny remain stable [for anyone who is] without action (karma)? The gods do not always lend their support to the pursuits of others. Fearing their own demise, they put great difficulties in the way of others. [In this way] there is constant rivalry between the gods and the sages. It is thus not true to say that *daiva* does not exist, since it is *daiva* that moves everything else. What, then, is the purpose of this (that is, human initiative) if it is *daiva* that moves everything? The answer is that it allows for the development of numerous designs, even in the heavenly spheres (lit. "the thirty-three worlds"). We are our own friend and our own enemy, and we are also the witness of what we have done and not done. Whatever happens in terms of good or ill is accomplished through work (karma). But work is not sufficient to achieve everything one desires. Merit is the refuge of the gods. Everything is attainable through good deeds. For a man of righteous behavior, what remains for *daiva* to do? (XIII.6.22–29)

By an ironic twist of *daiva,* it is just such petty jealousies that challenge us to cleanse the soul *(ātmaśuddhi)* with the moral acts *(puṇya)* that enhance our chances of success (through *puruṣakāra*) in the mundane and spiritual realms. This also suggests that the true measure of the "success" of any enterprise is not the outcome (for the act could fail) but the act's motivation and one's nonattachment toward the result. It is in this sense that we are "our own friend and our own enemy."

8

Action and Retribution

In spite of Yudhiṣṭhira's anomalous position for a *Kṣatriya* there seems little doubt that *puruṣakāra* is a valued asset for all four classes (including the majority of orthodox Brahmins) who, by their birth and natural disposition, are fitted for an active role in epic society *(pravṛtti)*. And for the king it is regarded as absolutely essential. Bhīṣma repeatedly warns Yudhiṣṭhira that a king cannot abandon his responsibilities without dire consequences. Nevertheless, as already noted from the remarks of Kṛṣṇa and from other more advanced souls, this obvious practical importance masks a doubt about its basis in reality. We are told that the soul *(puruṣa)* does not act; only the material component *(prakṛti)* of the personality *(jīva)* acts, conditioned by the qualities *(guṇas)*. The mythological material adds to the confusion by hinting at inner connections between *puruṣakāra* and *daiva*. The various gods who inhabit our bodies may enhance initiative (for example, "the Lord in the heart of all beings" [VI.40/BG.18.61]) or, more commonly, they may destroy it by provoking doubt, confusion, or inner conflict.[1]

We have also noted a constant shift of focus between the many who act in the world *(pravṛtti)*, and the few who seek to merge back into the all-embracing unity of the Divine Consciousness *(nivṛtti)*. From the unitary perspective, all action and desire is governed from on high: "He is that desire *(kāma)* that exists in every creature and every state of being, O king. He is the one who forever moves within the hearts of both gods and demons" (XIII. App. I. No. 6.164–165; cf. also VI.29/BG.7.11). From the personal perspective of the ego it is "I" who is responsible for moving me either toward the world *(pravṛtti)* or toward the Divine Source *(nivṛtti)*.

Finally, we briefly introduced the important role of the dharma as a guide to conduct, which included a role for the "gods" (that is, for

Daiva) in apportioning the debits and credits we accumulate as a result of our various moral choices. These choices are not always easy since the prescriptions of the Dharmaśāstras can take us only so far. It is then up to us to know what the dharma is in a given situation. Even Bhīṣma is forced to admit (and he should know) that this dharma is "subtle *(sūkṣma)* and has many branches without end."[2] The present chapter will examine some of the passionate debates on this subject for what they reveal of the progressive internalization of these gods to produce a more person-centered morality based on the doctrine of karma. Past behavior *(pūrvakarma)* is the new watchword that is substituted for the activity of the gods, leading the way to the emergence of a more morally autonomous "person" in classical India.

Puruṣakāra as Moral Autonomy

We begin with what, even for the epic, is an early period. In the famous story of the origins of the Kuru dynasty, Śakuntalā calls upon the gods in condemning Duḥṣanta's refusal to acknowledge their son Bharata:

> You think you are alone with yourself, but are you not aware of the ancient seer *(muni)* in your heart; the one who knows your evil deeds? It is before him that you speak this false testimony. An evil-doer always thinks, "no one knows me." But the gods and his own inner man know him. Sun, Moon, Wind, and Fire, as well as Heaven and Earth, Water, and his heart and Yama, and Day and Night, and Dawn and Dusk, and the dharma—all know the character of a man. When the knower of the field *(kṣetrajñā = ātman)*, the witness of all actions in the heart, is content with a person, Yama Vaivasvata destroys the evil that one has perpetrated. But when the *ātman* is not content with the wicked man [in whom it dwells], Yama snatches away the evil-doer himself. (I.68.27–31)

Here it is the *ātman* of the man himself who is the final judge. However, it is Yama who dispenses justice. Yama's role probably stems from the long-standing ritual idea that the gods return a share *(bhāga)* of what they receive in the sacrifice.[3]

It is not clear whether divine retribution would follow from a human action prompted by the very gods themselves, or by an impersonal *daiva*. However, the thought of humans paying the price for what, in effect, are divine manipulations, would be the height of injustice to an inquiring mind. The patent absurdity of such a situation may have contributed to the birth and growing popularity of a more logical solution; the notion that the vicissitudes of life are not due to the machinations of any god (or to *daiva)* but to our own actions in the past, whether performed in this or in some previous life: "Judged by historic standards, the Karma theory did much to raise man's status and to wean him from coaxing gods through sacrifice and prayer."[4] One of the earliest formulations of the effect of past action and behavior on present conditions, is the statement of the Bṛhadāraṇyakopaniṣad: "As a man acts, as he behaves, so does he become. Whoever does good, becomes good: whoever does evil *(pāpa),* becomes evil. By good works a man becomes holy *(puṇya),* through evil [works] he becomes evil" (Br.Up. IV.4.5). However, Haridas D. Bhattacharyya is no doubt correct in arguing that: "The doctrine of Karma had neither a single beginning nor a single growth. All through its history, it has assumed diverse forms according to the emphasis laid upon its different elements, and to-day it is difficult to say which is the pure form and which the debased."[5] In the "pure" form of this karma doctrine often found in the philosophical literature, it was accepted that

> every act, whether good or bad, produces a certain result or return which cannot be escaped. In the physical world there is the universal law of causation. The doctrine of Karma extends this inexorable law of causality to the mental and moral sphere. . . . This doctrine of Karma emphasizes three things; firstly it regards an existence as a sort of expiation for the doings of a previous existence or existences; secondly, an evil deed cannot be expiated by works of merit but its punishment must be borne; thirdly, the punishment for wrong is automatic and personal. Under the doctrine of Karma there is no such thing as chance or luck.[6]

It is evident from the epic material that there is a logical, if not perhaps strictly chronological, development of these ideas. Let us therefore proceed by looking first at a number of mixed formulations that recognize a link with past acts, but that introduce an external catalyst of some kind (a god, "Time," etc.) to precipitate the effects of past conduct into the conditions of the present. Bhīṣma, for example, introduces the natural elements *(bhūtas)* as the agent of retributive transmission: "At his death, the person obtains the pure and impure fruits [of what he has done], as witnessed by the 'elements.' The agent experiences the measure of the two of them [that is, virtue and vice]. It is thus that one may enhance one's fortune (lit. 'pure fruits') by charity, *tapas,* and [good] works, and that impure acts lead to misery" (XII.36.36–37).

The part of "Time" itself is cut back from a primary to a secondary role in this process. In discussion at XII.34, Vyāsa clearly states that "Know that a person is made up of actions; that he is the witness of pure and impure deeds; that 'Time' bestows the fruits of time, [that is to say] the alloted consequences in the form of happiness and misery" (XII.34.7). In another discourse Bhīṣma indicates that these past acts mature in their own time without external compulsion, after the manner of flowers and fruit:

> Whatever has been determined [that is, as a result of past acts] overtakes [the doer] however swiftly he runs. It sleeps when he sleeps and does whatever else he does. Like a shadow, the karma [of the past] rests when he rests, follows when he moves, acts when he acts. A man is always made to experience [the fruits of] whatever acts have accumulated in the past as a result of his own doing (lit. "ordained by himself"). "Time" severely afflicts all creatures [already] destined to be unsettled by the consequences of their past acts. Action undertaken in the past *(karma purākṛtaṃ)* matures in its own time without external compulsion, just as do flowers and fruits. At the end of their ordained course, actions undertaken *(pravṛtta)* are continuously transformed into honor and dishonor, gain and loss, growth and decay. A creature experiences the joy and suffering ordained as a result of his own doing in a former body while still in the womb. Whenever he does a good or a sinful act, whether in childhood, youth, or old age, he will always experience the results of it at the same period in every birth. The acts of a previous life *(pūṛvakṛtaṃ karma)* catch up with the agent like a calf that locates its mother among thousands of cattle. Drenched in water a garment is made clean. [Similarly], those who are burning as a result of their acts obtain endless happiness by abiding in a state of abstinence. Those whose sins have been destroyed according to the dharma, by taking up residence in the woods and performing *tapas* for a long period of time, succeed in obtaining the objects they desire. (XII. 174.8–18)

Life is now ordained by oneself *(ātmavihita)*, and it is only the retributive schedule that remains in the hands of "Time."

Tale of Gautamī and the Fowler

In a long conversation between Gautamī and the fowler Arjunaka, the previous acts of Gautamī's son (the murder victim in the story) catch up with him via the circuitous route of a second agent who escapes responsibility for his own (inherently culpable) act of killing. The onus is progressively shifted from the helpless agent (in this case the snake who stands accused of the death of the old lady's son) and the personified form of "Time" (Kāla—who also disclaims responsibility) to Gautamī and then to her son, both of whom must suffer the "fate" of their past acts. This story is one of a number designed to relieve Yudhiṣṭhira of his sense of guilt, and it therefore avoids reference to the influence of any previous acts by Yudhiṣṭhira. Why do you consider yourself (or your *ātman*) to be the cause, Bhīṣma challenges Yudhiṣṭhira (XIII.1.8), when your actions are dependent on other causes *(paratantra),* in this case the perfidy of Duryodhana? The fowler in the story that follows employs all the usual arguments against the obvious perpetrator of the crime. The serpent must die since it is guilty of the death of the old lady's son. Such punishment will provide a remedy for anger and grief (the argument for revenge) and also a protection for others who may otherwise be bitten in the future. Gautamī, however, pleads for release of the serpent, arguing that nothing will be gained by its death and certainly not the restoration of her son. Such an attitude may be appropriate for a self-contained person *(svastha),* replies Arjunaka, but hardly for one plunged in grief. The practical person *(arthavid)* seeks solace in revenge rather than assigning everything to the course of "Time." The argument then proceeds to trade the merits of forgiveness and compassion against those acquired by the serpent himself as a sacrificial victim.

While they are thus arguing back and forth, the serpent suddenly begins to speak in its own defense. It argues that the sin *(doṣa* and *kilbiṣa),* if there be any, is not his since he is not his own master and had no choice in the matter. Death (Mṛtyu) is responsible. But the fowler thereupon suggests that the serpent must at least bear part of the blame, since he is the instrumental cause in the same manner as the potter's wheel and rod and other instruments are instrumental causes of the pot. But such instruments are not independent causes of the pot, replies the serpent. If there be any sin in the death of the boy, it must somehow be shared among all the various causes.

At this point, Mṛtyu himself appears to reveal he was guided by Time *(Kāla),* and that neither he, nor the serpent are therefore responsible for the child's death. He continues:

> Just as the clouds are tossed about by the wind, I too, like the clouds, O serpent, am under the influence of "Time." All conditions of life related to *sattva, rajas* and *tamas* are governed by "Time" and operate in all creatures. All mobile and immobile creatures in heaven and earth, indeed this whole universe, O serpent, are influenced by "Time." Everything that happens in this world, whether tending to action *(pravṛtti)* or to quiescence *(nivṛtti),* and all changes *(vikṛti),* are said to be influenced by "Time." All existent and non-existent objects, including the Āditya and the Moon, Viṣṇu, Water, Wind, Indra, Fire, Sky, Earth, Mitra, plants and the Vasus, and rivers and oceans, are created and destroyed by "Time." (XIII.1.44–49)

Our very moods of joy and anger are determined by Time *(kālapracodita)*.

Finally, the personified form of "Time" himself appears before them, bringing the rather startling revelation that

> It was the karma of this child, O Arjunaka, that acted as the driving force in this matter. Nothing else was the cause of this child's death. He was killed by his own actions in the past *(svakarma)*. He met his death as a result of the other actions he performed. It is his karma that was the cause of his destruction. All of us are subject to our actions. Karma is inherited in this world, which is marked by the bondage of action. It is karma that drives the activities of the world, just as others drive us (to action). Men make their own destiny (karma) from actions performed in the past just as a person *(kartṛ)* may fashion whatever he wants out of a lump of clay. The agent *(kartṛ)* and his actions are bound together by his [previous] actions as sunlight and shadow are forever bound up with each other. (XIII.1.64–68)

Men cycle through the three worlds according to their own karma *(svakarma)*, Yudhiṣṭhira is told, and he should, therefore, free himself of responsibility for something that the Kauravas, through their own actions, brought upon themselves.

And in light of this clear disavowal by "Time," the tale ends on a decidedly contradictory note, however, when Bhīṣma concludes this passage by telling Yudhiṣṭhira that "What has happened was not your doing, nor, indeed, was it Duryodhana's. Know that it was "Time" (Kāla) that was responsible for the deaths of these kings" (XIII.1.75). This suggests either the possibility of interpolation of the words of "Time" about the responsibility of the child, or the existence of lingering doubts about the real location of responsibility. Bhīṣma himself entitles this whole discussion: "Doubts regarding the Subject of Morality" *(dharmārthasaṃśaya)*.

Mārkaṇḍeya's Discourse on Karma

The increasing emphasis on the role of past karma in the formation of current conditions inevitably calls into question the role of other agencies, including God Himself. Despondent at the rising fortunes of the Dhārtarāṣṭra, Yudhiṣṭhira (who is in exile at this point) thinks that "Man is the agent of his good and evil acts, and that he reaps the fruits. What then does the Lord do" (III.181.6)? In establishing a doctrine in the matter, Mārkaṇḍeya begins at III.181.9 (continuing to v. 33) by explaining how, in the beginning, Prajāpati created immaculate bodies for the housing of souls. However, as a result of lust and anger *(kāma* and *krodha),* greed and confusion *(lobha* and *moha)* overcame them, and they began to live by tricks and deceit *(māyā* and *vyāja),* whereupon the gods deserted them. Over time, this god-created body has become the repository of vast quantities of good and bad acts, and when it dies the person is instantly reborn together with all his previous acts. These follow him like a shadow to create the joys and sorrows of the new life. Those with a past history of good behavior are reborn with good characters into good families, grow up with little fear of illness or bondage, and are likely to encounter few obstacles in life. On leaving this world of acts *(karmabhūmi),* they proceed to the abode of the gods *(surālaya).*

Having established his theory, however, Mārkaṇḍeya immediately waters it down by concluding that: "Some is the result of destiny *(daiva),* some the result of chance *(haṭha),* and part of what men get is the result of their own acts *(svakarma),* O king. Think no more about it" (III.181.32). Yudhiṣṭira's original question about the role of the Īśvara is left hanging, except through this oblique reference to destiny *(daiva).* The emphasis is clearly on one's *svakarma* which, in addition to creating the conditions of the present, is also an important determinant of the future "world" in which the greatest happiness will be found. Those in pursuit of wealth will find it in this world and not the next; those in pursuit of Yoga (presumably leading to *mokṣa*) will find it in that world, not this; those in pursuit of dharma will find it both in this world and the next; while self-indulgent people who do nothing (implying dedication to *kāma*) will find it neither in this world nor in the next. Mārkaṇḍeya then assures the Pāṇḍavas that their fortunes will change, since their own acts, "determined by the purposes of the gods," will win them the highest heaven where good men dwell. We are left to wonder who is ultimately in charge here, the individual or the gods (presumably including Īśvara).

Tale of Kauśika and the Butcher

Less ambiguity is evident in Mārkaṇḍeya's account of the Brahmin Kauśika who is directed for spiritual guidance to a pious butcher, a most unlikely preceptor from the orthodox standpoint (though living in the perfect society of King Janaka of Mithilā). The Brahmin is initially ill at ease at finding himself in the presence of this loathsome form of livelihood (III.198.18), but the butcher explains that

> This occupation of mine is no doubt loathsome. However, the pressure (*vidhi* = "injunction") of our previous deeds is powerful and difficult to circumvent, O Brahmin. I am obliged to do this evil work as a result of evil acts performed in the past, and I make every effort *(yatna)* to

> kill it off. When such a thing has been ordained by previous injunction [that is, of his own acts], the killer is but the instrument. For we are but the instruments of these [previous] actions, O best of the twice-born. (III.199.1–3)

Nevertheless, a place is still reserved for "the one who bestows" the results of good and evil deeds (Dhātṛ) when he continues:

> This is my dharma; and this being so I will not give it up, best of the twice-born. I know that it is the result of my deeds in the past, and I earn my livelihood by this work. Here [that is, in this kingdom of orthodoxy that is Mithilā] it is considered contrary to the dharma to abandon one's own work. When one is engaged in one's own work it is considered to be the dharma [that is, the task of that person in life]. For an embodied being cannot escape the karma previously ordained for him. Dhātṛ looks upon this ordinance *(vidhi)* in a number of ways when determining one's work. A man who is working at a grisly task, O wise Brahmin, must find out how he can make it pure, how to avoid being destroyed by it. The final judgement on this gory job will [thus] be varied. (III.199.14–17)

He then provokes Kauśika to reflection by questioning whether anyone can be an absolute practitioner of nonviolence *(ahiṃsā)* in this cannibalistic world? There follows a number of examples of how difficult this is, punctuated by repeated admonitions of "and what do you think of that?" Even those most devoted to nonviolence such as the ascetics do harm to other creatures, for example, by simply walking about.

But the dharma is more than just difficult to follow; it is confusing (or subtle) by its very nature. Under certain conditions, a lie can become truth and a truth a lie, but whether the act is judged (by the Dhātṛ?) good or bad, "there is no doubt whatsoever about the inevitability of the resulting consequences for the man himself" (198.18.5). If the result of actions were not dependent on something over and above the current action, men would not experience the various difficulties and obstacles they meet in life. Or to put it another way: "If men were subject to their own wishes, no one would die, no one would grow old, all would have their desires fulfilled, and no one would experience any unpleasantness" (III.200.19). But, at death, the soul (*jīva* = here the *ātman* together with the subtle body) moves on, and

> No one else inherits the deeds that were done. The doer *(kartṛ)* himself has the share *(bhāga)* of good and bad. For he gets whatever karma he has done; there is no such thing as the destruction of what has been performed. The evil-natured man becomes good; the best of men be-

> comes an evil-doer. For the man in this world is followed by his own deeds [of the past]. His [new] existence is prepared by them in this manner, and then he is [re]born. (III.200.27–28)

One is thereby consigned to a life of "wandering through the *saṃsāra* as if on a wheel," suffering great pain, until one is freed from bondage by the performance of pure acts, and attains to the "worlds of the virtuous" where suffering is no more. Successful performance of one's own duties leads to tranquillity of mind, accompanied by meaningful personal relationships and worldly influence.

In the long run, however, even the fruits of this dharma are not satisfying, particularly when one has realized the fragile nature of the world. When this point comes, a person first undertakes to renounce everything, though he still does not abandon his duties, and "then strives for liberation, not by the wrong means but by the right," presumably through the punctilious performance of his duties. It is interesting to observe, from the Sanskrit text, the emphasis on effort in this process through use of the root √*yat* = "to strive, endeavor, etc."

Discourse of Parāśara to King Janaka

In light of the foregoing, it is easy to understand how destiny (in the form of *kāla* or *daiva*) eventually came to be synonymous with the results of past acts. A link with *daiva* is evident in remarks made by the sceptic *(pūrvapakṣa)* in the course of a long, and rather rambling, account of the matter given by Parāśara, the father of Vyāsa, in response to a question by King Janaka (XII.279). After explaining that the essence of the dharma for embodied creatures is contained in the scriptural ordinances laid down on the subject of action, the sceptic continues:

> As a pot when dipped into gold or silver [takes on the qualities of these precious metals], so do people become subject to their past karma *(pūrvakarma)*. Nothing grows without a seed. No one can prosper and enjoy life without action. On the destruction of the body, a person obtains happiness as a result of good acts. [It is only the sceptic who argues], "I do not, my dear sir, see anything that is the result of destiny (*daiva*—here equated with present circumstances as the result of past actions). There is no evidence that destiny has any cause. It is in consequence of their own nature *(svabhāva)* that the gods, the *gandharvas,* and the demons have prospered." (XII.279.10–12)

This conclusion (that is, that *svabhāva* is the cause) is then refuted by Parāśara who argues that, on the contrary, one inevitably experiences the consequences of past conduct, whether this be by the "eye," mind, speech, or by physical action:

> One receives an equal measure of whichever of the four kinds of action one performs, [action performed] in a suggestive manner (lit. "with the eye"), mentally, in speech, or in [physical] action. Karma always leads to mixed results, O king; but whether these tend to good or evil, these results are never destroyed. Sometimes, O good sir, the results of good acts are not apparent [lit. "remain as if hidden"] to one sinking in the [ocean of] the *saṃsāra* until such time as he is released from his sorrows. Once these sorrows have been exhausted, he begins to enjoy [the fruits of] his good acts. And know [also], O king, that the exhaustion of [the effects of] good acts are followed by those of evil. (XII.279. 15–18)

These verses were subsequently used by Śaṃkara to bolster the "pure" theory of karma expressed in his commentary on Vedāntasutra III.1.8.

Parāśara goes on to assure the king that the consequences of one's deeds do not last for ever; neither is one ever made to enjoy or suffer the deeds of another. The only way to control karma is to control the chariot of the body with the mind, by curbing the horses of the senses with the reins of knowledge (XII.280.1). In this manner, the wise man is able to "exert himself for the purpose of spiritual advancement by means of righteous acts" (XII.280.3). Numerous mythological examples are harnessed to the task of demonstrating the validity of what became the moral assumption of the great German philosopher Emmanuel Kant, namely that virtue (here practiced over the course of many lives) will ultimately lead to success and happiness (XII.281.12ff.). Parāśara concludes that if the dharma could be preserved, the whole world would be happy, and the heavens would rejoice (XII.282.13).

In addition to one's social duties *(varṇāśramadharma),* the practice of virtue also has an individual component. This consists in the performance of *tapas*—here regarded as an antidote to the erroneous belief that happiness follows from the gratification of the senses. As Parāśara points out: "Believing, as a result of attachment to pleasure, that life's accomplishments consist only in sensual enjoyments, the man who is devoted to pleasure cannot imagine that there is anything to be gained beyond sexual intercourse" (XII.284.6). But, as is well-known: "Happiness is obtained by those persons who are endowed with intelligence, who are always looking to the eternal Brahmā, who are devoted to pure conduct, and who abstain from actions driven by desire [alone]" (XII. 284.10). In the opinion of Parāśara: "Whatever objects of the world come of themselves (*aprayatna* = "without effort," that is, on our part) may be enjoyed without reservation by householders. However, it is my belief that their *svadharma* [that is, their social responsibilities] should be vigorously pursued (*prayatnena* = "with effort")" (XII.284.35). K. M. Ganguli refers, by way of a footnote, to the commentary by Nīlakaṇṭha in which he

> points out that the object of this Verse is to show that everything one owns or does is the result of the past acts. Spouses, food, drink, &c., one obtains as the result of past acts or "praravdha karma." In respect of these, "purushakara" or exertion is weak. Hence, to put forth exertion for their acquisition would not be wise. As regards the acquisition of righteousness, however, there exertion is efficacious. Hence, one should with exertion, seek to conform to one's own duties as laid down in the scriptures. Without such a distinction between destiny (praravdha) and exertion (purushakara), the injunctions and interdictions of the Scriptures would be unmeaning.[7]

The term "praravdha karma" (= *prārabdhakarma)* would here be synonymous with *pūrvakarma* which, as we have just seen, is associated with *daiva* (destiny that happens to one).

The body itself is part of the chain of effects flowing from desire-prompted actions of past existences: "As a result of its association with acts, this body is always [re]born under corresponding conditions [that is, conditions determined by these acts]. Furthermore, O king, whatever the circumstances of death, it is observed that the nature of the following birth is a product of [past] actions" (XII.286.17). And, contrary to Mārkaṇḍeya's view of instant rebirth: "The soul does not, O king, obtain a new birth immediately but wanders like a great cloud through the sky. Obtaining a new embodiment, O king, it is reborn once again. The soul *(ātman)* is superior to the mind, and the mind is superior to the senses" (XII.286.18–19).

Those whose souls have been perfected to the point of knowing the true condition of the *ātman* are never afflicted by the fruits of their acts (XII.287.8), the key being freedom from attachments: "The one who is free of attachments and who has conquered his anger is never affected by sin, though he be in the midst of worldly objects" (XII.287.10). Once this hankering after worldly enjoyments has been abandoned *(tyāga),* one is assured of happiness. By contrast, the sensualist (lit. "one devoted to his penis and his belly") goes around the cycle of births in a thick mist without seeing his way, like one afflicted with congenital blindness. Thus:

> As traders crossing the ocean make profits in proportion to their investment, creatures who ply this ocean of mortality attain to ends in proportion to the way they act. Death wanders through the days and

> nights of this world in the form of decrepitude, devouring all creatures like a snake devouring air. When born, a creature encounters the results of work previously performed. There is nothing, whether agreeable or disagreeable, that is obtained other than as a result of acts performed in the past. Whether lying or moving, sitting or dealing with the objects of the world, a person is always meeting the result of the pure and impure acts [of the past]. (XII.287.26–29)

And Parāśara summarizes his view in what appears to be a ringing endorsement of personal initiative:

> All the actions done in the past, whether pure or impure, return to the person himself. Knowing that everything that takes place [in the present] is the result of [past] action, the inner soul urges the mind *(buddhi)* to act accordingly. [In this manner], the different projects *(ārambha)* that may be undertaken will never fail, [provided that] one relies on one's own efforts *(vyavasāya)* and on such other assistance as there may be. The business of a worthy man of blameless soul, who acts without pride and anxiety, putting forth effort *(vyavasāya)* with the necessary skill *(upāya)*, is never lost. From the very outset in the mother's womb, a person is invariably responsible for all the pure and impure acts he has performed in the past. Death, which is irresistible and responsible for the destruction of life, together with "Time," leads all creatures to their end like sawdust scattered by the wind. As a result of pure and impure acts performed by himself in the past, the person obtains whatever he has and has accomplished in life, including his family and associates, his fame and fortune and everything else he has done of his own accord. (XII.287.39–40 and 42–44)

The only caveat in all of this would appear to be the activities of Death and "Time" from which there is no escape whatever one does.

This link between past karma and the *daiva* of present circumstances is also evident from remarks made by Bhīṣma at the very beginning of the Mokṣadharma section of Śāntiparvan, when he says: "The [results of] what has been done in a previous incarnation, whether pure or impure, are visited upon the wise and the foolish, as well as on brave persons, according to one's just deserts. It is even thus that living creatures have these good and bad experiences, together with joy and sorrow. Once aware of this, the man endowed with the qualities of his material nature lives happily" (XII.168.37–39a).

The Psychology of Transmission

The mechanism by which the acts of the past are transmitted to the present is dealt with in the Anugītā section of the Aśvamedhaparvan

(XIV.16ff.) where Kṛṣṇa recalls a dialogue between two Brahmins, one of whom, Kaśyapa, asks a number of questions about the psychology of karma in relation to the process of rebirth. J. Bruce Long has drawn attention to a disjunction in this text between a naturalistic account of death and rebirth (XIV.17; 18.1–13), and the theistic account of the original creation of bodies by Brahmā, which follows this (XIV.18.24–34).[8] It is in the first segment of this dialogue that the propensity of action to leave habit-forming traces in the mind is introduced. The entire process is driven exclusively by actions undertaken in the past, that is, by *pūrvakarma*: "Dissociated from the body, the *jīva* is surrounded on all sides by its own acts. It is endowed with marks *(aṅkitas)* of his pure and good and bad deeds. Brahmins endowed with knowledge, and duly conversant with the conclusions of scripture, know by these indications *(lakṣanas)* about their good and evil deeds" (XIV.17.28–29). The terms *aṇkita* and *lakṣana* are clearly equivalent to the *vāsanas* and *saṃskāras* that are given prominence in the later philosophical literature.

That the mind itself is the repository of these "marks" is made clear in what follows:

> Pure and impure actions ripen upon the attainment of body after body (*kṣetra* = a "field," that is, of action). They are not subject to destruction. As a fruit-bearing tree brings forth much fruit when the season comes, the actions performed by a pure mind result in much merit *(puṇya)*. And similarly, the actions performed by an evil mind are productive of sin *(pāpa)*. The soul *(ātman)*, led by the mind *(manas)*, sets itself to action. Hear then how the person who is governed entirely by his [past] acts, being overwhelmed by desire and anger, enters the womb. (XIV.18.1–4)

Furthermore, it seems that once cleansed *(śuddha)* of these mental habits (or "marks"), the mind would no longer be governed by past acts *(karmasamādiṣṭaṃ)*. It is asserted, for example, that "Whatever the acts, pure or impure, performed [by the person] in a former body, he will go through [the effects of] all of them, whether he likes it or not. By this means, [the effects of] former acts are exhausted, while others accumulate once again until such time as the person becomes aware of the dharma related to the Yoga of liberation [presumably *karmayoga*]" (XIV.18.11–12). This suggests that it is the acts themselves that are responsible for rebirth: "A living being thus always meets the action previously performed by him. All these [acts] constitute the cause by which he comes into this world in a debased form" (XIV.18.22). As noted once again by Long: "That the embodied state of being *(dehin)* is thought to be an abnormal condition for the *jīva* is indicated by the standardized use of the term *doṣa* (impurity, fault, or pollutant) in referring to the basic humors in the body."[9]

This karmic explanation of how a new human body is reproduced contrasts with the subsequent theistic account of the creation of the first macrocosmic body. This is the work of Brahmā-Prajāpati, who creates his own body before creating the *pradhāna* or material cause of all the other (microcosmic) bodies of mobile and immobile creatures. As in the Bhagavadgītā, an individual person *(puruṣa)* is a duality, consisting of a destructible body and an indestructible soul, which migrates from body to body. Instead of "Time," however, it is Brahmā himself who assigns the temporal limits to the exit from *(parivṛtti),* and return to *(punarāvṛtti),* each state of embodiment. Nowhere is there any mention of the contribution of the individual and his acts to this process. Long is thus moved to conclude that

> This passage supports a position midway between philosophical Vedānta and devotional Kṛṣṇa-ism, by attributing all primary causative action to god while, at the same time, identifying that Creator as Brahma-Prajāpati rather than Kṛṣṇa. We might be justified in assuming that the idea of karma is the underlying assumption of every statement on human destiny in the MBh., but taking this text as it stands, the responsibility for the creation of the world-order and the actualization of human destiny lies with the divine being, with no contribution of any magnitude from man himself.[10]

Vidura's "Wilderness of Life"

Perhaps the "purest" enunciation of the karma doctrine in the Mahābhārata is given by Vidura as part of his continuing efforts to lift the spirits of Dhṛtarāṣṭra. This time the blind king is grieving over what must be the most perfect example of the maturation of past action (or, in his case, failure to act) in the epic—the destruction of his entire family (XI.3.6–17). Willy-nilly, says Vidura, we must all accept responsibility for our own actions. It is in accord with such actions that creatures are born and destroyed, some while yet in the womb, some shortly after birth, some in youth, some in middle, and some in old age, just as pots produced by a potter may break at any time, even on the potter's wheel. Life's difficulties are all the result of past behavior, which, in turn, is governed by the degree of insight into the workings of the world. Those with little insight come under the dominion of greed *(lobha),* which brings them to ruin (no doubt Vidura has the king himself in mind). By contrast, those who are wise *(prājña),* established in truth, and conversant with the comings and goings of beings in this world *(saṃsāra)*, attain to the very highest end. The results of this past behavior *(pūrva-karma)* accompany the person at birth to produce (what we have come to regard as) "character." "Bound by the chains of the senses" to family, wealth, and the other sweet things of life, for example, that is to say, by attachments *(saṅga)*, he continues to act. The person is then paid out of this accumulated deposit of desire-prompted acts in the form of the various benefits and calamities encountered in this life, including his or her own death at the appointed time. This process is seldom seen for what it is on account of greed, anger, lust, and madness, which deceive the whole world, including ourselves. Others are then blamed for what we have brought on ourselves: "We speak of others as ignorant fools, but never take a look at ourselves. One is quick to instruct others, but has no wish to instruct oneself" (XI.3.13). One familiar with the nature of *mokṣa* thus looks at the world as a place to avoid.

Vidura continues by illustrating this disastrous karmic cycle in the allegorical terms of the famous "Parable of the Wilderness of Life" (XI.5.1–22), which recounts the wanderings of a certain Brahmin who enters a large forest teeming with beasts of prey. He has no apparent way of escape since the forest is surrounded by a net, and guarded on all sides by huge five-headed snakes reaching to the sky. A dreadful woman with arms reaching over the net is also to be seen. Running hither and thither to avoid these horrible creatures he inadvertently falls into a well by the side of a great tree. He ends up hanging by his heels halfway down the well, caught in a tangle of creepers that breaks his fall. But this is not all. Looking down he sees a large and powerful snake at the bottom of the well, and looking up he sees a gigantic elephant with six faces and twelve feet approaching the mouth of the well. Killer bees in the tree above are buzzing about a honeycomb that releases intermittent streams of honey into the well, while the roots of the tree are being gnawed away by a troop of black-and-white rats. His thirst is unquenchable even after repeated draughts of the honey that continues to fall into the well. In spite of his almost impossible predicament, however, the unfortunate Brahmin never abandons attachment to life, and even strives to prolong it.

This graphic imagery is clearly designed to open the eyes of the blind king (supposedly endowed with "the eyesight of insight") into the true nature of the human condition (XI.6.1–12). Such insight, says Vidura, is all that is needed to secure happiness in the higher worlds. The wilderness is the *saṃsāra* as a whole, he explains, while the great forest is the more limited sphere of one's own life. The beasts of prey are the various diseases to which we are subject, and the woman of gigantic proportions with arms outstretched is the prospect of decrepitude that awaits us. The well or pit is the physical embodiment into which we "fall," continually buzzed by desires (bees) that are never fully satisfied, no matter how much pleasure (honey) is available for their gratification. Our condition would seem hopeless, yet, suspended by creepers of hope, we continue to hang onto our pathetic ego-centered existence.

From the *nivṛtti* perspective of one who takes his stand in the Truth *(sattvastha),* human effort is of little consequence in the face of "Time," here represented in its threefold destructive aspect. The nights and days (black-and-white rats) are gnawing away at the very roots of the tree of life (of the embodied soul), clearing the way for the approaching elephant (of the years) with six faces (seasons) and twelve legs (months). And finally there is the embodiment of "Time" as Death in the form of a huge snake, who waits patiently at the bottom of the pit for the rats to complete their task. Suitably impressed and now fully roused from his former state of emotional collapse, Dhṛtarāṣṭra presses Vidura to continue.

The situation may be grim, but it is not entirely hopeless, Vidura hastens to reassure the king (XI.7.1–20). The course of existence can well take the form of a long journey through a forest of adversity, punctuated by frequent "falls" into different embodiments. However, this is only for the ignorant (like the king himself). Men of wisdom are aware that these fierce beasts are nothing but the concretization of their own *svakarma,* and are no longer disturbed by them. And he proceeds to illustrate the different degrees of control that may be exercised over one's life by the analogy of handling a chariot: "The body of creatures is called a chariot, and the driver is the living principle *(sattva).* The senses are represented by the horses, and our acts and understanding are the reins. Whoever is carried along by these impetuous steeds has to return to the *saṃsāra* in a perpetual round of rebirths" (XI.7.13–14). This is the "chariot of Yama" that confuses the ignorant. On the other hand: "Self-restraint, renunciation *(tyāga)* and vigilance are the three horses of Brahmā. Whoever controls the chariot of the mind to which the reins are firmly attached by good character *(śila),* casting off all fear of death, is destined, O king, for the world of Brahmā *(Brahmaloka)*" (XI.7.19b-20). The key to control of one's life and spiritual betterment, lies in control of the "mind," suggesting control of the emotions through knowledge (though it is not clear whether *puruṣakāra* is equivalent to the "power" of this mind). The alternative is to fall victim to the slings and arrows of outrageous fortune *(daiva)* in the manner of a Dhṛtarāṣṭra, dragged by his own emotional attachments from one disaster to another. Of course, full control of the mind is not necessarily synonymous with *mokṣa,* since the very need for control implies a state in which the horses of the senses are drawn—by attachment—toward their objects.

Krishna Chaitanya sees a curious parallelism between the karmic mechanics of epic events and the divine intentionalities of *Daiva.* He writes that "if for expressing his very subtle concept of a superordinate transcendental intentionality, Vyāsa indicates an event as designed from above, he carefully matches it with a Karmic causality that is self-sufficient in terms of the world's processes and human reactivities."[11] His examples are the destruction of the Yādavas, and the culpability of Arjuna in the death of Bhīṣma. In the first instance the divine intentionality is suggested by the willing submission of Kṛṣṇa to the fate meted out to him and his countrymen; in the second by the revenge of the Vasus in the (temporary) death of Arjuna at the hands of his own son (XIV.79–81). These events are also precipitated in karmic fashion, the former through the absence of Kṛṣṇa during the dice game (who otherwise would have put a stop to this foolishness); the latter through the killing of Bhīṣma perpetrated by Arjuna for his own advantage. The final demise of Duryodhana is a further example. As Chaitanya explains: "The reactions of the world, the objective situation, harden when the provocations continue and beyond a certain stage they become unalterable and confront the doer as his destiny."[12]

Chaitanya, with typical existentialist verve, also sees this deterministic thrust of past conduct as a necessary confrontation with a "destiny" that offers the necessary challenge to shape oneself and one's own future. He offers the example of Karṇa in this regard:

> The confidential dialogue with Krishna in the chariot was Karna's hour of illumination and perhaps it was even more profound than the illumination of Arjuna in the dialogue of the Gita. Life had throughout heaped misfortunes on him. But they ceased to have any significance for him at this hour; he does not even remember them. The empirical effects initiated by his past misdeeds—but not his own misdeeds alone, the web of causalities was too intricately woven for such simplist reading—had jelled into a situation which squarely confronted him with destiny. He could have become king; but he chose a different road, knowing full well that at the end of the road he chose, death would be waiting for him. But he has no thought for his own certain death either. He transformed what loomed up as a dark Karmic fatality into a personally wrought destiny and fulfillment. By the position he took up in his freedom in regard to the fruition of the past as the present on the empirical plane, he changed punishment into redemption.[13]

Chaitanya makes much of the ladder of human initiative implied in the different uses of the agricultural metaphor of sowing. He notes that in the Vanaparvan (III.33.45), the farmer fulfills his duty simply by sowing the seeds *(puruṣakāra)* in a field that has already been ploughed. Here the text simply suggests that he cannot thereafter be faulted if the monsoon fails. In the Udyogaparvan, however (V.77.1–5), Kṛṣṇa insists that the farmer should make further efforts to water the field by hand, implying that the husbandman should not just be resigned to his fate if the rains do not come. But, as mentioned earlier in chapter 7, this metaphor, which has previously linked *puruṣakāra* to the seed, is later completely transformed by Bhīṣma (XIII.6.7–8) when he suggests that

> man's initiative becomes the field and Daivam or the design of the webbed causalities of the world becomes the seed. Trials and tribulations can also thus become seeds that can yield splendid fruit, depending on the field, which is human initiative. Vyasa incorporates his theory of human actions and consequences into his overall conceptualization of a benign intentionality behind creation even while underscoring man's responsibility to strive.[14]

The objective conditions of life created by past behavior here confront the individual as an existential challenge to mobilize his or her inner resources for a quantum leap into new conditions of life. But just how far the epic heroes are responsible for this existential leap is a moot point that Chaitanya refers back to the assertions of the epic: "As to whether events are finally determined by human volition or the fortuitous patterns of the world's multiple and intricately webbed causalities (Daivam, or what we call act of God in legal parlance), there are repeated assertions that human volition is effective and that man must rely on his initiative."[15]

9

The Path of Self-Determination

Careful observation of the thematic material on destiny and human initiative in the Mahābhārata suggests that there are two ways of arranging and interpreting this material. The diachronic arrangement proposed in chapter 8 suggests the gradual emergence of a more autonomous "person" in classical India.[1] This has been corroborated by analysis of other texts. B. V. De Smet, for example, notes that the human endeavor of the early Vedic period was marked not by personal, but by a collective concern for the good order of things, particularly for the maintenance of *ṛta*—the physical and moral order of the world. This collective interest is later superseded by a Promethean quest for the *brahman,* the mysterious power behind the cosmic system, identified (in the Brāhmaṇa texts) with the sacrifice itself and later internalized in the Upaniṣads as being one with the *ātman,* the suprapersonal "self."[2] And the various epic gods residing in the human body are eventually reduced to the status of human functions (for example, XII.120.44; XII.316.16).

It is also possible to read these materials synchronically as simple expressions of patent differences in human beings that become particularly evident in times of crisis. Epic characters naturally tend to express their momentary states of mind in images and ideas drawn from the rich cultural lore available to them. From this perspective, what seems to be a haphazard collection of ideas may be interpreted as a reflection of the disparate confusions of individual minds struggling to make sense of the various predicaments in which they find themselves. We have noted the vast range of feeling involved, from experiences of complete powerlessness and/or frustration to various levels of control and responsibility for a given action or situation. Paralyzed by ties of greed and affection, King Dhṛtarāṣṭra is forced to accept what happens to him as fate *(daiva),* experiencing himself as the "blind" victim of cosmic forces over which he has no control. Other characters, too, reach back into the stock of traditional imagery to express helplessness or anger in cases of seemingly irreconcilable conflict of duty, or apparent injustice *(adharma)*. We can think of Yudhiṣṭhira when cornered into participating in the dice-game (II.52.18), or of Draupadī angrily contemplating the discomforts of a fourteen-year forest exile resulting from her husband's adherence to a dharma she fails to understand (III.31.21ff.). An outcry against *daiva,* or a particular god, or karma, could simply reflect the depth of infringement of the victim's own sense of autonomy or moral responsibility in a particular situation. A case for both of these readings can be made, depending on the collective or individual circumstances of the moment. It will be helpful therefore to step back at this point to contemplate the psychological and spiritual continuum that provides the mythological backdrop to human experience in the Mahābhārata. This will also highlight the key lessons to be learned from the material of former chapters.

The Spiritual Journey

The numberless things and beings in the Universe are pictured in the epic as so many stages in a spiritual journey along a continuum of conciousness. This is objectively represented as a journey through a hierarchy of seven "worlds" which, of course, are located as much in human experience as in ordinary space. As described in detail in chapter 3, a new Creation is envisioned as a sort of "fall" into manifestation; from Brahmā down to a blade of grass *(brahmādi tṛṇānta);* from subtle (*sukṣma* = sāttvic) to gross *(sthūla* = tāmasic) forms of existence, and also, more significantly for us, from knowledge to ignorance *(avidyā* and *moha)*. It occurs when the rippleless consciousness *(nirvikalpasamādhi)* of the Supreme Divinity shatters into a multiplicity of individual energy centers, all of which are imbued with a desire *(kāma)* to be reunited with their source. This leads to the notion of an eschatological journey through successive embodiments and states of experience *(loka)* (XII. 199.3; XII.271.36ff; XII.292.1ff; XII.296.47–49, etc.). The human level "so difficult to attain" is a key milestone along this evolutionary road, where the natural desire for unification is temporally sublimated into an ego-centered drive for autonomy and self-determination. When things get out of hand through ignorance, however, this drive, which is none other than *puruṣakāra,* is subverted into an expansionist need to have and to hold *(yogakṣema)* other things and beings.

This notion of a journey through time and space is, as J. Bruce Long has noted:

> clearly articulated in the Sanskrit term for metempsychosis, or rebirth. The term *saṃsāra* means literally the act of going about, wandering through, coursing along, or passing through a series of states or conditions, specifically the passage through successive states of birth, death, and rebirth. The basal universal energy *(tejas, tapas, śakti)* is a kind of élan vital, which creates, supports, and (according to certain "schools of thought") constitutes *substantively* all living things.[3]

A lowly worm may rise to become Brahmā as a result of spiritual advances over many lives (XIII.118–120).

The Earth is an ideal locale *(loka)* for the consciousness of this evolving *jīva* to emerge into the light of self-consciousness, including the faculty of conscience. It is the arena where the individual ego or I *(ahaṃkāra)* confronts the "other" of the world in frictional interaction, for which it is held to account by a set of rules or dharma. Our life "here below" has just the right mix of awareness (*prakāśa* or "light") and pain *(duḥkha)* to prompt us either, by action, to satisfy desire *(pravṛtti)* or, by reflection, to turn away from its objects *(nivṛtti)*. It is on this plane, and in this human form, that the evolving *jīva* becomes responsible for its own further evolution.

In the more philosophical mode of the Bhagavadgītā, this spiritual entelechy is characterized as the progression of nature *(prakṛti)* toward the possibility of the fully self-determined act, that is to say, toward control over the springs of action.[4] This possibility is illustrated (VI.30/ BG.7.4–5) where Kṛṣṇa makes the distinction between "the segmental processes of nature, which he generically groups as *Apara Prakrti,* and nature as a holistic and superordinate principle that manifests itself at every level of material organization, giving a directionality to the numerous components of material entities and processes that otherwise do not recognize each other or act in concert. At this creative level, nature is distinguished as *Para Prakrti.*"[5] Unfortunately, instead of abruptly disappearing with the advent of human life, most of the deterministic features of the lower *prakṛti* go underground "to create fantastic complications, though their ultimate indication still is that freedom is a reality even if it can be realized only by a great striving."[6] This inner drive is *puruṣakāra* or *yatna,* particularly when it is diverted into satisfying mundane desires in the external world.

The forces at work behind the human events of the epic may all be interpreted in light of this cosmic journey of the soul. Such a vision reveals the epic conflict as the climax, on the stage of action *(karmabūmi)* that is this world, of the drama of inner struggle that takes place on the field of values *(dharmakṣetra)* between our lower organic heritage, and our higher nature acting as proxy for the human spirit *(puruṣa)* who takes no active part in the war. This inner battle involves the constant attempt by the self-centered forces of desire *(kāma),* aversion *(dveṣa),* and anger *(krodha),* to usurp the throne of the higher values and ideals (dharma) that point the way to a transcendent mode of being. The stakes are nothing less than the future of human evolution and of human society to come. In contrast to the animals—governed by instinct, humans have the power to resist the atavistic drag of impulse, and this capacity for spiritual advance, in modern parlance, goes by the names of autonomy, self-determination, and "freedom" (implying a "freedom of doing"). The epic author would have no quarrel with Dr. Kalidas Bhattacaryya's definition of the (human) individual as one "who is not entirely an item of Nature, accepting unquestioningly what Nature offers and submitting blindly to its forces, but one who often resists it and initiates new actions, one, in other words, who is as much above Nature as in it. This over-natural status of man is called 'freedom.' "[7] While this modern sense of freedom has no direct equivalent in epic Sanskrit, it is clearly implied in the choice between the good *(śreyas)* and the pleasant *(preyas)* of Kaṭhopaniṣad II.1.2; in short the choice between a life of moral commitment and the pursuit of unbridled self-interest. Present satisfactions must be "sacrificed" in exchange for assurances of a higher state of existence in the future.

As we pointed out in chapter 5, this self-determination or autonomy is not complete freedom in the epic sense of *mokṣa* but is a progressive loosening of the net of attachments *(kāmajāla)* that bind the embodied soul *(jīvātman)* to the cycle of life *(saṃsāra).*[8] *Mokṣa* is not a freedom of the will related to the ego *(ahaṃkāra).* Nevertheless, we are assured by Indra (in the form of a jackal) that the human estate enjoys incomparable advantages that make it the envy and aspiration of all lower orders of being (XII.173.8ff.). Our humanity, flawed as it is, puts us on the staircase to heaven *(sopānabhūtaṃ svargasya*—XII.309.79; cf. also XII. 286.31–32). On the other hand we need not be reminded that these advantages also carry the risk of deviating from the path of spiritual evolution in a manner that has no parallel among the things and beings governed by the causal laws of the lower *prakṛti.* The human endeavor is "finer than the edge of a razor and grosser than a mountain" (XII.252.12). Humans have achieved a certain "freedom" to pilot their own evolution but, depending on how they use this, they may degenerate into the self-seeking demonic type or enjoy a meteoric rise to moral similarity *(sādharmya)* with the Supreme Being (VI.37/BG.XIV.2). Self-determination (or autonomy) is a necessary condition of the ultimate freedom of *mokṣa,* but it can also lead to a pernicious inflation of the ego, which makes it possible for a man like Duryodhana to resist the divine plan.

Moral Implications

This weakening of instinctual controls clearly poses a serious threat to the stability and well-being of society, particularly in the context of the progressive decline of the *yugas* (leading to Hobbsian conditions of *mātsyanyāya* in which the big fish eat the little fish). At the instigation of the lesser gods, Brahmā, so the story goes (XII.59.13–141; XII.91.16), is prompted to introduce moral standards (dharma), backed by a system of rewards and punishments, to control the libidinal *(kāma)* and materialistic *(artha)* excesses of the community. Regulation of social life (*loka-rakṣaṇakārika*—lit. "measures taken to protect the world," XII.59.77; cf. also XII.251.25) had, during the formation of the epic, become enshrined in complex formal codes of duties to be done *(kārya)* according to caste *(varṇa)* and stage of life *(āśrama)*. The *āśramadharma* is technically restricted to Brahmins (XII.62.2), though the epic is replete with examples of kings who retire to the woods when their social responsibilities have been fulfilled (Dhṛtarāṣṭra, the heavenly ascent of the Pāṇḍavas, etc.). It may be distinguished from the *varṇadharma* by the fact that: "Whereas the organization of Āśrama-dharma approaches life from the side of nurture (śrama), training it through successive stages; the organization of varṇa-dharma approaches life from the side of nature (guṇa), defining the role of the individual in society by virtue of natural tendencies and innate dispositions."[9] The "legal" aspect of relations between the individual and the group was part of the responsibility of the king *(rājadharma)*, to be enforced by means of the *daṇḍa* or "rod of chastisement" (XII.59.77–78).

However, these social norms are viewed in the epic within the much broader ethical context of human aspirations in general *(puruṣārtha)*, including the vital quest for inner harmony, and for a more meaningful integration within the cosmic system as a whole. In this context, emphasis on the regulatory aspect of the dharma tends to give way to normative disciplines designed to bring the mind to a greater radius of awareness and a finer grain of being. Thus, in addition to the fulfillment of one's social duties in a spirit of "sacrifice" (that is to say for the welfare of the community rather than one's own), more encompassing norms or *sādhāraṇadharmas*—such as nonviolence *(ahiṃsā)*, charity *(dāna)*, and truth *(satya)*—are encouraged as an integral part of spiritual and moral disciplines *(sādhana* and *abhyāsa)* directed to personal growth and self-realization. Thus (using a Mokṣaparvan example [XII.266.6–7]), the merits of patience *(dhairya)* are extolled as the antidote to desire *(icchā)*, aversion *(dveṣa)*, and lust *(kāma)*, and study *(abhyāsa)* is encouraged to dispel confusion *(bhrama)*, ignorance *(pramoha)*, and doubt *(āvarta)*.[10] The idea is to gradually transform these moral imperatives, through discipline, into the attitudes and behaviors attendent upon the spiritual passage of the individual from bondage to liberation *(mokṣa)*: "Where the dharma is, there is victory" *(yato dharmas tato jayaḥ)* is an oft-repeated expression that suggests spiritual as well as temporal victory.[11]

This passage from the social to the personal, from objective to more subjective standards of value, itself reflects a progressive social and psychological advance. As S. Cromwell Crawford points out:

> Objective Ethics constitutes the first stage of Hindu Dharma. On this stage morality is represented by social codes demanding external conformity. Psychologically understood, this is the stage of socialization and introjection. The voice of conscience is the interiorized voice of the group. The essence of conscience is a "must." The feel of conscience is that of fear of punishment for duties not done. Hindu Dharma further teaches that one should progress from the "must-consciousness" to the "ought-consciousness". . . . This is the Subjective stage known as *Citta-śuddhi* or purification of the mind. Subjective Ethics is an advance over Objective Ethics because "virtues are superior to duties." Whereas duty represents external sanctions, virtue represents internal sanctions. Duties are related to experiences of prohibition and fear, but virtues arise from experiences of preference and the feeling of self-respect.[12]

Of course this moral progression did not escape the ambiguities posed by the relativity and incommensurability of values built up layer upon layer since the Vedic period. By the time of the epic the dharma had proliferated into a confusion of "multiple doors" (XII.342.16), varying according to place and time *(deṣakāla)* (XII.297.16) and according to the respective capacities of human beings in different *yugas* (XII. 252.8): "The way of the dharma is subtle and has many branches without end"[13] is an oft-repeated complaint.[14] Not even the venerable Bhīṣma can say exactly what it is, as we have noted (p. 55). However, following its etymological meaning of "bear" or "support" (from √ *dhṛ)*, he defines it, in part, as "that which supports all creatures," its purpose being, "the growth and well-being of creatures." This suggests that the ultimate good is self-realization, but that this goal must wait upon the need for social regulation when the cause of justice or the life of the community as a whole is at stake (a particularly difficult lesson for Yudhiṣṭhira). This situation also reveals that the inner struggle is not restricted to the conflicting forces of dharma and *adharma* but may involve a conflict of different systems of value—different "dharmas."[15] This leads, finally, to the recognition that no act on this Earth is wholly good or wholly bad (VI.40/BG.18.48; XII.15.50).

The Vedic and Dharmaśāstra codes, reportedly based upon "the eyes of the virtuous" (XII.28.53), came to be supplemented by other voices of authority. These included the example of the good *(sadācāra),* the motive *(artha)* (XII.251.3), and finally the inner voice of conscience *(ātmatuṣṭi).*[16] The final judge of human behavior may be reserved for some god as already noted, or for "the Heart" (I.68.27). The latter is actually the inner voice of the *ātman,* "a particle of Myself in the world of the living" (VI.37/BG.15.7). We also find that these paradigms of behavior have been adapted, in many cases, to the needs of the nascent *bhakti* worldview, such as, the distinction between the traditional dharma of punishment and reward, and the so-called *sanātana dharma* of duties performed in a manner free of desire for reward (cf. XIII.150. 692*.7–8). Biardeau also suggests a connection between epic dharma and music and dance as the harmony of the Divine *līlā* that it is the duty of the king to maintain. Thus, Arjuna must learn the Veda of the *gandharvas* during his sojourn in *svarga* to prepare him for his royal duties.[17]

Humanity thus forms a bridge between the worlds of value and actuality, forever called to practice the good (or dharma) in face of the ever present possibility of evil (or *adharma*). In the context of the inexorable karmic law, the spiritual credits for what one accomplishes in this connection are progressively deposited to the account of the individual psyche in the subtle form of merit *(puṇya)* or sin *(pāpa),* with whatever consequences for future entanglements this may entail.[18] On the other hand, this is precisely what makes it possible to reverse the entanglement with the world by moving from the *pravṛttidharma* of the Veda (that is, the desire-prompted ritual activities that uphold the cosmic system) to the new renunciation at the heart of action itself, the renunciation-in-action, or *bhakti* form of *nivṛtti,* which purifies the mind by destroying these subtle accumulations of past karma *(pūrvakarma).* This radical change of direction is specifically designed to lead the aspirant away from the notion of my [action] *(mama)* in favor of one that is *nirmama* and *nirahaṃkāra* (that is, that is not related to the ego and its desires). As we shall see, these ideas are important for understanding the inner connection between *daiva* and *puruṣakāra* .

There are also symbolic hints that good and evil are endemic to this newfound human ability to chart the future (cf. VI.24/BG.2.33 and 38). The primeval ocean is churned by the demons as well as by the gods (I.15.5ff.). The creative churning brings prosperity (*Śrī* or Lakṣmī) and other good things but also a poisonous residue that has to be contained and controlled in the throat of Śiva to prevent the destruction of the cosmos.

> Due to the accession of freedom, man can rise to godliness or descend to be a devil. In that sense, and using the language of symbolic metaphor, there is a god as well as a devil in every man. But the world is the creation of deity and he ever abides with man; in fact he is the deepest self of the self of man that has been evolved by nature, again under the direction of deity, out of the materiality of the incarnate world, the world of becoming. Evil arises out of the denial of this indwelling deity, due to the abuse of freedom and the embracing of wrong self-images.[19]

The inner clash of dharma and *adharma* is thus projected into a mythology of cosmic struggle between divine and demonic forces, leading inevitably to the triumph of the superior legions of *adharma* were it not for the direct intervention of the avatar on the side of the dharma (cf. VI.27/BG.4.7–8). Thus the name of Kṛṣṇa is sometimes substituted for the term dharma in the adage that "Where the dharma is, there is the Victory" (for example, at VI.21.12 and 14). In some miraculous way the karmic energies that promote the good automatically spring into action to destroy evil whenever the divine spark within *(ātman)* is denied in favor of self-interest and self-indulgence. The defiance of a Duryodhana is inevitably "shattered against the throne of God, which is the world and its law."[20]

This self-determination—the freedom to choose evil as well as good, implies a power of moral discernment which, it is agreed in the epic, is exercised by the *buddhi,* a faculty with intellectual as well as moral overtones. In its sāttvic mode of operation, this *buddhi* distinguishes true and false as well as what ought to be done *(kārya)* from what ought not to be done (VI.40/BG.18.30). This dual role creates a blurring of the dividing-line between the theoretical and the practical reason, a phenomenon that goes back to the epic tendency to regard morality in relative terms as a necessary antidote to the fundamental error *(avidyā)* to which the *jīva* is subject. Action is prompted by *kāma* in the form of desire (XII.171.37), but the object of one's desires is a function of knowledge or lack of it (XII.246.1ff.): "Knowledge, the object of knowledge and the knower are the threefold source of action," says Kṛṣṇa (VI.40/BG.18.18). Action is hardly the result of a separate "act of will" (which has no direct equivalent in Sanskrit), but is seen to follow automatically upon a direct act of knowledge (in the sense of a "seeing" or *darśana*).[21] Knowledge (that is, "of the truth" = *satya*) becomes the highest virtue.

Indeed: "It is the virtue of virtues. If one is able, for instance, to *see* the absolute truth, there is little left for the will to do. The will is quieted. It is absorbed in the truth."[22] This intellectualized volition often makes it difficult to distinguish moral discernment (a function of *jñāna*) from moral decision (based implicitly on the exercise of *puruṣakāra*). Man in the epic is a "rational animal" (to borrow the definition of Aristotle).

On the other hand it cannot be said that the human endeavor is a matter of intellect alone, since it also involves a commitment of the whole person to action that is initially painful, but eventually becomes the source of enduring delight (VI.29/BG.6.21). Such a commitment spurs a progressive change in the system of identities to which the individual is bound (that is, his character) according to the meaning and insights he receives as he moves to successively higher vantage points. At the emotional level the aspirant learns to transform his functioning into "a motivation that does not have the compulsive, deterministic, obsessional power of a drive or a blind instinctual mechanism."[23] It is here that one is confronted with the struggles and confusions arising out of competing claims for allegiance. The human entity is neither a wholly spiritual being who would follow the imperatives of the dharma as essentially its own, nor a wholly physical being who would follow it unconsciously. He is always "tempted to defy its operation in him because he is neither wholly unconscious like the physical beings nor wholly conscious like the Supreme Being or God. It is for this reason that the moral law makes its power and presence felt in man as the categorical imperative."[24]

The highest categorical imperative of the epic is Kṛṣṇa's call to raise ourselves by our own efforts and to transform what looks like fate into a heroic self-affirmation. As he puts it: "One should uplift oneself by the self and not degrade the self. Thus the self alone is the friend of the self, and the self alone can be the enemy of the self. For he who has conquered his self by himself the self is a friend. But for him whose self is not conquered, the self is hostile, like an enemy" (VI.29/BG.6.5–6). And, G. W. Kaveeshwar adds that "In this self-uplift there need be no real impediment other than the weakness of the individual's own will *(sic)* and effort."[25] Moreover, an important corollary to this self-uplift is to act, through the redemptive possibilities inherent in one's particular situation, as an accessory *(nimittamātraṃ)* to the realization of the divine program for the world; in short, to rise to a moral similarity *(sādharmya)* with Kṛṣṇa himself (VI.37/BG.14.2).

This is made possible precisely through that victory on the field of dharma *(dharmakṣetra)* that frees the soul *(puruṣa* or *ātman)* from the residual determinisms of nature *(prakṛti)*. This "winning the battle of the mind" is later confirmed in the aftermath of the war when Kṛṣṇa warns Yudhiṣṭhira that

> The battle you now face is the battle which each must fight single-handedly with his mind. Therefore, O bull of the Bhāratas, you must be prepared to carry the struggle against your mind; and freeing yourself by your own efforts *(svakarma)* you must transcend the [powers of the] unconscious mind (*avyakta* = lit. "unmanifest"). In this war there will be no need for arrows nor for attendants or friends. The battle that is to be fought alone and single-handed is now upon you. And if vanquished in this struggle, you will be lost in [a flood of] emotion *(kāma)*. Knowing this, O son of Kuntī, and acting accordingly, you will fulfill the purpose of your existence. And acknowledging this wisdom *(buddhi)* and the way of all creatures, and in accordance with the conduct of your ancestors, you should properly administer your kingdom. (XIV.12.11–14, echoing similar advice by Bhīma at XII.16. 20–23)

Like Arjuna before him, Yudhiṣṭhira at last finds in his own crisis of conscience the inner strength to triumph over his lower nature and see where his duty lies—to administer the kingdom that Arjuna and the others have won back for him. Vyāsa has already told him that if he wants to rule in complete nonattachment, he can dedicate the realm to God and administer it as a servant (XII.32). On the other hand, the ambiguity about Kṛṣṇa's role in the fighting leaves one wondering whether this victory can, in the epic's view, be won without the tacit alliance or Grace *(prasāda)* of God Himself.[26]

The Evolutionary Ladder

The great range of spiritual dispositions *(svabhāva)* among people also testifies to the huge stakes that are gambled in this struggle for human betterment. As we have seen, we may arrange the winners and the losers in this game of life on a great evolutionary ladder leading from complete moral blindness and identification with nature, those who, in the words of Kṛṣṇa (VI.32/BG.9.8), are "powerless by the forces of nature," to successively higher states of moral awareness and emotional detachment *(vairāgya)*, culminating in freedom *(mokṣa)* from the determinations that come from false identification with the causal system of nature. The line of this evolution is traced by the various combinations of the *guṇas* or "modalities of nature." Those with a preponderance of the quality of *tamas* (from √ *tam* = "to faint") show a tendency to drift as a result of a failure to be in touch with reality: "*Tāmasika* movements are biological and therefore uncontrollable and unfree."[27] Dhṛtarāṣṭra is the prime example of such a type, a man so governed by unconscious drives that he acts (or fails to act) "as if mounted on a machine" (VI.40/BG.18.61). He acknowledges the authority of the dharma (or of his conscience in the form of Vidura) but can do nothing about it and falls victim to circumstances (that is, to *daiva*). According to V. S. Sukthankar: "he is the perfect symbol of the vacillating ego-centric self, pandering to its own base passions and weaving its own evil designs, engrossed in self-esteem and bent on self-aggrandization, alternately gloating over transient gains and moaning over inevitable losses."[28]

The conventional order of humanity is marked by a predominance of *rajoguṇa*—activity directed to the satisfaction of libidinal-æsthetic *(kāma)* and material *(artha)* ends of life based on attachment to the fruits of its endeavor *(phalākāṇkṣī)*:[29] "Rājasika movements are propelled by strong passions of love *(rāga)* or hate *(dveṣa)* and are therefore also unfree even through *[sic]* the person knows these actions to be his own."[30] The progressive type accepts the moral order of the world (dharma), while the deviant form is the demonic type *(āsursaṃpad)* (VI.38/BG.16.7–21) that falls away from the line of evolution. The first type is exemplified by the person of Arjuna who listens to the advice of his guide. He is (in V. S. Sukthankar's reading): "the symbol of the jivatman, not indeed of the ordinary mortal, the ego-centered personality, but the Superman (Narottama), who by practice of self-control and discipline, has purified himself, conquering the baser part of his own nature."[31] The asuric type is exemplified by Duryodhana who pays lip service to the dharma while ruthlessly pursuing his quest for power *(bhogaiśvarya)*.[32] Sukthankar sees him and his ninety nine brothers as symbolizing "in their aggregate the brood of ego-centric desires and passions like lust, greed, hatred, anger, envy, pride, vanity, and so on, to which the empirical ego is firmly attached and to which it clings desperately."[33].

The higher form of humanity is characterized by a predominance of *sattvaguṇa*. Actions undertaken under the influence of *sattva* are characterized by freedom to the extent that they incorporate detachment *(vairāgya)*. This *sattva* is the intellectual acumen of the spiritual seeker *(mumukṣu)* who, by adopting a program of self-discipline *(sādhana* or *abhyāsa)*, gradually becomes free of attachment *(muktasaṇga)* and egocentricity *(anahaṃvādī)*, steadfast *(dhṛti)* in his determination *(utsāha)*, and unshaken whatever the outcome (VI.40/BG.18.26). This ladder of awareness and freedom is portrayed by Kṛṣṇa in the following manner: "It is said that the senses are high; greater than the senses is the mind *(manas)*; greater than the mind is the intellect *(buddhi)*; but greater than the intellect is he [that is, the *puruṣa*]" (VI.25/BG.III.42; cf. also XII.

240.2; XII.267.16). Commenting on this verse, S. Cromwell Crawford remarks that "The outward life of sense is least free because consciousness is constricted by the sway of senses. Freedom emerges when the senses are made dependent on the mind. Freedom is enhanced when the mind is yoked with intelligence. Greatest freedom is achieved when intelligence is informed by the consciousness of the Self."[34] In addition to saints and sages this type is represented by famous *kṣatriya* kings of yore, such as Janaka.

The epic ideal of human autonomy is perfectly captured in the image of the charioteer (symbolizing the *ātman*) who is able to guide the chariot of the body by taming the wild horses of the senses with the reins of the *buddhi* (XI.7.13–14; XII.280.1; XIV.50.4–5; cf. also III.202.21 and V.34.57, which use the same image without referring to the reins). This image is, of course, duplicated by the presence of Kṛṣṇa (the *ātman* or *puruṣa* who is nominally not an active participant in the fighting) as the charioteer and guide of the embodied soul, represented by Arjuna. Returning to the image of victory *(jaya)*, the epic view of self-determination is the victory of the rational element *(buddhi)* over the self-seeking impulses of desire and aversion *(rāgadveṣau)* for the objects of the senses, marked by enhanced self-sufficiency and control.

The epic would not contest that involuntary bodily movement is governed by natural causality *(prakṛti)*. However, action prompted by desire or aversion is driven, in turn, by the accumulated *puṇya* and *pāpa* resulting from the desire-prompted activities *(kāmyakarma)* of past lives, currently maturing as the existing personality. We are only "free" to the extent that we can resist *(vairāgya)* patterns of behavior contrary to the path of evolution (regarded as "sin"). Without this capacity, however, the sense of freedom that accompanies our activities is really only an illusion rooted in the sense of agency involved in viewing the action as "mine." Commenting on Kṛṣṇa's psychological treatment of this topic, Crawford notes that the Gītā

> does not fall into the customary traps of modern Behaviourists or Existentialists who argue either for freedom or determinism. Instead of taking a polaristic position, the Gītā tries to do justice to all ranges of human experience. On the lowest range, it concurs with Behaviouristic thought that nature is determined. But, unlike the Behaviourists, the Gītā does not stop there. In existentialistic fashion it proceeds to qualify the determinism of nature by man's mental and spiritual capacities to control nature. The lower self is progressively brought under the control of the higher Self, but in so doing, the lower is not abrogated by the higher. Instead, the interests and activities of the empirical self

are sublimated, so that all aspects of personality are made to function helpfully and harmoniously.[35]

At some point along this evolutionary road we arrive at that key crossroads of choice between the broad (easy) avenue of pleasure and power *(bhogaiśvarya)* and the narrow path of nonattachment leading to true freedom *(mokṣa)*. As we have noted in the case of Arjuna, the acquisition of power through the performance of *tapas* is a legitimate—indeed, a necessary path for the *Kṣatriya* to follow, but in the interests of society rather than of self. Bhīṣma argues strongly for the selfless exercise of power as guarantor of the dharma (XII.132). On the other hand (VI.24/BG.2.41–44), this quest for power can easily turn demonic when pursued by desirous natures *(kāmātma)* concerned only with what they can appropriate for themselves *(yogakṣema)*. One should therefore strive, by constant spiritual practice *(abhyāsa)*, to act without attachment to the fruits of action (*phalākāṇkṣī, niṣkāma,* etc.). Cultivation of such an attitude purifies and prepares the mind for the essential freedom that "consists in my accepting or not what stands determined for me, whether by Nature itself or by scriptures, saints, sages, and others."[36]

This ultimate realm of freedom is no longer the "freedom of doing" that stands on this side of good and evil and is capable of either, but the higher "freedom of being" in which the individual (if we can still describe him as such) aligns himself with the cosmic teleology of the avatar, and indeed no longer enjoys the freedom to be good or bad. Paradoxically, it is only the imperfect will that needs to be free to choose between good and bad courses of action: "The transition to the perfect will, which no longer has an Ought over it, takes place in freedom. But in this unique and final act of freedom the will 'exhausts' its capacity, it 'uses up' the substance of its freedom; and then for it there is 'at the root of its Being no freedom left over.' According to this view, man's true act of freedom is the self-annihilation of the ego and of the Ought."[37] This is clearly the view of the epic author (albeit without the notion of "will" as such).

This self-annihilation of the ego raises a key question: whether a freedom "beyond good and evil" may not also transcend our commonly accepted (Western) notions of the human person. We have already learned from the Gītā that *mokṣa* involves the sacrifice of the affective bonds of the little ego-self in favor of a larger system of identities that enables one to progressively expands one's perspectives and ego-boundaries to the point at which one is able to identify one's self with the self of all beings (the *sarvabhūtātmabhūtātmā* of VI.27/BG.5.7). The dharma clearly has no value or purpose at this point, since behavior is no longer governed by external prescription or inner imperative but is the spontaneous expression of a being whose actions are no longer his or her own. Like flowers or the sun that scatter their splendors freely according to their nature, such a person has become, in every respect, God's instrument *(nimittamātraṃ)* on earth (XII.276.28–30).

In psychological terms, the ego with its deficiency needs is replaced by a plenitude of being *(niṣkāma)* and a feeling of companionship with all life *(samatva)* that seeks the welfare of the world *(lokasaṃgraha)*. This is the dissociation of the *puruṣa* from the *prakṛti* that comes from calming the restless mind by means of the various spiritual practices *(abhyāsa)* recommended in the Bhagavadgītā (VI.28/BG.6.35). Discrimination *(viveka)* and detachment *(vairāgya)* are the "two wings of the bird" that provide the sāttvic bridge from the world of causal determinism (which is the *saṃsāra)* to the transcendental freedom of *mokṣa*. This reveals the strange paradox that what was the source of the bondage of the soul (that is, nature herself) becomes, in her higher teleological mode of operation *(sattva)*, a means of releasing the *puruṣa* from its previous attachments and spurious identifications with itself (VI.35/BG. 13.21).

Only by this relativisation of the human personality can we reconcile the apparent contradictions between the so-called Free Will statements and the determinism of the Gītā. As S. K. Belvalkar has noted, it is evident that Arjuna "does not doubt for a moment that he is a free agent, free to fight or not to fight."[38] But this is only because he identifies so completely with his nature *(prakṛti)* in the form of a particular body, mind, and intellect *(buddhi)*. He regards what he does as "my actions" whereas, in reality, they do not derive from his true self at all (the *ātman*) but from the modalities of nature *(guṇas)* expressed through him. What he regards as his personality *(svabhāva)* is a product of the past (VI.28/BG.6.43), and his habitual modes of thinking and acting are therefore completely determined by the causal energies of nature (VI.25/ BG.3.5; 3.27–28; 3.33; VI.27/BG.5.14; VI.35/BG.13.20; 13.29; VI.36/ BG.14.19; VI.40/BG.18.59–61).

The only way out of this impasse, as noted in chapter 6, is to abandon this identification with the *guṇas* by purifying the *buddhi* of its habitual mode of thinking "I am the doer" (VI.25/BG.3.27). And Kṛṣṇa introduces some practical techniques on how to accomplish this. Arjuna should first seek to renounce the fruits of his actions either by offering these fruits as "a sacrifice" or *yajña* (VI.26/BG.4.23), or by dedicating his actions and their fruits to the Lord who dwells in the heart (VI.25/ BG.3.30; VI.27/BG.5.10; VI.34/BG.12.6; 12.10; VI.40/BG.18.57). But the significant further suggestion is that he replace the thought of himself as a "doer" with alternatives more in keeping with the reality of things such as, "the *guṇas* work among the *guṇas*" (VI.25/BG.3.28), "I do nothing at all" (VI.27/BG.5.8), "the senses work among the objects of the senses" (VI.27/BG.5.9), "Vāsudeva is all" (VI.29/BG.7.19), or "it is only the *guṇas* working" (VI.36/BG.14.23). These seeds are all planted to cultivate in him the idea that he (that is, the *puruṣa* or *ātman*) is not really the actor, and thus untouched by the actions of *prakṛti* (VI.35/BG.13.32). These practices combine with meditation and others to sever all ties to nature's field of activity *(kṣetra)* until he gets to the point at which he knows with the eye of knowledge *(jñānacakṣusā)* what it is to be free of nature *(bhūtaprakṛtimokṣa)*, and can then proceed to the supreme state (VI.35/BG.13.34).

10

Conclusion

It has become evident that the quest for essential freedom leads the soul *(jīvātman)* to abandon its own self-identity in favor of a greater identity as *puruṣa* (spirit) or *ātman* (self). This *puruṣa* or *ātman* is identified or associated in some manner with the Supreme Person *(puruṣottama* and *paramapuruṣa)* or the Supreme Self *(paramātman)*. Although the exact status of this *puruṣa* became an important topic in later commentaries, the Mahābhārata itself is not definitive as to whether there is ultimately only one or a multiplicity of *puruṣas* (cf. VI.37/BG.15.16–17; XII.338). Our task in what follows is to focus on the implications of this psychological passage from one form of self-experience (as the *jīvātman* or *puruṣa* associated with *prakṛti*) to another (as *puruṣa* disassociated from all determinations by *prakṛti*) for what we noted at the beginning of this investigation (p. 5) regarding the dichotomy of ideas about the role of *puruṣakāra* and *daiva* in the conduct of life.

We are referring here to the two distinct categories of learned opinion (XII.224.50–52; restated at XII.230.4–6) regarding the factors contributing to worldly success. In our translation these were characterized as those who take their stand in action *(karmastha)* and, those who take their stand in the truth *(sattvastha)*, respectively. What is involved in these two points of view on action may be now gleaned from what we have learned so far about the differing [opinions] (*viṣama* = lit. "uneven"; "not uniform") faced by those who argue from the perspective of action. Even the ancient bards are confused *(mohita)* about the mysterious course of action *(gahanā karmaṇo gatiḥ)* (VI.26/BG.4.16–17).

The "Fate" of Human Action

A major complexity is the succession of stages (or "moments" in Paul Ricoeur's terminology) involved in the course (the *gati*) of a voluntary action, each of which is liable to determination by karmic or alien forces, *daiva* (fate) or *haṭha* (chance) as the case may be. Perhaps the clearest outline of the etiology of action is offered by the following exposition to Bṛhaspati attributed to Manu-prajāpati:

> Just as plants in the soil are dependent on the one earth, the intellect *(buddhi)*, with the inner self as witness, [is dependent upon] the actions associated with it [that is, on past conduct]. [Just as] the propensity to act *(abhisaṃdhitā)* is born of past desire *(lipsāpūrva)* [and] desire is born of prior habits of thought *(jñānapūrvodbhavā)*, the fruit [of action] *(phala)* is rooted in action *(karma)*, and action in a prior propensity to act. One should know that the fruit is produced by the action, action is produced by the intention (*jñeya* = "intended object"). The intention is made up of concepts *(jñāna)*. One should know that these concepts consist of truth and error. The destruction of [this chain of] actions, intentions, results of action and concepts [leads to] the establishment of that divine fruit called the [true] object of knowledge [that is, Brahman]. (XII.199.5–8)

The human predicament thus arises as an effect of past conduct, producing a "personality" with a tendency to perpetuate these past patterns of conduct into the future.

This also reveals what we have suspected all along, namely that *puruṣakāra* is but *daiva* in disguise. Whether the driving force behind this cycle is a god, demon, or karmic causation (the *daiva* of unconscious motivations) would make no difference. As Maṅki muses on losing all his worldly wealth to the waywardness of a camel: "If there should occur anything that might be called exertion *(pauruṣa)*, on being examined, it would, in fact, turn out to be destiny *(daiva)*" (XII. 171.13).

Although these determinations may intervene at any point in the cycle of action, those moved by desire for worldly gain naturally tend to focus on the *daiva* of unforeseen or untoward events in the external social or natural environments. Kṛṣṇa counts this form of *daiva* among the contributory causes involved in the accomplishment of all actions (VI.40/BG.18.14), and Nārada wryly comments that "Were it not that the results of action were governed by other circumstances persons would obtain whatever object they desired" (XII.318.9). The aging process and other human calamities would be unknown. Unlike Nārāyaṇa (who is able to fulfill his plans without the least impediment), the fruits of our endeavors do not always conform to our desires (XII.337.905*). Furthermore, there is the suggestion that our control over nature is proportional to the degree of control we are able to exercise over our own natures: “The powers *(śakti)* gained by the practices of virtue and Yoga enable one to roam the heavens at will, to realize all one’s purposes and to attain the highest state of existence” (XII.263.53). This is because the *prakṛti* controlled from within (own nature) is the stuff of the world itself (external nature). However, since power corrupts, there is an acute danger of inflation of the ego leading to an abuse of power and eventual destruction at the hands of the avatar (exemplified in the cases of Duryodhana, Jarāsaṃdha, Śiśupala, and other epic characters).

From Manu’s description, the only possibility of escape from this vicious circle is by breaking the chain of causality. However this introduces additional complications arising out of the conflicting Vedic injunctions to perform action! *(kuru karma)* and abandon action! *(tyaja karma)* respectively (cf. XII.233.1). For if the chain of action can be broken only by renouncing all active social involvement (the *nivṛttidharma* of the Brahmin *saṃnyāsin),* what are the prospects for the salvation of the *kṣatriya* king, or for anyone else called to active social duty *(pravṛttidharma)*? This conflict is greatly intensified in the case of Yudhiṣṭhira, when he finds himself forced by circumstances *(daiva)* to exercise the most deadly force *(daṇḍa; hiṃsā)*—among the most negative values of the Vedic tradition—with all the vigor (*puruṣakāra, utthāna,* etc.) at his command.

The genius of the solution proposed by Kṛṣṇa in the Bhagavadgītā—namely *karmayoga* and its higher amplification in the form of *bhakti,* is that *puruṣakāra* becomes the hallmark of a successful endeavor that is no longer judged for its outward form or function but for the inner spirit that animates it. This implies a revolution of traditional values that may be understood in cosmic as well as in psychological terms. Cosmically, the world and its driving forces are no longer depreciated as a “fall” from the pristine Consciousness but become objects of worship as the wonders *(vibhūtis)* of God’s Creation (VI.32/BG.10.19ff.). The model for the *nivṛttidharma* of the Upaniṣadic *saṃnyāsin* was the cosmic *pralaya* in which the processes of the world are dissolved into the yogic quiescence from which they came. In the ritual of entry into *saṃnyāsa* the Brahmin aspirant formally “abandons” the world of action *(karmabhūmi)*. Summarizing the analysis of Madeleine Biardeau, Alf Hiltebeitel describes how the “one who performs this ceremony symbolically renounces the three sacrificial fires and the three saṃsāric worlds and enters into the enlarged universe in which there are four additional worlds beyond those of the ordinary person, there to find himself in the company of the Devas and the Pitṛs, ‘all of these, like himself, being admitted to deliverance at the moment of the cosmic *pralaya.*’ ”[1] Human activity (karma) and initiative *(puruṣakāra)* thus tended to be devalued. In place of the external ritual of the sacrifice the *saṃnyāsin* is enjoined to perform a libation of his senses and mind into the fire that dwells in his own heart (XII.237.28).

But this *pralaya* model is abandoned by *bhakti* in favor of a new model of salvation based on the creative phase of the cosmic cycle. Practically and psychologically, the promise of *mokṣa* is not only extended to all members of society (including women) but may be realized at the heart of the most abject activities, including the "reprehensible duties" of a king (XII.32.22) and those of a "killer" butcher (III.198.20ff.). By replacing the physical abandonment of actions *(karmasaṃnyāsa)* with actions (that is, *pravṛtti)* undertaken with an inner attitude of renunciation (that is, *nivṛtti*) the aspirant can have the best of both worlds. The unconscious mind is gradually purified of the atavistic pattern of identifications *(saṃskāras)* that fetter the human spirit *(puruṣa)* to the causal cycles of nature *(prakṛti)*. *Puruṣakāra* is thereby rehabilitated in the vigor of duties performed without self-involvement *(nirmama* or *nirahaṃkāra)* (VI.24/BG.2.71) and self-interest *(naiṣkarmya)* (VI.25/BG.3.4), dedicating all actions and fruits to Kṛṣṇa (VI.25/BG.3.30). *Karmasaṃnyāsa* remains open to the Brahmin, and is even preferred over the traditional *pravṛttidharma* of a Vedic ritualism motivated by a desire that perpetuates the cycle of rebirth (cf. XII.233.6–8). However *karmasaṃnyāsa* must be closed to the *Kṣatriya* king since it is opposed to his *svadharma* as a warrior (VI.25/BG.3.35). It is also beyond the competence of a rājasic personality such as Arjuna (VI.27/BG.5.6).

We must recognize, however, that while *puruṣakāra* becomes a leading virtue of the active life, and perfectly consistent with the quest for true freedom, it is clearly fated to dissolve with the dissolution of the ego *(ahaṃkāra)* and its sense of agency *(kartṛtva)*. In the last analysis, the perspective of those who take their stand in action *(karmastha)* is the perspective of a *puruṣa* particularized by a given body, mind, and intellect, in short the perspective of the human personality *(jīvātman)* entangled in the causal cycles of *prakṛti*. However, the actions themselves are no illusion (as Śaṃkara is later to assert in his introduction to SBG.5), since the world of *bhakti* is an objectification of the Lord Himself, and He works tirelessly to sustain it (VI.25/BG.3.22–23). On the other hand, the activities of the human personality are truly "self"-determined (by the *puruṣa*) only to the extent that the notion of "I do" has been shed; that is to say that the attitude of the agent is *nirahaṃkāra*—without the feeling that his or her actions are mine *(nirmama)*.

The Problem of Agency

The question then becomes: who is the real agent? This subject is not addressed directly in the Mahābhārata itself, but important later commentators of the Bhagavadgītā suggest that, ultimately, it is the Supreme Divinity *(puruṣottama)* who is the agent. Although this is in line with the cosmogony of the Divine Yoga, it does leave the twin issues of human responsibility and the status of the Vedic injunctions very much in limbo. Śaṃkara and Rāmānuja both approach the issue in the context of their respective theories about the relationship between the *puruṣa* and the *puruṣottama*. Arguing from the relative standpoint *(vyavahārika-satya)* in Brahmasūtrabhāṣya II.III.42, Śaṃkara reverts to the traditional mode of thinking that the *jīva* is driven by a god. The major difference is that, in this case, the god in question is the manifested form of the Lord (Īśvara), acting in accordance with the previous efforts *(pūrvaprayatna)* of the *jīva* itself: "For though agency *(kartṛtva)* is derived from above, the *jīva* really does act. As he acts so also does Īśvara make him act. Furthermore, Īśvara makes him act in the present in accordance with his [the *jīva*'s] previous efforts *(pūrvaprayatna),* and He caused these acts [earlier] in accordance with even earlier efforts. Thus, since the *saṃsāra* is beginningless *(anādi),* this view is above reproach" (Śaṃkara: BrSBh. II.III.42). From the ultimate standpoint *(paramārthikasatya),* however, the *jīvātman* and all else are products of the divine projection of the world, which is *māyā*.

In Śrībhāṣya I.III.41 Rāmānuja too, argues that the Lord is the source of all agency. However, more conscious of preserving the integrity of the Vedic injunctions, he wishes to salvage some responsibility for the individual by falling back on his theory of qualified nondifference *(viśiṣṭādvaita)*. But though the *puruṣa* is independent *(svatantra)* of the Supreme Self and thus can act on its own, it is still the latter who, by means of granting permission *(anumatidānena)* to the *jīvātman* to act, must be allowed the final say in the matter. This idea of *anumati* is clearly inspired by what is stated at VI.35/BG.13.22. This reads: "The *puruṣa* in this body is called the witness *(upadraṣṭṛ),* the permitter *(anumantṛ),* the sustainer, the enjoyer, the Great Lord, and the *paramātman*" (VI.35/BG.13.22).[2]

The initial direction of human development is thus toward a "freedom of doing" made possible by increased self-control and insight into the truth about the abject state of the embodied *puruṣa (jīvātman)*. But this enlargement of vision also brings a progressive shift in self-identity and sense of agency, from the characteristic "I do" of the *ahaṃkāra,* to the realization that the real "I" (the *puruṣa*) is inherently free of the prākṛtic encumbrances of body, mind, and intellect, all of which are governed by natural causality. Whether divine particle *(amśa)* or divine totality, this *puruṣa* is, in reality, the passive subject of experience, the witness *(upadraṣṭṛ)* and enjoyer *(bhoktṛ)* of the cosmic play of name and form. Embodied as the *jīvātman*, its task is to dissociate itself, that is to say, to sacrifice the *ahaṃkāra* and to offer the body as a pure channel for the higher divine agency to express through it. This renunciation of attachment to self-interest *(nirahaṃkāra)* brings the essential freedom of *mokṣa*.

True "self-determination" thus involves the mutation of the ego-bound personality whose claim to autonomy and freedom is ultimately founded on a misconception of its own true nature. All that may be claimed for the freedom of one who takes his stand in action *(karmastha)* is a freedom-in-bondage that reminds us very much of the only human freedom *(liberté seulement humaine)* of Paul Ricoeur. Such freedom necessarily falls short of the ideal limit—the limit that lies beyond the limitations of space and time and the frictions of matter, beyond all particularity of existence and limitations of knowledge. In the epic context such an ideal can only be realized by one who takes his or her stand in the truth *(sattvastha)*, that is to say, by a "self" that no longer identifies with the body-mind-intellect complex of personality (or with Ricoeur's incarnate cogito) but with the Grand Design of Kṛṣṇa. It is no longer the *ahaṃkāra* that acts but the Lord who uses this body as His instrument—*nimittamātraṃ bhava savyasācin* (VI.33/BG.11.33). This is the essential freedom *(mokṣa)* beyond identification with the causal system of *prakṛti*. From this higher vantage point of liberation, the *puruṣa* freely accepts the determination of the "Lord in the heart of all beings," whose form of agency is *daiva*.

From the perspective of the *ahaṃkāra* the course of action is a mystery *(gahana)*, since it moves from the necessities received from the past toward an uncertain future state determined by a mix of individual and cosmic forces. Here we sense the only too human condition of the incarnate will as the unity of the voluntary and the involuntary, and Ricoeur's analysis offers tantalizing parallels to epic notions of the *ahaṃkāra* as the unity of *puruṣa* and *prakṛti*. The Bhagavadgītā is, of course, quite clear in relating *prakṛti* with the realm of the involuntary. In contrast to Ricoeur's person, however, the epic "person" is moved not so much by a will as by atavistic impulses (*kāma, krodha,* etc.) modulated by a power of insight *(viveka)* into the nature of the *puruṣa* and its human predicament. Although not directly the actor, the witnessing *puruṣa* is nevertheless a sort of "catalytic agent" of human activity in proportion to the visionary insight sparked in the *buddhi*. This *buddhi* progressively reins in the runaway horses of the passions, producing more sāttvic modes of behavior and a shift in the focus of attention from mundane striving *(puruṣakāra)* to the quest for liberation *(mumukṣu)*. In sum, the epic personality is a mental fiction that dissolves in the visionary insight, together with the cycle of desire *(lipsā; kāma)*, propensity to act *(abhisaṃdhitā)*, action (karma), and fruit *(phala)* that fuels the eternal round of human initiative *(puruṣakāra)*.

Here, too, the parallel with Ricoeur is instructive. The complexities involved in the passage from *decision*, to *movement*, and finally to *consent* to the conditions of "absolute necessity" in human life (his equivalent of *daiva*) reveal a hierarchy of freedoms based on the reciprocity of the voluntary and the involuntary, action and condition for action:[3] "Deciding is the act of the will which is based on motives; moving is the act of the will which activates abilities or powers; consenting is the act of the will which acquiesces to a necessity—remembering that it is the same will which is considered successively from different points of view: the point of view of legitimacy, of efficacy, and of patience."[4] And do not our epic characters, too, enjoy these contingent freedoms? They enjoy a "freedom of choice" in which they are motivated (that is to say conditioned, determined, circumscribed) by the horizon of reasons and values represented by their *svadharma;* they exhibit a "freedom of movement" (or of doing) in which they are governed by the limits of their various capacities as human beings; and they are urged to a "freedom of consent" by which they can (potentially at least) say a final "yes" to the karma inherited from the past in the form of character *(śīla)*, the unconscious tendencies of the mind *(vāsanas* or *saṃskāras)*, and "the necessity that comes from living in a particular place, being born on a particular day"[5] (rendered by the absolute karmic necessities of *jāti*—birth, *āyus*—length of life, and *bhoga*—our preordained quanta of pleasure and pain). Each stage is marked by a polarity of activity and receptivity. In decision, for example, "there are choices which tend toward a simple obedience to reasons not questioned at the moment of choice, and other choices which, in confusion of motives, tend toward a risk, even the throw of the dice."[6] We are reminded of Yudhiṣṭhira's decision to participate in the dice game, and of Śiva playing dice with Pārvatī (I.189.14ff.), dice being the symbol of *daiva* par excellence. Human effort itself *(puruṣakāra)* is a measure of the resistance of self and world that must be overcome. The ebb and flow of all aspects of life are both willed and endured; we are all "fated" to act from given conditions.

Ricoeur also makes the further point that this only human freedom "responds to the no of condition with the no of refusal. . . . In effect, *what* we refuse, is always, in the last analysis, the limitation of character, the shadows of the unconscious, and the contingence of life."[7] Whether in the form of surrender or a Promethean defiance: "At the core of refusal is defiance and defiance is the fault. To refuse necessity from below is to defy Transcendence. I have to discover the Wholly Other which at first repels me. Here lies the most fundamental choice of philosophy: either God or I."[8] The figure of Duryodhana is surely a prime example of the demonic drive for absolute sovereignty that comes from his refusal to accept any limit to his human condition. His last words are a magnificent demonic gesture of defiance before the awesome power of Divinity. Significantly, this defiance is greeted by a heavy rain of fragrant flowers out of heaven, accompanied by the music and song of *gandharvas* and *apsaras* (IX.60.47–53; XI.63.18–39).[9]

Of course we must be careful not to carry these parallels too far in view of the obvious differences between the epic *ahaṃkāra* and Ricoeur's *cogito* (which is no mental fiction but the prime datum of consciousness). In particular, his notion of consent falls far short of the *bhakti* transformation of human agency and identity, yet he sees no possibility of its achievement: "Who can say *yes* to the end, without reservations? Suffering and evil, respected in their own shocking mystery, protected against degradation into a problem, lie in our way as the impossibility of saying an unreserved *yes* to character, the unconscious, and life, and of transforming the sorrow of the finite, the indefinite, and of contingence perfectly into joy."[10] But this is precisely the achievement of the *sattvastha* who, from the sublime heights of their vision, can freely consent to this divine agency—*daiva*—at work in themselves and in the world around them.

The Solution to the Antinomy of Providence

The antinomy between *puruṣakāra* and extrahuman agencies such as *daiva* or *haṭha* can only be reconciled in the light of this quantum shift of self-identity that takes place at the vanishing point of the *ahaṃkāra*. This symbolic "death" of the I-center is the prelude to a new birth in which the play *(līlā)* of the sense objects ceases to evoke the incessant demand to be "mine" *(mama)*. No longer directed to filling a lack, human striving *(puruṣakāra)* gets transformed into a plenitude of divine energy that may be viewed as the *daivalīlā* of Kṛṣṇa playing in the world through the flute of the human body. Seen from the macrocosmic perspective of the mythology, the combinations of *puruṣa* and *prakṛti* follow the Supreme Spirit *(paramapuruṣa)* through His triple states as Brahmā—creator of the cosmic *ahaṃkāra* and Lord of *pravṛtti*, Viṣṇu—

supporter of this process in time, and Śiva—who returns the process to a state of quiescence *(nivṛtti)*. The gulf that separates the *karmastha* from the *sattvastha* is thus a gulf between two views of the universe and human nature, as the movement is toward *pravṛtti* or toward *nivṛtti*. This, in turn, constitutes the basis for two views of self-identity and human agency. Limited by their own confusions, the *karmastha* can only struggle toward the limits of their "only human freedom"; while the *sattvastha* abandon this useless struggle for the greater freedom that comes from freely *consenting* to the part they are given to play in the divine drama of the world.

This dichotomy of view is also reflected in the two distinct connotations of the word *daiva* in the epic, the first constituting a mark of self-centeredness, the other based on the true state of things *(sat)*. From the self-centered perspective of the *ahaṃkāra,* the term is typically used to express the sense of powerlessness that emerges as a result of untoward reversals of fortune. The *daiva* (with a small *d*) that continually thwarts the cherished hopes and plans of King Dhṛtarāṣṭra provides an eloquent example of someone who falls victim to his all-too-human attachments. On the other hand, the cosmic "Time" referred to by the various sages and reformed demons met with in the Śāntiparvan (Bali, Namuchi, Vṛtra, etc.) points to a transcendent *Daiva* (with a capital *D*) that governs the course of things as a whole, including human society and the microcosmos of embodied existence. The world process is an expression of the one divine power that works not only beyond us but also through us. From this perspective everything is seen "with an equal eye" *(samadarśin),* that is to say as an expression of the one cosmic power of *Daiva*. Under these conditions the only course is to align oneself—like Arjuna after the divine theophany in the eleventh chapter of the Gītā, with what we know of the cosmic purpose, and to accept what comes in the knowledge that success and failure, victory and defeat, and pleasure and pain, are endemic to the temporal cycle of *saṃsāra*.[11]

On the other hand, the epic author himself does not appear to be aware of the basic contradiction posed by the juxtaposition of a finalistic teleology that permeates the course of the world, and our God-given freedom to choose between the good *(śreyas)* and our own self-indulgence *(preyas)*. In the light of the cosmic determinism of *Daiva,* human self-determination is reduced to a groundless phantom. This is Nicolai Hartmann's "antinomy of providence" in which the ethos of man "is annihilated, his will paralyzed. All initiative, all setting up and pursuit of ends is transferred to God. . . . In this way the finalistic determinism of divine providence abolishes ethical freedom. But if we grant validity to personal freedom, it inevitably abolishes the finalistic determinism of divine providence. Each stands in contradiction to the other, as thesis to antithesis."[12]

It was left to the medieval commentators to wrestle with this nagging tension, a tension that could only intensify with the *bhakti* emphasis on the life-affirming values of human activity in society. This led to a spirited defense of the Vedic injunctions and the traditional structure of the *varṇāśramadharma* against the world-denying tendencies of the Upaniṣadic *saṃnyāsa*. Human life is exalted when the individual is made accountable for transgressions against *svadharma*, the complex system of religious duties and obligations to which he or she is subject. Without the human power to effect results, says Yudhiṣṭhira (III.32.25–27), there would be no reason why the *ṛṣi* or anyone else should follow the dharma. Age-old prescriptions regarding *tapas, brahmacārya, yajña, svādhyāya, dāna,* and *ārjavam* would go down as the greatest hoax of all time *(vipralambhātyanta)*. And recalling her statement on p. 89, Draupadī concurs that human advancement must depend on freedom of choice: "One [first] makes up one's mind *(manas)* on what one wants (the *artha*) and then acts on it. Basing himself on prior deliberation *(buddhipūrva)*, the cool-headed man *(dhīra)* is thereby the cause (*kāraṇa*, that is, is responsible) for what follows. While it is not possible to provide an exact accounting of the [chain of] acts involved, social progress is the result of human choice" (III.33.23–24). This echoes the oft-repeated claim (for example, at V.130.15–16; XII.92.6; XII.139.7; already noted on p. 90) that it is the conduct of the king that determines the conditions of the time *(kāla)* and the different ages of the world *(yuga)*.

Once again we are faced with the antinomy of providence. What may be true for a world of human agents is hardly consistent with a mythology of *yugas* determined by the strictest periodicities of time. But are we asking too much of our epic author, as Biardeau suggests?

> The difficulty we have is only conceptual and would not be a problem for the mythographers. . . . At times we are told that *daiva* is all-powerful to the point where no one is responsible for the great carnage of the battle, at other times however it is Dhṛtarāṣtra or Duryodhana, or even Yudhiṣṭhira who bear the burden of the catastrophe. The intervention of the avatar, invariably set at the meeting point of two *yugas,* is necessarily a product of inexorable *daiva* which any attempt to avoid would be useless. If on the other hand, we take the point of view of the king who, by his action, introduces the reign of this or that *yuga,* thereby imposing a human causality on the course of time, *daiva* can be overcome and the role of the king is to turn it to the advantage of his kingdom. When the epic narrative is set at the meeting point of two *yugas* it is the first perspective that prevails. When on the other hand,

> attention is centered on the war to be declared or avoided, it is the human drama that is the main issue. But it is in the nature of this double myth to keep these two types of causality together whatever difficulty we might have—conceptual once again—of thinking them together.[13]

This "double-myth" explanation of the two perspectives does not go nearly far enough; for it misses the deeper ambivalence of the epic view of human nature, based on the two antithetical views of self-identity just discussed. It is to these two forms of self-identity exemplified by the *karmastha* and the *sattvastha,* that the ultimate source of this dichotomy of opinion on the subject of human agency must be traced. The antinomy is solved by Śaṃkara by losing humanity and the world to the divine illusion *(māyā)*. In his view, human beings *(jīvas)* are fictional self-identities performing unreal activities out of attachment for the objects, emotional states, and ideas about a world that never really was. Commenting on VI.37/BG.15.7 he writes:

> [In the verse beginning with the word] *"mama,"* [the words] *"mama eva"* [refer to] Myself. [The word] *"aṃśa"* [is glossed as] "a portion of Myself," the Paramātman, Nārāyaṇa who, in a state of turmoil, appears in *"jīvaloka,"* [that is to say] in the world of embodied souls, [which is] the *samsāra,* as one of them, eternal. [The words] *"jīvabhūta sanātana"* [refer to the embodied soul] manifesting as the eternal and age-old doer and enjoyer. [He is like] a reflection of the sun in water, which is a portion of the [real] sun; and on removal of the immediate cause, the water, goes back to the original sun, and does not return. In the same way, the soul goes back [to its origin] and does not return. Or, it is like the space *(ākāśa)* in a jar etc., which is limited by the form *(upādhi)* of the jar. On the destruction of the jar this portion *(aṃśa)* of space becomes one with [infinite] space and does not return. (SBG. 15.7)[14]

Rāmānuja, on the other hand, seeks to save the world and its karma with a Divine Power that "permits" the self-centered activity of real individual entities until the proper order of things (which is the dharma) deteriorates to the point at which the Divinity is forced once more to intervene, in the form of the avatar, to destroy the perpetrators of social chaos *(adharma),* and reestablish a new order of society upon the ashes of the old. In this reading—much closer to the spirit of the text, the things and beings of the world are fully real. The source of human misunderstanding is not with objective reality as such, but with the relationships that apply between the entities involved, namely the *paramapuruṣa* (or *paramātman* or Īśvara), the individual souls or *puruṣas,* and the material evolutes of *prakṛti.* A living being is a real composite of soul and body involved in a real cycle of change: "This *prakṛti,* active from time immemorial, having evolved into a field of experience *(kṣetra),* and being in association with the *puruṣa,* becomes the cause of the bondage (of the *puruṣa)* through its own modifications such as desire *(icchā)* and aversion *(dveṣa)*. This (same *prakṛti),* through other modifications such as humility *(amānitva)* etc., becomes the cause of salvation of the *puruṣa*" (RGB.13.19).

Biardeau is more correct in her belief that the epic author would have tended to see this issue in the context of the practical needs of his reader/listeners, not as a problem to be solved intellectually. His message is directed, not to the scholar, but to the ordinary men and women of his day. This is born out by the stirring exhortation of the Bhāratasāvitrī (the "Essence of the Bhārata") with which the epic concludes—clearly designed to galvanize the *puruṣakāra* of the nameless multitudes traveling his vision of the great human journey:

> Thousands of mothers and fathers, and hundreds of sons and wives come and go in this world. Others too [will similarly come and go in the future]. There are thousands of occasions for joy and hundreds of occasions for fear. These come day after day to the ignorant but never to the wise. With uplifted arms I cry aloud but nobody hears me. Dharma is the foundation for *artha* and *kāma*. Why is it not respected? For the sake of neither pleasure nor of fear nor greed should anyone cast off dharma—not even for the sake of life itself. Dharma is eternal but pleasure and pain are not eternal. The *jīva* is eternal but its cause [that is, ignorance] is not eternal.[15]

Appendix: Some Notes on Scholarship

The extraordinary scope and complexity of the Mahābhārata, and the apparent doctrinal divergences to be found there, present methodological difficulties for scholars interested in the study of specific themes. Norbert Klaes puts the matter succinctly when he writes that

> one of the main difficulties of scholarly work on this immense poem up to now has been how to approach it and with which method to criticize the various sections. In other words, before discussing single episodes, one should first know, whether the whole Mahābhārata is conceived according to a single literary design, whether central ideas or purposes govern it and justify the collection of multifarious elements, or whether the poem is just a more or less accidental collection of both very old and new material.[1]

Individual components or particular themes can only be understood in terms of one's understanding of the poem as a whole. The history of scholarly examination has shown that this understanding tends to depend, in turn, on one's view of the process of composition that made the Mahābhārata what it is today.

Prior to the Second World War scholarly opinion tended to polarize between those who saw the text as a confused assemblage of heterogeneous material originating from various sources and belonging to different historical and philosophical strata, and those who saw it as the expression of some central guiding agenda.[2] The first view regarded the text as consisting of two fundamentally incompatible elements, an original epic core and an undigested mass of later accretions that could be weeded out by the surgical skills of higher criticism. For this first group, the Mahābhārata problem

> reduces itself to the discovery of criteria which will enable us to analyze the poem and to dissect out the "epic nucleus" from the spurious additions with which it is deeply incrusted. This is the "Analytical Theory" of the origin and character of the Mahābhārata, which was espoused by the majority of the Western critics of the Great Epic of India, chief

> among them being Lassen, Webber *(sic),* Ludwig, Sörensen, Hopkins and Winternitz.[3]

To this list we must add the name of Adolf Holzmann the Younger who propounded an extravagant "Inversion Theory" (subsequently discredited) to explain the so-called sins of the Pāṇḍavas, arguing that it was, in fact, the Kauravas (that is, rather than the Pāṇḍavas) who were the embodiments of righteousness in the original epic.

The second group of scholars, led by Joseph Dahlmann around the turn of the century, propounded what was later dubbed (by Hopkins) as the "Synthetic Theory" of the origin and character of the poem:

> This theory categorically repudiates as utterly fantastic the modern notion that the Great Epic is but a haphazard compilation of disjointed and incoherent units. It insists on the other hand—as the name of the theory already suggests—that the Mahābhārata is primarily a synthesis, a synthesis of all the various aspects of Law, in the widest sense of the term covered by the Indian conception of Dharma, cast by a master intellect into the alluring shape of a story, of an epic. . . . The poem is, as Indian tradition has always implied, a conscious product of literary art *(kāvya)* of the highest order, with a pronounced unity of conception, aim, and treatment.[4]

Instead of separating the narrative from the didactic portions of the epic as the first group attempted to do, this synthetic view saw the didactic material, including the Bhagavadgītā, as an essential part of the poem—indeed so essential that the story itself could well have been invented for the purpose of illustrating the moral and ethical ideas of the author(s).[5]

While Dahlmann himself had toyed with the idea of symbolism as a key to the inner meaning of certain aspects of the plot (for example, the polyandrous marriage of Draupadī), it was not until the postwar work of Stig Wikander and Georges Dumézil in the field of comparative mythology that attempts to explain the poem as a reflection of historical events gave way to the opposite conception, namely that the poem constitutes a sort of historicized mythology.[6] Thus, for Dumézil: "The problem is not to explain how the poem developed from a nucleus of real events for which no evidence remains, but to determine how, at what point of the story, at what generation of the heroes, the link with history was forged."[7] The poem itself is not modeled after historical events but on an alleged eschatological myth dating from Indo-European times, and featuring a trifunctional hierarchy of gods.[8] Dumézil argues that

> In essence, the Mahābhārata is the transposition of a vast system of mythic representations into the world of men. The principal gods, centered on the hierarchy of the gods of the three functions, as well as a number of demons were related to the main heroes not as an afterthought but as their models, and the conceptual links between these gods were transferred to the heroes in the form of ties of kinship (brothers, wife) or of alliance, friendship, hostility. The storyline of the poem is itself the transposition of a myth related to a great world crisis: the confrontation of the forces of Good and the forces of Evil develops to a paroxysm of destruction which results in a renaissance. . . .
>
> The transposition was a well thought out literary project, rigorously followed with no deviation by skillful and talented technical specialists, who fully explored the possibilities inherent in the mythic material. A team working along the same lines and under firm direction, is the hypothesis that best takes account of the scope and success of the operation. And not only a team: a school, since, with the exception of out-of-context interpolations, of innumerable narrative or philosophical excursions that are easily detached, we recognize revisions, associated variations, certain proliferations (such as the fourth book), which attest to the successive efforts in this direction, and in support of the transposition.[9]

In his view, the transition from myth to history is not made until the very end of the epic when rule passes from Arjuna—the mythical transposition of the warrior-god Indra, to his grandson Parikṣit.

The emerging Western view of the Mahābhārata as a symbolic whole is in keeping with the traditional conception of the epic espoused by Indian commentators such as Madhva in the thirteenth century and V. S. Sukthankar in the twentieth, as already reported in chapter 2. Krishna Chaitanya also follows tradition in adopting an aesthetic view of the author(s) intentions (albeit with Western existentialist overtones). The poem, as he sees it, is a unique literary product

> which tried to discover, through art, what philosophical thinking and related modalities had tried to find out: how man can realize the greatest possible meaning, the maximum value, in his living, in the conditions of incarnate existence. The most liberated state of being *(moksha)* can be attained only if one exists first. And existence has evolved on earth through the tremendous impulsion of an *elan vital,* surfacing in man as his libido *(kama)* which gives him the drive for acquiring the resources of a secure material existence *(artha)*. But the drive of the libido and the desire for economic means have to be tempered by the discipline of normative living *(dharma)* if man is to attain liberation. These are the hierarchically arranged goals of man outlined by

> prior thought and the epic explicitly states that it is in one respect the science of these goals (I. 62). But the tremendous thrust of the libido, which isolates man and sets him against his brethren and nature, had to be grasped in its fullness and intensity with far greater understanding than in the rather bloodless speculations of philosophy. Vyasa lays bare the structural violence that is deeply embedded in the life of this world, the role it plays in creating balances, before he proceeds to explore ways of securing harmony in less ruthless ways. The germinal metaphor of the wood and the tigers expands to colossal dimensions in the carnage of the Kurukshetra battle-field. But solutions that can end this type of carnage are also offered in the great discourse in the very same field. A comprehensively conscious artistic intelligence is behind the creation of this work.[10]

This Indian exegetical tradition has since inspired Western readers such as Ruth Cecily Katz, who interprets the epic and the character of Arjuna at the heroic, human, and devotional levels. In her view: "the creation of order by sacrifice seems to be the heroic meaning of the Kurukshetra War and the epic as a whole."[11] The human dimension is marked by the moral ambiguities involved in fulfillment of this task, while the devotional imperative is the "sacrifice" by which the hero abandons his ego in acceptance of the divine plan of Kṛṣṇa (equivalent to his "fate").[12] She explicitly acknowledges her debt to Sukthankar (going back to Madhva) by noting: "The three levels of Arjuna's personality correspond in part to those noted by Vishnu Sitaram Sukthankar as running through the epic as a whole." She acknowledges the existence of a "metaphysical" (in contrast to devotional) dimension but feels that this is better illustrated by the character of Yudhiṣṭhira than by that of Arjuna who is "never strictly a philosopher in the epic."[13]

Ritual has also received attention in recent years as a symbolic repository of the inner meaning of the text, for example, Heino Gehrts sees the Mahābhārata as "the consequent development of one central idea: the consecution of events as well as the characters and the distribution of its heroes are regulated by the form of one of India's ancient rituals of royal consecration, by the *rājasūya* . . . the author of the Mahābhārata is convinced, that the *rājasūya* is a dangerous ritual, that it may lead—under the influence of demoniacal perturbations—to the extermination of the warrior caste."[14] Alf Hiltebeitel is also attracted by the sacrificial model.[15] Starting with the trifunctional Indo-European model of Georges Dumézil, Hiltebeitel concludes by proposing a somewhat different view of the relation of myth (concerning the gods) and epic (concerning the heroic exploits of men). The way in which the epic poets composed/compiled the Mahābhārata "would seem to have been not so much through a process of 'transposition' as through a process of correlation between two levels of continually changing and growing tradition: myth and epic. The epic poets would thus emerge not so much as programmers, transposing one set of information into another form, but as *ṛṣis,* in this case the *ṛṣis* of the 'Fifth Veda' whose 'school' is covered by the name of the elusive but ever-available *ṛṣi* Vyāsa."[16] In this context, he sees the sacrifice of battle *(raṇayajña)* as the fundamental symbolism shaping the Mahābhārata war, with Kṛṣṇa performing the role of sacrificial priest.[17]

Recently, Hiltebeitel has been influenced by the French structuralist Madeleine Biardeau, to whom we owe perhaps the most thoroughgoing analysis of the Mahābhārata as a whole.[18] Her path-breaking examination of the poem has clarified a number of anomalies of form and content, casting the epic as the product of an emerging "Hindu" devotional *(bhakti)* worldview. Like Dumézil, she treats the events themselves as pure myth, without any necessary basis in historic fact.[19] Although there may well be a germ of historical truth in the central narrative, she argues that the work as a whole is driven by what she calls a "mythical necessity." This prompts her to argue against a factual treatment of the material: "The perspective must be reversed; when describing a *sal* or wine palm, the reason is not that it is part of the environment familiar to the poet—clearly a cultivated man, a Brahmin rather than a bard. On the contrary, it may be because it is part of his mental landscape by virtue of the symbolic meaning(s) attached to it. More generally, different landscapes are portrayed, not for their actual location on the map *[sic],* but for the positive or negative values they carry."[20]

Under these conditions, it is not the historical facts, or even how the various materials were assembled to form the text we now have, which are exegetically important. Rather it is the intentionality and preoccupations of the Brahmin composers-compilers that count and how this basic agenda has transformed the original materials (whatever they may have been) to give them new meaning and value. Although these preoccupations and materials no doubt have a history, they must be used without their history for the most part, "stripped of their date, of their origin, but organized and hierarchized according to a system of values drawn from inside the atemporal vision which the Hindu has of the universe. . . . "[21]

Biardeau reveals how the symbolic form of the Mahābhārata is modeled after the cyclic eschatology of the traditional Purāṇic accounts of divine incarnation known as *avatāra.* However, it is not an avatāric myth per se but a conscious attempt by a disaffected Brahmin hierarchy to extend the possibility of salvation to the king. This effort turns out to be revolutionary in its impact on subsequent events. In recognition of its primary intent she calls it a royal myth, "a teaching given to kings where the ideal sovereign appears indissolubly linked to the *avatāra* for whom he is a substitute."[22] In her view, the curriculum for this royal instruction was designed by orthodox Brahmin priests, the spiritual custodians of the community and its rulers, at a time when the Indian principalities were being undermined by a growing ascetic trend on the part of the ruling caste of warrior kings *(Kṣatriyas)*.[23] She explains:

> For an individual Brahmin there is no real problem: a simple change from the status of householder to that of renunciate is all that is required. But what becomes of the kingdom if the king abandons the sacrifice to seek his personal salvation? In short, the choice between life in the world and renunciation cannot be left free of all constraint. What is needed is to reconcile the eternity of the world—that no one wishes to see end—with the discovery of the possibility of a definitive personal salvation.[24]

A path to salvation for a king who remains within the world could only be found by somehow incorporating the functions of the king. This could not but raise the issue of ritual impurity associated with the use of violence *(hiṃsā)*, for while the problem of the ritual killing of animals had already been solved in the legal texts known as the Dharmaśāstras, the Brāhmaṇic priesthood of the time still faced the delicate matter of the royal killing of human beings in defense of the social order.[25] Somehow, a religious sanction had to be found for the royal exercise of *daṇḍanīti*, the duties incumbent upon the king in the administration of justice (leading to the possibility of salvation for the king). This was eventually accomplished by extending the notion of "sacrifice" to include even the most abject functions of the king (such as war), provided this activity was undertaken in a spirit of Yoga, that is, with an attitude of non-attachment, ready to lose all—even life itself.

This notion of renunciation *in* action (in contrast to the Upaniṣadic renunciation of action itself) eventually opened the door to salvation for the lower caste strata *(varṇas)* as well. Ultimately, human activities could be undertaken as a form of worship by dedicating the fruits to the Lord, typically in the form of the divine incarnation *(avatāra)* who acts for the welfare of the world *(lokasaṃgraha)*. This involved a virtual revolution in values leading to the rise of a new religion of devotion *(bhakti)* toward a Supreme God (who may be conceived in personal terms). *Bhakti* salvation could henceforth be open to men and women alike, and even to those who had been evildoers (VI.31/BG.9.32).

Although Biardeau acknowledges her debt to Dumézil, she thus views the Mahābhārata, not as the transposition of a pre-Vedic mythology of social *function,* but as a transformation of orthodox Brāhmaṇic *values* of Upaniṣadic sacrifice and renunciation into the values of this new *bhakti* religious system (of which the epic may be regarded as the "founding charter").[26] This transformation of values is nowhere more evident than in the imagery and symbolism surrounding the "sacrifice" of the eighteen-day war itself, regarded as the centerpiece of a triad of sacrifices that includes the *rājasūya* (royal consecration) and the *aśvamedha* (horse) sacrifices.[27] "In other words, this episode of the central myth seeks to transpose the ritual values into a truly epic key. We are not dealing with a reduction of the myth (concerning the gods) into an epic (with respect to heroes), but with a new reading of ancient values, where what was not sacrifice, becomes sacrifice."[28]

The work of recent Western scholarship thus serves to confirm, in a more methodical manner, what generations of Indian readers have intuitively understood; that despite its enormous bulk and diversity, the Mahābhārata does indeed constitute a single literary design with unity of purpose and continuity of meaning. However, because the work as we have it is myth rather than historical fact (though possibly based on distorted memories of some distant fratricidal conflict), this meaning is couched in a complex symbolism. Clearly, the epic is not a "horizontal" unity of a single strata but the unity of a vertically arranged hierarchy of strata, of which the narrative (or "historical") dimension is the least important, particularly from the Indian point of view. In order to understand these levels it is necessary to delve below whatever surface contradictions may be found in the poem to the symbolic keys that provide access to the hierarchy of levels that reveal the unity of the whole. This was, essentially, the guiding assumption of the present book.

Unfortunately, this task is complicated by two characteristic features of Hindu religious tradition. In the first place, the need to preserve the sanctity and priority of the Vedas leads to a hermeneutic in which the concepts and ideas of prior forms of thought are never rejected, but simply reevaluated and reworked into new hierarchies of meaning and value. As Chaitanya has noted:

> The concepts of all the systems are closely studied; but because of their insufficincies *(sic),* they are radically transformed, deepened in meaning, integrated into a unitary system of great stability, a world-view to which the most advanced modern thinking in a multiplicity of fields becomes a foot-note. Vyasa's Purusha and Prakrti are not the Purusha and Prakrti of Samkhya; his Karma is not the Karma of the Mimamsakas; his Yoga is not the Yoga of Patanjali. His treatment of the four

> ends of human existence *(Purushartha)* is radically new. And here we come to the profundity of his final achievement.[29]

The view of Hiltebeitel is that "the epic narrative itself has been structured in part to bridge the gap between the Vedic and Purāṇic mythologies, conserving the former (and conserving pre-Vedic themes as well) and embracing it within the new 'universe of *bhakti*' of the great gods of epic and Purāṇic Hinduism."[30]

This task is further complicated by what we noted earlier; that the very intent of the poem is to foster the progressive spiritual insights that bring the mind to a liberating vision of human existence as a whole. The fact that the epic was originally designed as a work of kingly instruction should not lead us into thinking that what it instructs is of no concern to the ignorant masses: "Everyone is king in his own home" (XII.308. 147) as far as the epic is concerned, and the epic view is clearly that we experience a kaleidoscope of different "perspectives" or *darśanas* according to the meaning and insights we (as spiritual seekers) receive as we move to successively higher vantage points. Hiltebeitel has observed how, through various devices, the epic poets are able to present "countless *darśanas*, perspectives, on the drama that forms its core."[31]

Far from denying the overarching unity of the epic as a whole, therefore, I take the view that these hierarchies of content and perspective *(darśanas)* form part of its very structure. The diversity of different levels, and the juxtaposition of didactic and narrative sequences, elusive and ambiguous as they may appear on the surface, conceal a remarkable coherence of aim and plan. This has prompted Biardeau to acknowledge that "Even fifteen years of (good) housekeeping is not enough to grasp the complexity of such a partner, but I see it rising before me as an increasingly coherent monument, astonishing in its unity, dizzying in the depth of meaning and level of detail that is achieved"[32] This unity is, of course, the unity of the new "Hindu" devotional universe of meaning and value, forged—by mythical necessity—out of traditional religious didactic and narrative material.

Notes

Preface

1. Wendy Doniger O'Flaherty, *Hindu Myths: A Sourcebook Translated from the Sanskrit* (Harmondsworth: Penguin, 1975), p. 17. She bases her estimate on a review of the works of previous authors such as J. N. Farquhar, Jan Gonda, Frederick Pargiter, A. D. Pusalkar, and Moritz Winternitz. Needless to say, the dates for the *terminus a quo* and the *terminus ad quem* are the subject of continuing controversy. Pāṇini (fourth century B.C.?) teaches the formation of the word Mahābhārata in *sūtra* 6.2.38 of his *Grammar*. However, the Greek traveler Megasthenes, who was in India about 315 B.C., makes no mention of the epic. Weber found that it was known to Dion Chrysostom in the second half of the first century A.D. (though whether in its present form is unclear). We do know from epigraphic evidence that by the fifth century A.D. the epic was already recognized as a work of one hundred thousand stanzas composed by a great *ṛṣi* by the name of Vyāsa. As William Dwight Whitney warns: "All dates given in Indian literary history are pins set up to be bowled down again. Every important work has undergone so many more or less transforming changes before reaching the form in which it comes to us, that the question of original construction is complicated with that of final redaction." Cf. Whitney, "Brief Account of the Indian Literature." In *Sanskrit Grammar* (Cambridge, Mass.: Harvard University Press, 1973), p. xix.

2. For a good discussion of this issue, see Ruth Cecily Katz, *Arjuna in the Mahābhārata: Where Krishna Is, There is Victory* (Columbia, S.C.: University of South Carolina Press, 1989), pp. 10–15. In *The Mahābhārata* (Chicago: University of Chicago Press, 1973–1978), vol. III, p. 19, J. A. B. van Buitenen writes that "there is organic growth in the Mahābhārata, in the sense that an interpolation was not extraneous to the text but was attracted, even at times provoked, by an incident in the 'original."' A. K. Ramanujan is of the opinion that, in order to enhance the symbolic integrity of the whole: "new incidents are added only in certain places where there seems to be a need for them, one thinks of such an analogy with crystal growth." See Ramanujan, "Repetition in the Mahābhārata." In *Essays on the Mahābhārata*, Arvind Sharma, ed. (Leiden, Netherlands: E. J. Brill, 1991). pp. 441–442.

3. As will be clear from the discussion in chapter 6, the Bhagavadgītā serves to highlight important issues intrinsic to epic ideas of destiny and human effort. Opinion is nevertheless divided as to whether this key text is an integral part of the Mahābhārata or a later interpolation. The present author favors the view of van Buitenen (supported by many recent scholars, including Biardeau, Hiltebeitel, Katz, etc.) who believe that "The Bhagavadgītā was conceived and created in the context of the Mahābhārata. It was not an independent text that somehow wandered into the epic." J. A. B. van Buitenen, *The Bhagavadgītā in the Mahābhārata* (Chicago: University of Chicago Press, 1981), p. 5. However, for a recent contrary view, see Georg von Simson, "Die Einschaltung der Bhagavadgītā im Bhīṣmaparvan des Mahābhārata," *Indo-Iranian Journal XI* (1968–1969): 159–174. Various formulations of the interpolation theory are proposed by former scholars such as E. Washburn Hopkins and Winternitz.

4. V. S. Sukthankar, "Critical Principles Followed in the Constitution of the Text." In Prolegomena to Book I of *The Mahābhārata for the First Time Critically Edited* (Poona, India: Bhandarkar Oriental Research Institute, 1933), p. 103. See also pp. 76–77 for reasons behind the rejection of traditional Western methods of text reconstruction, and pp. 86–92 for details of the criteria on which the final text is based. It should be noted that not all scholars agree on the merits of the Critical Edition. Thus Madeleine Biardeau, following Sylvain Lévi, believes that "What appears to many people as an unmanageable overgrowth of myths in epics and Purāṇas is actually an invaluable source of information for a better understanding of each of them." Cf. her "Story of Arjuna Kārtavīrya without Reconstruction." *Purāṇa* 12, 7 (July 1970): 293. The article illustrates her method of revealing the inner meaning of the epic by means of a comparative analysis of different versions of text. In her view: "Any kind of variation is possible, provided the intended significance of the whole remains clear" (p. 299).

5. Evidence for Indo-European epic roots may be found in Georges Dumézil, *Mythe et épopée: l'idéologie des trois fonctions dans les épopées des peuples indo-européens*, 3 vols. (Paris: Éditions Gallimard, 1968). Cf. also the works of Stig Wikander, particularly "Pāṇdavasagan och Mahābhāratas mytiska förutsättningar." In *Religion och Bibel, Nathan Söderblom-sällskapets Årsbok* (1947), vol. VI, pp. 27–39. More recently, Alf Hiltebeitel, *The Ritual of Battle: Krishna in the Mahābhārata* (Ithaca: Cornell University Press, 1976).

6. This spiritual and devotional function of poetry is illustrated in a colorful fashion by Abhinavagupta, writing around 1000 A.D. Scripture, he says:

> teaches after the fashion of a master, by giving direct commands. The story literature edifies us more gently, after the fashion of a helpful friend, by presenting interesting examples of what fruits befell the actions of others in the past. And poetry instructs us in the most effective way, after the fashion of a beloved woman, by so delighting us that we are scarcely aware of an underlying purpose.

Quoted by Gary A. Tubb, "Śāntarasa in the Mahābhārata." In *Essays on the Mahābhārata,* Sharma, ed., p. 172.

7. Cf. XIV.51.45. "I am the guru, O mighty armed one, and know that the mind is my pupil."

8. For Ānandavardhana, the great Sanskrit literary critic of the ninth century A.D., the Mahābhārata

> teaches man ultimately to renounce the vanity of earthly glories and attain *dharma* (truth and righteousness), *vairāgya* (renunciation), *śānti* (eternal peace), and *mokṣa* (salvation). Vyāsa himself remarks in his epic that he has sung the glory of the Lord and that his epic is the Nārāyaṇa Kaṭhā, "The Story of the Lord", thus clearly indicating what the message of his epic is; for the story of the Pāṇḍavas is only an occasion, the purpose being to reveal the greatness of the Lord.

From Swami Prabhavananda, *The Spiritual Heritage of India* (Hollywood: Vedanta Press, 1979), p. 94, quoting a passage from Ānandavardhana's *Dhvanyāloka*. Tubb, *Śāntarasa in the Mahābhārata,* p. 199, also quotes from the Dhvanyāloka to the effect that the true purpose of the Mahābhārata is "the highest human aim characterized by liberation, and, from the poetic point of view, the flavor *[rasa]* of peace *[śānti],* characterized by the fostering of the happiness produced by the extinction of craving *[tṛṣṇa],* as the predominant *rasa.*" On Mahābhārata commentary, see V. S. Sukthankar, "Notes on Mahabharata Commentators." In *Critical Studies in the Mahābhārata.* Vol. I of Sukthankar Memorial Edition, P. K. Gode, ed. (Bombay: Karnatak Publishing House, 1944), pp. 263–267. The most noteworthy of these commentators were Arjunamiśra (c. 1450–1500 A.D.), Caturbhujamiśra (c. 1350–1550 A.D.), Devabodha (?), Nīlakaṇṭha (c. 1700 A.D.), Ratnagarbha (?), Sarvajña-Nārāyaṇa (c. 1100–1300 A.D.), and Vidyāsāgara (c. 1350 A.D.).

9. Sukthankar, et al., eds. *Mahābhārata.* 1933–1966.

10. Van Buitenen, trans. and ed., *The Mahābhārata* and *The Bhagavadgītā in the Mahābhārata.* I also consulted the English text by Kesari Mohan Ganguli, trans., *The Mahabharata of Krishna Dwaipayana Vyasa,* 2nd Edition, 12 vols. (Calcutta: Oriental Publications Co., 1952–1962).

Chapter 1. Introduction

1. Paul Shorey, trans., "The Republic." In *The Collected Dialogues of Plato* Bollingen Series LXXI, Edith Hamilton and Huntington Cairns, eds. (Princeton: Princeton University Press, 1973), 517c, p. 749.

2. George Thompson, trans., "Agamemnon." In *Aeschylus: The Oresteia Trilogy* (New York: Dell Publishing Company, 1974), p. 62.

3. See, for example, Isa. 40.22.

4. See, for example, II Cor. 8.9.

5. In addition to the sacrifice, the powers of the cosmos may be harnessed by means of various ascetic practices *(tapas)* and by use of appropriate *mantras* and incantations.

6. Koshalya Walli, *Theory of Karma in Indian Thought* (Varanasi, India: Bharata Manisha, 1977), p. 277.

7. E. Washburn Hopkins, "Modifications of the Karma Doctrine." In *Journal of the Royal Asiatic Society* 38 (1906): 584–585.

8. The word for "god," that is, *deva,* comes from the sanskrit root √*div* which means "to shine"—though also, significantly, "to gamble." Its correlate, *puruṣa,* is used in two senses. It often simply connotes a "human being," but in the more philosophical sections of the epic (for example, in the Bhagavadgītā) it is used to indicate the spiritual essence of human nature to be realized by each and every individual man and woman. The word *jīva* may be used for any embodied creature.

9. Georges Dumézil, *Mythe et épopée,* vol. I, p. 170.

10. *kecitpuruṣakāraṃ tu prāhuḥ karmavido janāḥ| daivamityapare viprāḥ svabhāvaṃ bhūtacintakāḥ || pauruṣaṃ karma daivaṃ ca phalavṛttisvabhāvataḥ| traya ete'pṛthagbhūtā na vivekaṃ tu kecana || evametacca naivaṃ ca yadbhūtaṃ sjate jagat| karmasthā viṣamaṃ brūyuḥ sattvasthāḥ samadarśinaḥ* || (XII.224. 50–52).

11. Commenting on these verses Nīlakaṇṭha portrays the *sattvastha* as holding the orthodox *(siddhāntha)* position of the Vedānta against heterodox opponents *(pūrvapakṣa)*. Among these latter he includes mīmāṃsakas, astrologers *(daivajña), sāṃkhyas, ārhats* (= Jains) and various non-Vedic thinkers *(bāhya)*. Cf. also XII.230.4–6 for a similar exposition. *(pauruṣaṃ kāraṇaṃ kecidāhuḥ karmasu mānavāḥ| daivameke praśaṃsanti svabhāvaṃ cāpare janāḥ || pauruṣaṃ karma daivaṃ ca phalavṛttisvabhāvataḥ| trayametatpṛthagbhūtamavivekaṃ tu kecana || evametanna cāpyevamubhe cāpi na cāpyubhe| karmasthā viṣamaṃ brūyuḥ sattvasthāḥ samadarśinaḥ||)*. The different emphases given to the relative strengths of *daiva* and *puruṣakāra* have been partially cataloged by P. V. Kane. According to him, *daiva* is represented as all-powerful at I.1.186–87; I.84.6–9; II. Appendix I, no. 30, line 33; II.43.32; II.52.14; III.176.27–28; V.8.35; V.40.30; V.156.4; V.187.17; and at XV.16.2. *Puruṣakāra* is useless against it. A golden mean is advocated at I.114.15; II.15.11; V.77.4–5; X.2.3; and also at XII.56.14–15. However, many other passages—(specifically those at VII.127. 17; XII.27.30; XII.58.13–16; XII.149.46; XIII.6.1ff.; X.2.12–13; and X.2.22–23)—indicate that *puruṣakāra* is superior to *daiva*. Kane, *History of Dharmaśāstra III* (Poona, India: Bhandarkar Oriental Research Institute, 1968–1977), p. 168.

12. Sukthankar, *On the Meaning of the Mahābhārata* (Bombay: Asiatic Society of Bombay, 1957), p. 109.

13. The problem faced by the epic author is somewhat analogous to the conflict faced by Kant between "the starry heavens above and the moral law within," namely, how to explain the apparent paradox of our participation in two worlds, the world of Nature with its deterministic system of causalities, and the world of moral obligation that implies freedom? The presuppositions about human nature, world, moral obligation, and freedom are, of course, entirely different in the two cases.

Chapter 2. Hermeneutical Perspectives

1. In his Mahābhārata tātparya nirṇaya. Quoted in A. D. Pusalkar, "The Mahābhārata: Its History and Character." In *The Cultural Heritage of India,* 4 vols., 2nd Edition, Haridas Bhattacharya, eds. et al. (Calcutta: Ramakrishna Mission, Institute of Culture, 1953–1962), vol. II, "Itihāsas, Purāṇas, Dharma and Other Śāstras," p. 68.

2. Sukthankar, *On the Meaning of the Mahābhārata,* p. 30. Significantly, Sukthankar draws his "meaning" not from the Critical Edition, but from the Bombay Edition of the text, a fact seized upon by Biardeau in support of her views on textual reconstruction in the Indian context. See Biardeau, "Story of Arjuna Kārtavīrya without Reconstruction," note 14, p. 302.

3. O'Flaherty, *Hindu Myths,* pp. 21–22.

4. Not forgetting that as a Vasu in *svarga,* he gives a cow—source of a Brahmin's power, to an earthly princess.

5. Biardeau, "Études de mythologie hindou (IV)." In *Bulletin de l'École française d'Extrême-Orient* 63 (1976): 172–173.

6. Biardeau, "Conférence de Mlle Madeleine Biardeau." In *Annuaire de l'École pratique des Hautes Études: Viéme section-Sciences religieuses* 85 (1976–1977): 165.

Chapter 3. Cosmic Destiny

1. The Three Worlds *(trailokya)* include the Earth *(bhūrloka),* heaven *(svarloka* or *svarga),* and the intermediate *(bhuvarloka)* or, later, the nether regions *(naraka)*. They form part of a hierarchy of seven worlds or *lokas* (although thirty-three are also mentioned [III. 247.25]). The cosmography of the seven *dvīpa* of the earth with their various countries *(varṣa)* is detailed in the Bhīṣmaparvan (VI.6–13).

2. Viṣṇu is featured as the highest Divinity, the one who maintains, and also as one of the *ādityas* (cf. I.59.17).

3. The reference is taken from Appendix 27 of Book III that follows after III.256.30 in the Critical Edition.

4. Evidence for a similar view in the Mahābhārata is not hard to find, as in the following description of the secondary absorption *(pralaya)*: "Brahmā is

the mind. This mind, which is the soul of the manifest, though itself unmanifest, withdraws what has been manifested by mind" (XII.225.10). In an earlier account by Bhṛgu (XII.175), this creative source is actually personified as Mind *(manas)*.

5. It must be remembered that the epic is not specifically interested in cosmogony and cosmology per se, in contrast to the Purāṇas. However, as Biardeau has indicated: "If, from one perspective it is true to say that the epic is anterior to the Purāṇas, this is certainly not true of its doctrinal content." See Biardeau, "Études (IV)," p. 135.

6. Biardeau has drawn attention to the fact that the *yugas* are not related to the life of the avatar in the same manner as the *mahākalpa* and the *kalpa* are related to the two higher forms of the Divinity. The link is with the moral life of the *trailokya* rather than to the life of the Divinity as such. In fact, he could just as well be absent:

> We thus realise that in fact, we can describe the succession of the *yuga* without any reference to an avatar. It was impossible to describe a creation or end of the world without introducing the corresponding form of the divinity. With the *yugas,* the harmony is broken. The state of the earth is described but in fact it is the triple world that is at stake since the dharma does not allow us to dissociate the earth from heaven and the hells. As far as the supreme divinity is concerned, he can simply be absent. This means that his presence is not absolutely essential to the temporal structure of the *yugas* and to the idea of a progressive decline of the dharma. It is true that this is often connected with time, the destructive role of which is well known, but this reference only adds to the difficulty of reconciling individual karma and the cyclic socio-cosmic process." See Biardeau, "Études (IV)," pp. 122–123.

The apparent contradiction involved in accommodating a collective sociocosmic process unrelated to human conduct to the karma of individual action is never fully resolved.

7. It must be admitted that "Time" is not a factor in all accounts. A later story (XII.283.7–18) puts the blame on the demons for the decline of the dharma. After multiplying on the earth in the bodies of men, the deities decide to impart their collective energies to Śiva, who thereupon destroys the main culprits in the form of desire, anger, and greed, as well as the Great Delusion *(mahāmoha)* who is the chief among them. The Śāntiparvan myth of XII.337. 28–32 explains that after creating the world Nārāyaṇa (Viṣṇu) suddenly realized that poor Earth (here personified as a goddess) would suffer under the increasing weight of creatures. Furthermore, the asceticism *(tapas)* of the demons *(asuras)* would so inflate them with power and pride that they would begin to threaten the sages *(ṛṣis)* and the deities (and presumably also the dharma, the sociocosmic moral order controlled by them). Nārāyaṇa thereupon

promises to rescue the earth by returning in whatever animal or human form the situation demanded. Bhagavadgītā chapter 4, verses 7–8 is more direct in describing the decision as a personal one of the Lord himself: "Whenever the dharma falls away O Bhārata, and *adharma* rises up I give myself forth. From *yuga* to *yuga* I come into being for the protection of the good, the destruction of the wicked, and the re-establishment of the dharma."

8. The van Buitenen translations of the *yugas* are useful in conveying the sense of the dice. Thus, the Golden Age *(kṛtayuga)*—"Age of the Winning Throw," *tretāyuga*—"Age of the Trey," *dvāparayuga*—"Age of the Deuce," and *kaliyuga*—"Age of Discord."

9. Biardeau, "Études (IV)," p. 135.

10. The Greek myth of the "fates" is duplicated in the epic image of the two (rather than three) women who weave the threads of past and present, night and day (I.3.147ff).

11. Kesari Mohan Ganguli, trans., *The Mahābhārata of Krishna-Dwaipayana Vyasa*. Published by P. C. Roy (Calcutta: Oriental Publishing, 1952–1962), vol. XII, p. 293.

12. The Earth is the world of acts *(karmabhūmi)*, while heaven is regarded as the world of the fruit. Cf. III.247.36 and XII.185.19. Biardeau has noted that, considered in practical terms, this higher influence is no longer completely in the hands of a Brāhmaṇic orthodoxy (represented by the traditional Vedic gods). It must call on the assistance of the Supreme Divinity of *bhakti* (Viṣṇu) to restore the dharma. It should also be noted that the seven worlds *(lokas)* of the cosmos that culminate in Brahmaloka are more than just locations in space. They constitute the soteriological hierarchy of human experience *(saṃsāra)* representing seven states of experience through which the soul must wander for a period of ten *kalpas* before reaching the final resting-place beyond all name and form, merged into the Supreme Divinity at the final dissolution of the Universe (XII. 280). These worlds are thus worlds of experience that form an integral part of the psychology of the egocentric personality *(jīva)*. In the course of this spiritual journey, the *jīva* displays various spiritual powers and is subject to a graduated mix of happiness and misery in its numerous embodiments "from Brahmā to a blade of grass" (III.2.68). A worm can become Brahmā himself, provided he always practices the dharma of his particular status in this celestial ladder of being (XIII.118–120). Prior to final liberation (which occurs as a collective event according to Biardeau's analysis of the Purāṇic material), these various bodies appear to be subject to *daiva* in inverse proportion to their spiritual merits. Those in the blissful worlds of heaven enjoy luminous bodies "born from ones deeds" (III.247.14).

13. There is some confusion here. Mention is made of a boon by Śiva at I.103.8, but by Vyāsa at I.107.8. By contrast, the birth of the Pāṇḍavas is ulti-

mately the work of Śiva through his representative Durvāsas. This paradox is noted by Biardeau.

Chapter 4. Personal Destiny

1. Nicolai Hartmann, *Ethics,* 3 vols. (London: George Allen & Unwin, 2nd Impression 1951), vol. 3, "Moral Freedom," p. 31

2. There is no clear-cut Manichæan opposition of good *(dharma)* and evil *(adharma)* in this process, where the gods are necessarily on the side of the good. A number of them are even represented on the "demonic" Kaurava side. There is an apparent "cosmic concern" to maintain some sort of balance between these two moral forces.

3. P. Lal, *The Mahabharata of Vyasa* (Delhi: Vikas Publishing House, 1980), p. 8.

4. We have already drawn attention to the association in the Indian context with the "law of the fish," equivalent to our "law of the jungle," a premonition that the big fish will soon start eating the little fish.

5. Biardeau, "Études de mythologie hindou (V)," in *Bulletin de l'École française d'Extrême-Orient* 65 (1978): 223. In the Mahābhārata itself, this dilution of responsibility is justified in the conversation between Gautamī and the Fowler Arjunaka recounted in chapter 8 (XIII.1.8–76).

6. Bhīṣma is the son of Śaṃtanu by the goddess Gangā who is cursed by the sage Vasiṣṭha to endure an earthly existence as an expiation for the celestial folly of stealing the cow of plenty.

7. Biardeau, *Annuaire* 84 (1975–1976): 183.

8. Biardeau, "Études (IV)": 223.

9. We sense more than a touch of irony in these epithets—Dhṛtarāṣṭra was neither wise nor "highly fortunate." It may be noted in his defense that Dhṛtarāṣṭra was not a deserving victim through any fault of his own, but had to pay the price for "the fault of his mother and the wrath of a sage" (I. 61.78).

10. Dumézil claims that Dhṛtarāṣṭra and Pāṇḍu are, in fact, the respective incarnations of the pre-Vedic gods Varuṇa and Bhaga, and that Vidura is the incarnation of Aryaman (cf. *Mythe et épopée,* vol. I, p. 156). However, this is not born out by the facts of the story itself. Dhṛtarāṣṭra is an incarnation of a *gandharva* king.

11. This is the first of a traditional three-part division of the Mahābhārata. The other two are war *(yuddha)* and the eventual victory *(jaya)* of the new dharma that rises out of the ashes of the old world order (cf. I.54.19). This bringing of a new dharma by the avatar could only result in the inauguration of a new Golden Age *(kṛtayuga),* probably symbolized by the reign of Parikṣit. Of course, the Purāṇic tradition locates the Mahābhārata war at the junction of the

dvāpara- and the *kaliyugas*. But how can the avatar inaugurate a *kaliyuga*? Biardeau has made an extensive analysis of this issue.

12. Sukthankar, *Meaning of the Mahābhārata,* pp. 44–45.

13. Krishna Chaitanya, *The Mahābhārata: A Literary Study* (New Delhi: Clarion Books, 1985), pp. 184–185. We would substitute the word *daiva* for nemesis in this instance.

14. Biardeau, "Études (V)," p. 104.

15. This is described at II.46 of Biardeau's preferred Citrashala Press Edition and at Appendix I, No. 30 of the Critical Edition.

16. Biardeau, "Études (V)," p. 105.

17. Ibid., p. 103. The salvivic tone is suggested by the parallel she finds between the death of Śiśupala, particularly the manner in which his *tejas* "salutes" *(√vand)* and is "absorbed" *(viveṣa)* into Kṛṣṇa prior to the ceremony (II. 42.23–24), and the absorption of the worlds into Kṛṣṇa described in chapter 11 of the Bhagavadgītā.

18. The second game is symbolically required to provide for a "remnant" to ensure the renaissance of the world and of the dharma. Cf. Biardeau, *Annuaire* 80 (1971–1972): 132.

19. Biardeau, "Études (IV)," p. 206.

20. Biardeau points out that from the point of view of the Kauravas, the Pāṇḍavas are the sacrificial victims that have been released instead of being killed. Cf. *Annuaire* 80 (1971–1972): 130.

21. Biardeau, "Études (IV)," pp. 206–207 and "Études (V)," pp. 101–106.

22. The gods and the demons were both fathered by Kaśyapa, the demons being the older brothers (cf. I.60.33 and III.34.58).

23. Both the *rājasūya* and the dicing have their counterparts heralding the ultimate demise of Duryodhana/Kali. Thus the *goharaṇa* or cattle raid—also an integral part of the *rājasūya* ceremony, will result in the humiliation of Duryodhana in Book IV. Cf. *Annuaire* 86 (1977–1978): 152. The events of the dicing will be reenacted during the mace duel between Duryodhana and Bhīma in Book IX. This time, however, Duryodhana is the one who fights alone while Yudhiṣṭhira is represented by Bhīma who wins by a single "throw" of the mace—also involving a ruse. Cf. *Annuaire* 90 (1981–1982): 147.

24. Biardeau, *Le Mahābhārata* (Paris: Flammarion, 1985), vol. I, p. 206.

25. It may be noted that he also has allies in the underworld in the form of Ulūpī, daughter of the king of the snakes—he has a child by her (I.206.34); and he has mastered the *gandharvas* (in a night battle with Citraratha, king of the *gandharvas,* who gives him a clairvoyant power [I.158.40]).

26. Biardeau, *Le Mahabharata* (Paris: Flammarion, 1986), vol. II, p. 138.

27. "On the contrary, Satyaki—whose name denotes the totality of things—is that aspect of the presence of Kṛṣṇa in the Pandava camp by which he prepares for the renewal of the world and of the dharma by protecting a "remnant" of human existence. Bhūriśravas on the other hand, is a Kuru, grandson of a younger brother of Śaṃtanu and son of Somadatta." Cf. Biardeau, *Annuaire* 86 (1977–1978): 145.

28. Biardeau, *Annuaire* 90 (1981–1982): 151. She notes that the name Bhūriśravas translates as "a strong sound of neighing," evoking the name of Uccaiḥśravas, the horse that was produced from the churning of the milky ocean.

29. Because of this falsehood, Yudhiṣṭhira's chariot, which had always floated a few inches above the ground, now comes down to the earth.

30. Biardeau, "Études (IV)," p. 252.

31. Biardeau, *Annuaire* 86 (1977–1978): 143.

32. The first curse denies him the brāhmaṇic power and the second takes away the royal powers he obtained from Duryodhana (and later also from Jarāsaṃdha).

33. Biardeau, "Études (V)," pp. 174–175. Dumézil regards this combat involving the son of the Sun and the son of Indra as the earthly transposition of the old myth where Indra himself triumphs over the Sun by "tearing off" or "stealing" or "sinking" one of the wheels of his chariot. Cf. Dumézil, *Mythe et épopée,* vol. I, p. 137.

34. Chaitanya, *Mahābhārata,* pp. 444–445.

35. Biardeau, *Annuaire* 89 (1980–1981): 249.

36. The *avabhṛtha* bath mentioned by Kṛṣṇa here is the final bath undergone by the person performing the sacrifice.

37. Biardeau, *Annuaire* 84 (1975–1976): 171–172.

38. It may also be noted that, although supporting the Pāṇḍavas as a result of a wise decision by Arjuna, Kṛṣṇa has already seen to it that his *gopī nārāyaṇa* army will fight—highly successfully as it turns out, on the side of the Kauravas.

39. Cf. Biardeau, *Annuaire* 87 (1978–1979): 150.

40. Biardeau, *Le Mahabharata,* vol. II, p. 321.

Chapter 5. Destiny and Human Initiative

1. It is worth noting in this connection that the "evil" responsible for this downfall is more of a social than of a personal nature. Duryodhana was certainly "evil" in his greed, ruthlessness, hunger for power, etc., but he also had a number of redeeming qualities. As a ruler he was generally well-liked by the citizenry of Hāstinapura. Blame for the social mayhem affecting the body politic

of Hāstinapura is mostly laid upon the evil *(adharma)* associated with the perceived breakdown of the traditional functional relationships of society, particularly those between the Brahmin and warrior castes. Instead of fulfilling their leadership role as kings and protectors, warriors were wont to abandon their responsibilities for lives of partial renunciation (for example, Bhīṣma) or pleasure (for example, Pāṇḍu). Brahmins such as Droṇa and Aśvatthāman also deviate from their appointed roles by employing their spiritual energies for the accumulation of material wealth and to achieve supremacy in the art of weaponry, both traditional preserves of the warriors.

2. Dumézil, *Mythe et épopée,* vol. I, p. 166.

3. *bhāga, bhāgya, bhāgadheya,* etc.

4. Van Buitenen notes that *haṭha* literally means "violence," that is, a violent interference in the established pattern. Cf. van Buitenen, *Mahābhārata,* vol. II, p. 822.

5. Dumeźil. *Mythe et eṕopée,* vol. I, p. 254. The evidence for this link is somewhat tenuous, however, particularly in view of the statements made on at least two occasions in the Mahābhārata that Dhṛtarāṣṭra is the incarnation of a king of the *gandharvas* (I.61.77 and XV.39.8).

6. Yudhiṣṭhira later admits to a less commendable motive, his own desire for power and prestige (cf. III.35.2 and XII.1). Balarāma also puts the blame on Yudhiṣṭhira, even suggesting that it was he who initiated the challenge (cf. V.2.9–11).

7. It may be noted that the Pāṇḍavas themselves are not destined for *mokṣa* in this life. Even before their death Bhīṣma informs them that their sojourn in *devaloka* will be followed by rebirth in human form. It is only in the next creation *(visarga)* that they will attain to the status of a perfected soul *(siddha)* among the gods. Cf. XII.272.68–69. On the other hand, as Norbert Klaes and Krishna Chaitanya have shown in the cases of Yudhiṣṭhira, Karṇa, and others, there is clear evidence of character development, the realization of the potentials of a person contained, in germ, at birth.

8. Rollo May, *Freedom and Destiny* (New York: Norton, 1981), p. 55.

9. May compares freedom to "a flock of white butterflies bestirred in front of you as you walk through the woods: rising in cluster they flit off in an infinite number of directions." Ibid., p. 52. Paul Ricoeur approaches the subject by asking: "Where is freedom? In the removal of all dependency? In the lack of determination? In the anxiety of choosing oneself? Or does it coincide with the discovery and understanding of an inner necessity, deeper than any choice and any kind of autonomy? In a word, does the highest degree of freedom consist in the surging up of an absolute power of choosing or in the love of fate?" Ricoeur, "Philosophy of Will and Action." In *The Philosophy of Paul Ricoeur: An An-*

thology of His Work, Charles E. Reagan and David Stewart, eds. (Boston: Beacon Press, 1978), p. 65.

10. R. N. Dandekar. "Man in Hindu Thought," *Annals of the Bhandarkar Oriental Research Institute,* 43, 1–4 (1962): 54.

11. In the Anuśāsanaparvan (XIII.143.24) there is mention of the four weapons *(caturastras)* attached to the body (represented as Kṛṣṇa's chariot), identified in the English translation by Ganguli as, for example, Destiny.

12. This means that, much like ourselves, epic characters are potentially "free" in terms of axiological determination but bound with respect to ontological determination. As Nicolai Hartmann observes:

> only so long as the struggle is active does there exist a free being. With the victory of the one or the other, man becomes determined by one side (monistically), and thereby positively unfree. If the causal nexus in him controls the end posited, mechanism rules completely, and man, as Lamettrie would have it, is converted into a "machine." But if the finalistic nexus dominates the natural processes, then the cosmic ends, ruling with almighty power, stand over against the weak, finite purposive efforts of man, who can make no headway against them." Hartmann, *Ethics,* vol. III, p. 85.

13. One should note that Yudhiṣṭhira is not permitted by his *rājadharma* (royal obligations) to be "free of the triple system" of the *puruṣārthas*. Cf. chapter 7 for further elaboration of this topic.

Chapter 6. Action and Contemplation

1. Biardeau, "The Salvation of the King in the Mahābhārata." In *Contributions to Indian Sociology* (New Series), 15, 1–2 (1981): 92.

2. Chaitanya, *Mahābhārata,* p. 449.

3. M. Hiriyanna, *Popular Essays in Indian Philosophy* (Mysore, India: Kavyalaya Publishers, 1952), p. 36.

4. Biardeau, "Études (V)," p. 196.

5. Cf. Julian F. Woods, "The Doctrine of Karma in the Bhagavadgītā," *The Journal of Studies in the Bhagavadgītā,* vols. VIII–IX, 1988–1989, pp. 47–81. Śaṃkara's views are clear enough. In the introduction to chapter 5 of his Gītābhaṣya he states, for example, that "it is impossible to imagine, even in a dream, that a realized being *(ātmatattvavid)* would derive any benefit from *karmayoga,* so opposed to right knowledge *(samyagdarsána),* and entirely based on illusory knowledge *(mithyājñāna)*" *(kartavyatvopadeśāt ātmatattvavidaḥ samyagdarśana-viruddhaḥ mithyājñānahetukaḥ karmayogaḥ svapne'pi na sambhāvayituṃ śakyate).* All karma is a product of *avidyā* since it is only possible in a pluralistic world of individual actors and instruments of action. For him, therefore, Kṛṣṇa's emphasis on action in chapter 3 of the Gītā is significant only in comparison

to the kind of false renunciation of action described in VI.26/BG.3.4 as "mere renunciation" and again at VI.26/BG 3.8 as nonaction *(akarma)*.

6. In contrast to the *adhyāsa* theory of Śaṃkara, this trick of the mind takes effect at the individual *(vyaṣṭi)* rather than at the collective *(samaṣṭi)* level of reality. Furthermore, the resulting human estate is considered by Rāmānuja as "real" in the sense that it is a real (that is, not illusory) composite of soul *(ātman)* and body *(śarīra, deha, piṇḍa,* etc.).

Chapter 7. The Path of the Warrior

1. In describing the five key ingredients of any action (VI.40/BG.18.14) Kṛṣṇa himself presents an interesting mix of inner and outer factors. These ingredients are a material basis *(adhiṣṭhāna)*, an actor or doer *(kartṛ = ahaṃkāra)*, the necessary external accessories *(karaṇa)*, an energy source *(pṛthak ceṣtā)*, and destiny *(daiva)*. Destiny is no doubt included as the "wild card" in the success of the enterprise.

2. Cf. Bhīṣma's graphic description of his character (XII.76.18–20). Yudhiṣṭhira is kind *(ānṛśaṃsa)*, soft *(mṛdu)*, patient *(dānta)*, very noble *(atyārya)*, highly principled *(atidhārmika)*, unmanly *(klība)*, and addicted to righteousness and mercy *(dharmaghṛṇāyukta)*.

3. Norbert Klaes, *Conscience and Consciousness: Ethical Problems of Mahābhārata* (Bangalore, India, Dharmaram College, 1975), p. 96.

4. Biardeau notes here: "This is already the teaching of Kṛṣṇa in the Gītā, the teaching given to Arjuna by the avatar of Viṣṇu who does not directly take part in the action. The role of Yudhiṣṭhira is therefore very close to that of the avatar, a logical one for the son of Dharma, but he must above all count on the activity of Arjuna in conformity with the ideal he proposes." Biardeau, "Conférence de Mlle Madeleine Biardeau" *Annuaire* 81 (1972–1973): 138.

5. J. Bruce Long. "The Concepts of Human Action and Rebirth in the Mahābhārata." In *Karma and Rebirth in Classical Indian Traditions,* Wendy Doniger O'Flaherty, eds. (Berkeley: University of California Press, 1980), p. 47.

6. "The Lord in the form of the Dhātṛ ordains one's role in life as a result of a chain of causes, and distributes the fruits of the previous actions performed by men" (III.33.19).

7. Biardeau. "Conférence de Mlle Madeleine Biardeau," *Annuaire* 81 (1972–1973): 136.

8. Klaes, *Conscience and Consciousness,* p. 113.

9. Chaitanya, *Mahābhārata,* p. 281.

10. "When Bhīṣma introduces Yudhiṣṭhira to the subject of *rājadharma,* the "duty of kings," he begins by breaking the subject down into four topics:

attendance on gods and Brahmins, truth *(satya)*, exertion *(utthāna)*, and the maintenance of prosperity *(śrī)*. Hiltebeitel, *Ritual of Battle*, p. 214.

Chapter 8. Action and Retribution

1. Examples we have already met include the Dhātṛ who operates within our bodies (II.52.18, II.67.3, and III.30.30), the seven celestial custodians of the *pravṛttidharma* who control our acts and course of life (XII.327.72), the god Śiva (XII.149.112), and various others (II.72.8–11 and XII.120.44). The spiritual ambitions *(tapas)* of forest sages are a major cause for concern among the gods. Luckily, these *ṛṣis* can usually be distracted by the charms of a celestial maiden *(apsara)*.

2. Cf. III.200.2; also XII.108.1, XII.109.9–11, XII.254.35–36, XIII.10.2, XIII.10.32, etc.

3. See, for example, III.200.27 where the word *bhāga* is used explicitly in this connection. ("The agent himself has the *bhāga* of good and bad.")

4. T. G. Kalghatgi, *Karma and Rebirth* (Ahmedabad, India: L. D. Institute of Indology, 1972), p. 43.

5. H. D. Bhattacharyya, "Vicissitudes of the Karma Doctrine." In *Malaviya Commemoration Volume* (Benares, India: Benares Hindu University, 1932). Quoted in Benoy Gopal Ray, *Gods and Karma in Indian Religions* (Santiniketan: Center of Advanced Study in Philosophy, Visva-Bharati University, 1973), p. 89.

6. Kane. *History of Dharmaśāstra*, vol. II, p. 1561.

7. Kesari Mohan Ganguli, trans., *The Mahabharata*, Vol. IX, pp. 390–391.

8. Long, "Concepts of Human Action and Rebirth in the Mahābhārata," pp. 52–57.

9. Ibid., note 39, p. 56.

10. Ibid. p. 57. Unfortunately, the article is too short to provide the necessary support for his "underlying assumption" about the contribution of karma to human destiny.

11. Chaitanya, *Mahābhārata*, p. 337. However, I am not sure that he could demonstrate such a parallelism in every case.

12. Ibid., p. 338.

13. Ibid., pp. 341–342.

14. Ibid., p. 343.

15. Ibid., p. 342.

Chapter 9. The Path of Self-Determination

1. The term *autonomy* comes from the Greek *autos* (self) and *nomos* (law). Hence the reference is to "that which gives law to itself," or "that which is its

own law." We use the word interchangeably with the term *self-determination* (the determination of one's actions by oneself without compulsion). The term *person* is from the Latin *persona,* a translation of the Greek *prosopon,* both words signifying the mask worn by actors onstage. The term is appropriate since, as we have already learned from chapter 6, the epic "person" is ultimately a case of mistaken identity.

2. R. V. De Smet, "Early Trends in the Indian Understanding of Man," *Philosophy East and West* 22: 3 (July 1972): 259–268.

3. Long, "Human Action and Rebirth in the Mahābhārata." In *Karma and Rebirth in Classical Indian Traditions,* pp. 57–58.

4. R. Kane defines moral self-determination as the sole or ultimate dominion of the agent over the choice

> in the sense that (i) the agent's making the choice at t rather than doing otherwise, or vice versa (that is, choosing from duty or self-interest), can be explained by saying that the agent "rationally willed at t to do so" in the sense of "endorsed reasons or motives at t for choosing as he or she did choose rather than doing otherwise" (the motives of duty or of self interest as the case may be), and (ii) no further explanation can be given for the agent's choosing rather than doing otherwise (or vice versa), or for the agent's endorsing the set of reasons he or she did endorse at t, that is an explanation in terms of conditions whose existence cannot be explained by the agent's choosing or rationally willing something at t. Kane, *Free Will and Values* (Albany: State University of New York Press, 1985), p. 153.

5. Chaitanya, *Mahābhārata,* p. 237.

6. Ibid., p. 256.

7. Kalidas Bhattacharyya, "The Status of the Individual in Indian Metaphysics." In *The Indian Mind: Essentials of Indian Philosophy and Culture,* Charles A. Moore, ed. with the assistance of Aldyth V. Morris (Honolulu: East-West Center Press and University of Hawaii Press, 1967), p. 300. It is generally agreed today that the highest expression of freedom is to be found in moral choice.

8. As Kaṭhopaniṣad II.1 shows, even the choice of the good is able to "chain a man" *(puruṣaṃ sintaḥ).* The epic uses the image of the net (for example, I.110.2, XII.289.11ff., and XII.295.23) as well as that of the cocoon that the embodied soul, in its ignorance, spins about itself (cf. XII.136.28–29, XII.212.47, XII.309.14, and XII.316.28–29).

9. S. Cromwell Crawford, *The Evolution of Hindu Ethical Ideas* (Calcutta: Firma K. L. Mukhopadhyay, 1974), p. 216.

10. These two functions are contrasted at III.149.34–36. Of course the *sādhāraṇadharmas* go far beyond the virtues of sacrifice, study, and charity promoted here.

11. Cf. V.2.14, VI.21.11, VI.61.16, VI.117.33, IX.62.58, XI.13.9, XI.17.6, and XIII.150.8, etc.

12. Crawford, *Hindu Ethical Ideas,* p. 223.

13. Cf. III.200.2. Cf. also XII.108.1, XII.109.9–11, XII.254.35–36, XIII.10.2, XIII.10.32, etc.

14. According to Katz, these moral ambiguities or impasses of dharma are a mark of the "human" dimension of the epic heroes, particularly of Arjuna. In addition to Bhīṣma's problem, examples include the battlefield dilemna of the Gītā (VI.23/BG.1.24ff.), Arjuna's self-doubt prior to the death of Bhīṣma (VI.102.36–37), his dubious assistance to Sātyaki (VII.116–118), deceit associated with the killing of Jayadratha (VII.121) and Karṇa (VIII.66), as well as moral issues surrounding the deaths of Droṇa (VII.164) and Duryodhana (IX.57).

15. According to the case built by Klaes (cf. *Conscience and Consciousness*), Yudhiṣṭhira's problem is of this nature. Thus, he is caught between the categorical imperative of his own conscience and the demands of the traditional *varṇāśramadharma* espoused by Kṛṣṇa.

16. The mark of a good action, viz., that it be undertaken in a spirit of detachment *(vairāgya* or *niṣkāma)* for the welfare of others *(lokasaṃgraha),* cannot be left to individual judgment unless he or she is already in a state of detachment. Hence the need for written codes.

17. Biardeau, "Études (V)," p. 190.

18. However, the epic has no sense of "radical evil." For a discussion of the origins of *puṇya* and *pāpa* see C. L. Prabhakar, "The Idea of Pāpa and Puṇya in the Ṛgveda," *Journal of the Oriental Institute of the University of Baroda* 24: 3–4 (March–June 1975): 269–283.

19. Chaitanya, *Mahābhārata,* p. 305. The churning process may well be modeled after the pressing of the *soma* juice during the Vedic Soma sacrifice. See Katz, *Arjuna,* p. 75.

20. Ibid., p. 364.

21. The closest Sanskrit equivalents of "will" would perhaps be *saṃkalpa* (purpose, intention, or resolution), or *abhisaṃdhitā* (decision).

22. G. R. Malkani, "Philosophy of the Will." In *World Perspectives in Philosophy, Religion and Culture,* Ram Jee Singh, ed. (Bombay: Bharati Bhawan, 1968), p. 196.

23. Chaitanya, *Mahābhārata,* p. 272.

24. Balbir Singh, *The Conceptual Framework of Indian Philosophy* (Delhi: Macmillan Co. of India, 1976), p. 50.

25. G. W. Kaveeshwar, *The Ethics of the Gītā* (Delhi: Motilal Banarsidass, 1971), p. 173.

26. After performing awesome austerities *(tapas)* in his quest for divine weapons (symbol of the self-control needed to accomplish the "work of the gods"), Arjuna is attacked by a wild boar (symbol of untamed nature?) which he shoots at the same instant as a *kirāta* (tribal or "savage") who had suddenly appeared out of the forest (III.40.16). When his claim to the dead animal (actually a *rākṣasa* in the form of a boar) is challenged by the *kirāta,* his heroic efforts fail him and he is reduced to a sacrificial oblation *(piṇḍa)* in the dramatic encounter that follows. The *kirāta* turns out to be the god Śiva who restores his powers and "grants him eyesight" (III.40.54). When Arjuna thereupon falls to the ground and worships him, his powers are immeasurably multiplied by the gift of the dreaded *brahmaśiras* and by various other divine weapons.

Possession of a weapon by the name of *brahmaśiras* suggests to Biardeau that Arjuna has supplemented his *kṣatra* powers with the divine potentials embodied in the power of the *Brahman,* a truly lethal combination which, she argues, reveals his association with the avatar. Biardeau regards this episode as a consecration *(dīkṣa)* for the battle with the *asuras* that Arjuna will undertake on behalf of the gods in heaven *(svarga).* She notes that Kṛṣṇa himself incorporates the *kṣatra* and *brahman* powers through his line of descent from Yadu, eldest son of Yayāti and Devayānī, daughter of the Brahmin Śukra, priest of the demons (and grand-daughter of Indra on her mother's side). The *brahmaśiras* is the power inhering in the part of the sacrificial victim that is offered in the sacrifice. The awesome extent of this power may be measured by the fact that it is equivalent to the *paśupata,* the instrument that "kills" the sacrifice of Dakṣa. According to Biardeau, this story refers to the cosmic death of the sacrifice itself: "a monstrous sacrifice, the end of all others, a cosmic funeral," equivalent to the end of the world. Cf. Biardeau, "Études (V)," pp. 154–156. Katz notes the death/rebirth structure of this encounter with the *kirāta* that she views as a *shamanic* initiation emphasizing the ascetic side of Arjuna's "heroic" character. Cf. Katz, *Arjuna,* pp. 90–104. But just how much of this is his own doing is debatable. Commenting on this episode, Chaitanya asks rhetorically: "Can man's action have fruition, if the intentionality behind the working of the world does not endorse it?" adding that the total inadequacy of the Gāṇḍiva on this occasion, "indicates the deep spring whence flows the efficacy of all the instrumentalities and processes of the manifested world." Chaitanya, *Mahābhārata,* pp. 203–204.

27. Crawford, *Hindu Ethical Ideas,* p. 224.

28. Sukthankar, *Meaning of the Mahābhārata,* p. 104.

29. Described by Kṛṣṇa in the Bhagavadgītā at VI.40/BG.18.34.

30. Crawford, *Hindu Ethical Ideas,* p. 224.

31. Sukthankar, *Meaning of the Mahābhārata,* p. 107.

32. Neither Duryodhana nor his father can claim any measure of personal autonomy. The difference is that the former seemingly escapes the pain of moral conflict (though not the pain of defeat) while the latter is subject to recurrent bouts of "fear and trembling."

33. Sukthankar, *Meaning of the Mahābhārata,* p. 105.

34. Crawford, *Hindu Ethical Ideas,* p. 129.

35. Ibid., p. 129–130.

36. Bhattacharyya, "Status of the Individual in Indian Metaphysics." In the *Indian Mind: Essentials of Indian Philosophy and Culture,* Charles A. Moore, ed., with the assistance of Aldyth V. Morris (Honolulu: East-West Center Press and University of Hawaii Press, 1967), p. 319.

37. Hartmann, *Ethics,* vol. III, "Moral Freedom," p. 116.

38. S. K. Belvalkar, "The Bhagavad-gītā: A General Review of Its History and Character," in *Cultural Heritage of India,* vol. II, "Itihāsas, Purāṇas, Dharma and other Śāstras," p. 140.

Chapter 10. Conclusion

1. Hiltebeitel, *Ritual of Battle,* p. 115.

2. In discussing the complexities of the Hindu dharma Paul Hacker observes that

> Der Hindu-Theismus hat sich zwar auf verschiedene Weise bemüht, dem höchsten Gott einen Einfluss auf das Karmangeschehen einzuräumen. Aber so wenig wie der Hindu in der Lage war, den Dharma konsequent als Willen Gottes zu verstehen, ebensowenig konnte er die Auswirkung des getanen oder verfehlten Dharma als Belohnung oder Bestrafung von Verdienst oder Schuld auffassen. Die Rolle des höchsten Gottes in dem Mechanismus der Dharma-Adharma-Kausalität blieb die eines eigentlich entbehrlichen Aufsehers. (Hindu theism has sought in various ways to find a place for the highest God to influence the process of karma. But it was as difficult for the Hindu to conceive of the dharma as the Will of God as it was to imagine the consequences of dharmic or adharmic acts as reward for merit or punishment for sin. In practice, the role of the highest God in the causal mechanics of dharma-adharma remained that of a virtually dispensable supervisor).

See Hacker, "Dharma im Hinduismus." In Hacker, *Kleine Schriften* (Wiesbaden, Germany: Franz Steiner Verlag Gmbh., 1978), p. 506.

3. Paul Ricoeur, *Freedom and Nature: The Voluntary and the Involuntary,* Erazim V. Kohak, trans. (Evanston, Ill.: Northwestern University Press, 1966).

4. Ibid., p. 341.

5. Ricoeur, "The Unity of the Voluntary and the Involuntary as a Limiting Idea." In *Philosophy of Paul Ricoeur,* p. 16.

6. Ibid., p. 19.

7. Ricoeur, *Freedom and Nature,* p. 463.

8. Ibid., p. 477.

9. Ricoeur's view is that ultimate consent must pass through this stage of refusal as one of two "Copernican revolutions." In his introduction to *Freedom and Nature,* Ricoeur's translator writes that "While the first Copernican revolution won the Cogito by placing man at the center of the universe, the note of adoration makes consent possible by replacing man with Transcendence as the center of reality. Only because the first revolution won the Cogito can the second revolution be a consent rather than a surrender." Cf. Erazim V. Kohák, "The Philosophy of Paul Ricoeur," Introduction to Ricoeur, *Freedom and Nature,* p. xxviii.

10. Ibid, pp. 479–480.

11. Katz would appear to be in substantial agreement. However, she casts the issue in light of the decline of the *yugas*, the onset of the *kaliyuga* being the signal for a transition from the "heroic" to more "human" modes of conduct. Human effort and "fate" work in harmony with each other at both the heroic and devotional levels of interpretation, the former giving the priority to effort the latter to 'fate.' "At the heroic level, there is no doubt that effort will succeed: fate and effort will not be in opposition to one another. At the human level, the *kaliyuga* represents the interference of fate." Cf. Katz, *Arjuna in the Mahabharata,* p. 179. From the transcendent perspective of the Kṛṣṇa theophany (VI.33/ B.G.11.32) she notes that "The fate-effort opposition of the human level is thus transcended in favor of a fuller recognition of fate" (p. 228). This is the devotional mode in which "the significance of all actions taken throughout the Mahabharata is altered radically: action is no longer seen as something apart from fate or opposed to fate; fate is supreme, but action harmonizes with it to fulfill the Mahabharata's paradoxical conception of united fate and effort as the components of success." Ibid., p. 234. The way to transcendence, whether along the path of knowledge or the path of devotion to Kṛṣṇa, thus involves a devaluation of the ego and its efforts: "Clearly, in underrating the role of the individual ego, both [that is, paths] underrate the role of individual accomplishment" (Cf. p. 227).

12. Hartmann, *Ethics,* vol. III, p. 267.

13. Biardeau, "Études V," p. 87–88.

14. For more information on Śaṃkara's conception of human nature see Hacker, "Śaṃkara's Conception of Man." In *Kleine Schriften* (Wiesbaden, Germany: Franz Steiner Verlag Gmbh., 1978), pp. 242–251.

15. *mātāpitṛsahasrāṇi putradāraśatāni ca | saṃsāreṣvanubhūtāni yānti yāsyanti cāpare ‖ harṣasthānasahasrāni bhayasthānaśatāni ca | divase divase muḍham āviśanti na paṇḍitam ‖ urdhvabāhur viraumyeṣa na ca kaścicchṛṇoti me | dharmādarthaśca kāmaśca sa kim arthaṃ na sevyate ‖ na jātu kāmān na bhayānna lobhād dharmaṃ tyajejjīvitasyāpi hetoḥ | nityo dharmaḥ sukhaduḥkhe tvanitye jīvo nityo heturasya tvanityaḥ* ‖ (XVIII.5.47–50).

Appendix: Some Notes on Scholarship

1. Klaes, *Conscience and Consciousness,* p. 2.

2. We are indebted here to the excellent summary of modern scholarship on the Mahābhārata contained in "Lecture I: The Mahābhārata and its Critics" in his *Meaning of the Mahābhārata,* pp. 1–31. Cf. also A. D. Pusalker, "Twenty-five Years of Epic and Puranic Studies," R. N. Dandekar, ed., *Progress of Indic Studies 1917–1942* (Poona, India: Bhandarkar Oriental Research Institute, 1942), pp. 101–152.

3. Sukthankar, *Meaning of the Mahābhārata,* p. 11.

4. Ibid., pp. 19–20.

5. This idea had appeared in India by the seventh or eighth century A.D. in the works of the philosopher Kumārila. Cf. Barend A. van Nooten, *The Mahābhārata Attributed to Kṛṣṇa Dvaipāyana Vyāsa* (New York: Twayne Publishers, 1971), p. 87. It would seem from the quotation from *Dhvanyāloka* that this was also Ānandavardhana's view (cf. note 8, p. 163).

6. Both sides of the ongoing debate on the historicity of the central story are represented among articles contained in D. C. Sircar, ed., *The Bhārata War and Purāṇic Genealogies* (Calcutta: University of Calcutta, 1969). Cf. also S. P. Gupta and K. S. Ramachandran, eds., *Mahābhārata: Myth and Reality: Differing Views* (Delhi: Agam Prakashan, 1976); and Ram Chandra Jain, *Jaya: The Original Nucleus of Mahabharata* (Delhi: Agam Kala Prakashan, 1979). The position of the present author is well summarized in the view that "The historical character of the persons celebrated in epic poetry is not in question. But their historicity does not long resist the corrosive action of mythicization. The historical event in itself, however important, does not remain in the popular memory, nor does its recollection kindle the poetic imagination save insofar as the particular historical event closely approaches a mythical model." Mircea Eliade, *The Myth of the Eternal Return or Cosmos and History,* Willard R. Trask, trans. Bollingen Series, 46 (1954; rpt. Princeton: Princeton University Press, 1974), p. 42.

7. Dumézil, *Mythe et épopée,* vol. I, p. 242.

8. Ibid., p. 222 ff.

9. Ibid., pp. 238–239.

10. Chaitanya, *Mahābhārata,* pp. 23–24.

11. Katz, *Arjuna in the Mahabharata,* p. 118.

12. Ibid., p. 234.

13. Ibid., note10, p. 21.

14. Heino Gehrts, *Mahābhārata: das Geschehen und seine Bedeutung* (Bonn: Bouvier Verlag Herbert Grundmann, 1975), p. 292. For the *rājasūya* as a model for Book II, see van Buitenen, *Mahābhārata,* vol. II, pp. 5–6; and "On the Structure of the Sabhāparvan of the Mahābhārata." In *India Maior* (Festschrift J. Gonda 1972), pp. 68–84.

15. Hiltebeitel, "The Mahābhārata and Hindu Eschatology." *History of Religions* 12, 2 (November 1972): 95–135.

16. Hiltebeitel, *Ritual of Battle,* p. 359. On the trifunctional nature of the Pāṇḍavas, cf. p. 195.

17. Ibid., p. 318. Cf. also p. 9. Katz takes a similar position from within her interpretation of the epic at the heroic level: "The metaphor of the Kurukshetra War as a sacrifice captures the central meaning of the epic at the heroic level, which is built upon the structural opposition of order and disorder, both represented by the imagery of fire and sacrifice." See Katz, *Arjuna,* p. 115.

18. Ibid., p. 140 where he writes: "I have tried to suggest here, although in Part Three I will steer a middle course between them, that the Indo-European perspective of Dumézil and the Purāṇic, one might say 'Hindu,' perspective of Biardeau are both valid, and that, to borrow from a Sāṃkhya similitude, they may at some points be as necessary to each other, in making a way through the Mahābhārata forest, as the blind man and the lame." Cf. also Katz, *Arjuna,* note 21, p. 120.

19. Van Buitenen has criticized her for this. He claims a middle position: "Although I have much sympathy for those who argue that a text like the Mahābhārata should not be cut up in pieces but should be viewed as a work that, whatever its various origins, functioned as a whole, I do think that a middle position can be taken. It is only after we have learned to discern what disparate parts have gone into the making of the Mahābhārata that we are allowed the question why these parts were felt to be compatible so that the text as a whole made sense." *(Mahābhārata,* Introduction to Book IV, p. 20. Cf. also his detailed critique in Introduction to Book V, pp. 142–184.)

20. Biardeau, *L'hindouisme: anthropologie d'une civilisation* (Paris: Flammarion [Champs], 1981), pp. 15–16.

21. Ibid., p. 21.

22. Biardeau, "Études de mythologie hindou (IV)," *Bulletin de l'École française d'Éxtrême-Orient* 63 (1976): 173. Cf. also "The Salvation of the King in the Mahābhārata." *Contributions to Indian Sociology* (New Series) 15 (January–December 1981): 75–97.

23. J. N. Farquhar believes that this occurred during the Śunga dynasty, a period of brāhmaṇic revivalism, which arose after the collapse of the Buddhist-leaning Mauryan Empire in the second century B.C. Cf. Farquhar, *An Outline of the Religious Literature of India,* (1920, rpt. Delhi: Motilal Banarsidass, 1967), p. 78.

24. Biardeau and Jean-Michel Péterfalvi, *Le Mahābhārata: Livres I à V* (Paris: Flammarion, 1985), p. 29.

25. See *Laws of Manu* V.39–40: "Svayambhū [the 'Self-existent'] himself created animals for the sake of sacrifices; sacrifices [have been instituted] for the good of this whole [world]; hence the slaughtering [of beasts] for sacrifices is not slaughtering [in the ordinary sense of the word]. Herbs, trees, cattle, birds, and [other] animals that have been destroyed for sacrifices, receive [being reborn into] higher existences." Quoted from Georg Bühler, trans., *The Laws of Manu, The Sacred Books of the East,* vol. XXV (1886; rpt. Delhi: Motilal Banarsidass, 1984), p. 175.

26. "Every Hindu knows at least implicitly, that in relying officially on the Veda and keeping it as the supreme reference, the MBh is in fact the foundation charter of what in India is called the religion of bhakti, of devotion, and that the Vedic texts hardly lend themselves to this new interpretation." Cf. Biardeau and Péterfalvi, *Mahābhārata*, p. 28. It should be noted that this *bhakti* is not the mystical exuberance of the later sectarian cults but a religious system based on a more positive valuation of the world and the activities that keep it in place. No longer is salvation to be had only through the abandonment of society and its rituals *(karmasaṃnyāsa)* but may be found at the heart of any and all activity, provided this is undertaken in a spirit of detachment and service to the Lord *(karmayoga)*.

27. The so-called three sacrifices *(trimedhā)* announced by a celestial voice at the birth of Arjuna (I.114.33). The *rājasūya,* specifically the dicing episode, is the "sacrifice" of the Pāṇḍavas by the forces of Duryodhana/Kali. Instead of being killed they are banished to the forest for thirteen years. The *brahmāstra* episode and the *aśvamedha* symbolize the restoration of the Dharma and the re-creation of a golden age with the recovery of the sovereignty by the royal line (cf. pp. 212–217).

28. Biardeau, "Conférence de Mlle Madeleine Biardeau," *Annuaire de l'École pratique des Hautes Études: Ve section-Sciences religieuses* 81 (1972–1973), p. 136.

29. Chaitanya, *Mahābhārata,* p. 449.

30. Hiltebeitel, *Ritual of Battle,* p. 139.

31. Ibid., p. 140. Cf. also his note 33, p. 127. See also the general statement quoted from Sukthankar, p. 6.

32. Biardeau and Péterfalvi, *Mahābhārata,* p. 14.

Family Connections in the Mahābhārata

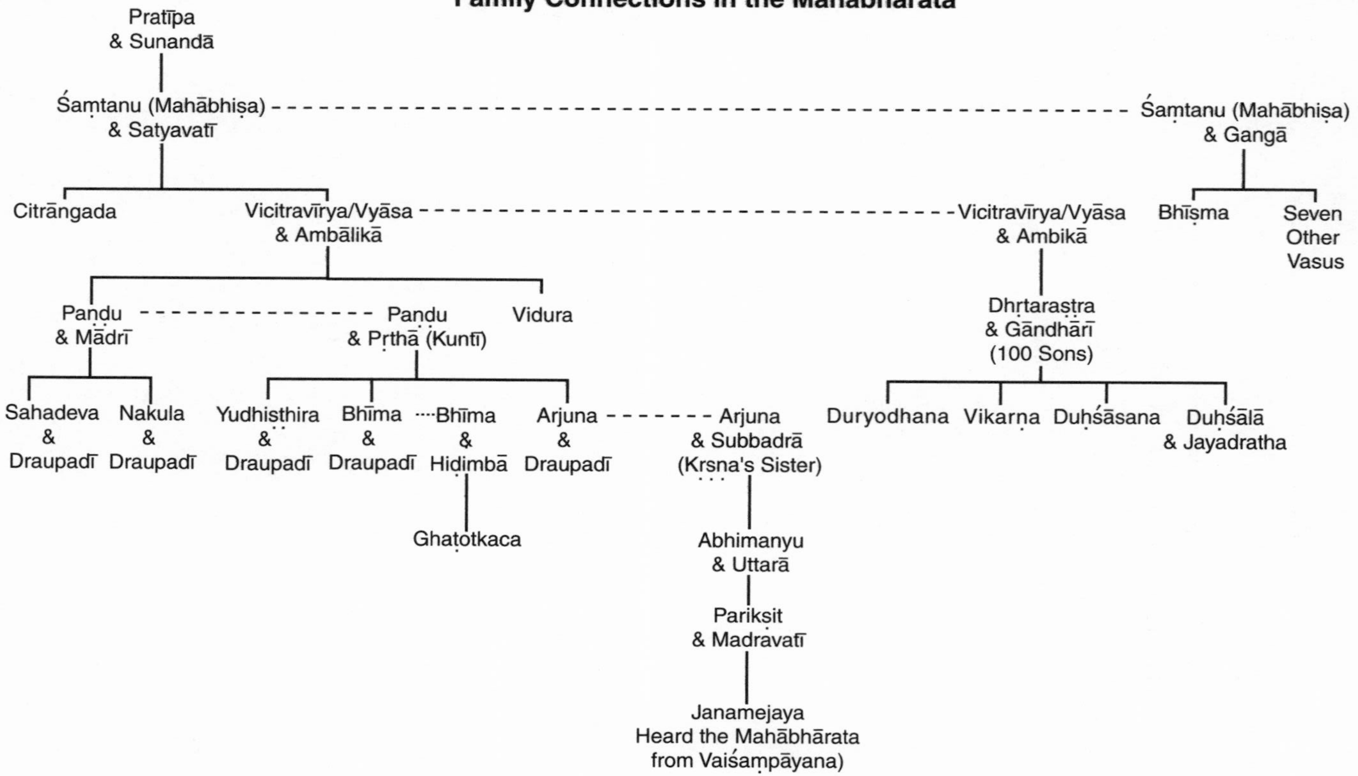

Glossary of Proper Names

The following index of family and place names is not exhaustive—the Mahābhārata story has a cast of thousands. The objective is simply to offer the reader some idea of the relationships of the main characters mentioned at various places in the course of this book.

Abhimanyu Arjuna's son by his fourth wife Subhadrā and also Kṛṣṇa's nephew. As the incarnation of the Moon (Soma) and the father of Parikṣit, he was a key link in the survival of the Lunar dynasty *(Candravaṁśa).* He was killed by Duḥśāsana on the thirteenth day of the battle.

Ādideva (lit. "primordial god") an epithet applied to Kṛṣṇa as Supreme Godhead.

Āditya the name of a group of twelve Vedic gods (that includes Viṣṇu as the dwarf).

Agni the god of the sacrificial fire. He appears in the epic both as god and human incarnation (Dhṛṣṭadyumna, the son of Drupada).

Ambā the eldest daughter of the king of Kāśī and one of the three wives of King Vicitravīrya. She is reincarnated as Śikhaṇḍin, another son of Drupada, who kills Bhīṣma.

Ambālikā the youngest daughter of the king of Kāśī and wife of King Vicitravīrya. She fathers the "pale" King Pāṇḍu with the help of the sage Vyāsa.

Ambikā the second of the three daughters of the king of Kāśī and wife of King Vicitravīrya. She fathers the blind king Dhṛtarāṣṭra with the help of the sage Vyāsa.

Andhakas the name of a tribe related to the Vṛṣṇis.

Antaka the personified form of Death (that incarnates in Aśvatthāman).

Anugītā a subsection of the Aśvamedhaparvan (Book XIV) in which Arjuna asks Kṛṣṇa to recall the lessons of the Bhagavadgītā. Kṛṣṇa does the best he can by recounting a three part dialog of instructions for a Brahmin; instructions for a Brahmin wife; and instruction by a guru to his disciple.

Arjuna one of the five sons of King Pāṇḍu (though technically the "son" of Indra, King of the gods) and the youngest to be born to Kuntī. He is the de facto leader and major combatant on the Pāṇḍava side. As Nara he is the eternal friend of Kṛṣṇa (as Nārāyaṇa). He marries Draupadī, Ulūpī, Citrāngadā, and Subhadrā (Kṛṣṇa's sister), though only the first and the last are important. He fathers one son on each of these wives, Śrutakīrti by Draupadī, Irāvan by Ulūpī, Babhruvāhana by Citrāngadā, and Abhimanyu by Subhadrā, though only the latter is important. His identity is evoked by well over sixty synonyms or epithets throughout the epic (for example, Bībhatsu, Dhanaṃjaya, Pārtha, Guḍākeśa, Jaya, Jiṣṇu, Kirīṭin, Phālguna, Savyasācin, Śvetavāhana, and Vijaya).

Arjunaka the Fowler (hunter) in the story of Gautamī and the Fowler.

Aśmagītā the discourse between the Brahmin sage Aśma and King Janaka on the causes and cure of sorrow. It forms part of the Śāntiparvan (XII.28).

Aśvamedhaparvan the title of Book XIV of the Mahābhārata dealing with the Horse Sacrifice of Yudhiṣṭhira.

Aśvatthāman the son of Droṇa and Kṛpī. He is the collective incarnation of Mahādeva (Śiva), Antaka (Death), Kāma (Desire), and Krodha (Anger). He is a fierce supporter of the Kauravas, and following the battle itself goes with Kṛpa and Kṛtavarman to the Pāṇḍava camp and single-handedly slaughters Dhṛṣṭadyumna and most of the remaining Pāṇḍava heroes. Later, he kills the embryo of Parikṣit in the womb of Uttarā, until the unborn baby is restored to life by Kṛṣṇa. Aśvatthāman is condemned to roam the earth for three thousand years for his crimes after being forced to give a magic jewel on his head to the Pāṇḍavas.

Badarī the name of the hermitage of the *ṛṣis* Nara–Nārāyaṇa (that is, Arjuna–Kṛṣṇa) in the Himālayas.

Bāhlika the name of a tribe in the Kingdom of Madra.

Baka a demon who is killed by Bhīma.

Balarāma the incarnation of the cosmic serpent Śeṣa and elder brother to Kṛṣṇa. Also known as Baladeva and Balabhadrarāma. He was the seventh son of Vasudeva and Devakī (followed by Kṛṣṇa as the eighth).

Bali a "good" demon in the line of Hiraṇyakaśipu who once defeated the gods and rose to the position of Indra, King of Heaven. However, he was tricked into losing his sovereign position by agreeing to a request by a hermit boy (who was really Viṣṇu as the dwarf Vāmana) for "three steps" of land. Vāmana thereupon grew in size to measure the whole earth with his first step, the whole of heaven with his second, and with the third he pushed Bali down into hell. A chastened Bali eventually acknowledged the sovereignty of Viṣṇu after being reborn in the form of an ass.

Bhaga one of the twelve Ādityas (that is, sons of Aditi). He lost his eyes to Rudra (= Śiva) until the latter was offered his rightful "share" of the sacrifice. In addition to being the distributor of the "shares" Bhaga is acknowledged as the lord of general good fortune.

Bhagadatta a demon and king of Prājyotiṣpura who was killed by Arjuna.

Bhagavadgītā a famous section of the Bhīṣmaparvan (Book VI) in which Kṛṣṇa gives spiritual advice to Arjuna who is despondent at the thought of warring against his own family and gurus.

Bharadvāja a Brahmin *ṛṣi* who fathered Droṇa on the celestial woman Ghṛtācī.

Bharata a famous king of the Lunar dynasty *(Candravaṃśa)* and the son of Duḥṣanta and Śakuntalā. The Mahābhārata is the great story of the Bhāratas, that is to say, the "descendants of Bharata." Arjuna is often called "Bhārata."

Bhārgava a descendant of the great Brahmin sage Bhṛgu (for example, Rāma Jāmadagnya).

Bhīma also known as Bhīmasena; one of the five Pāṇḍavas and the second to be born to Kuntī. In reality he is the son of Vāyu, the wind god. As a result he was endowed with great strength. He killed a number of demons and also Duryodhana after delivering a low blow with his mace and kicking him in the head.

Bhīṣma the son of King Śaṃtanu and the goddess Gaṅga (the river Ganges). He is an incarnation of Dyaus (one of the eight Vasus). Respected as the "grandfather" of the Pāṇḍavas and the Kauravas, he is, in reality, only their great uncle. He supported the Kauravas in the war and was killed by Śikhaṇḍin. His real name was Devavrata, the name of Bhīṣma referring to the "terrible" vow he took to remain a bachelor for life.

Bhṛgu a son of Brahmā and founder of an important line of *ṛṣis* called the "Bhārgavas."

Bhūmidevī a goddess who entreats Brahmā to save the earth from being overrun by the incarnating demons. Brahmā thereupon asks all the gods to incarnate with a part of themselves to help her, thereby setting the stage for the Mahābhārata.

Bhūriśravas the son of Somadatta and the grandson of a younger brother of Śaṃtanu. He fought for the Kauravas and was killed by Sātyaki after Arjuna had cut off his left arm in a singularly ungallant act.

Brahmā the first of the three forms *(trimūrtis)* of the Supreme Being as "Creator," the two others being Viṣṇu (the Preserver) and Śiva (the Destroyer). In the Mahābhārata Brahmā orders the lesser gods to incarnate themselves on the earth to rid it of the scourge of demon kings. *See also* Viṣṇu and Śiva.

Brahmadatta the name of a king who has a conversation with the bird Pūjani on the subject of trust (in Book XII.137).

Brahman the impersonal Absolute; the unmanifested Source or "God" from which all things emanate; the Supreme Reality or "God" in His formless state. In the Upaniṣads and in certain portions of the Mahābhārata Brahman is equated with Ātman (the universal "Self").

Brāhmaṇas prose sections of the Veda *(śruti)* dealing mainly with matters pertaining to the sacrifice, over which the Brahmin priests have gained control. There are eight of them in all.

Brahmā–Prajāpati Brahmā as "Lord of creatures."

Bṛhadāraṇyakopaniṣad a celebrated Upaniṣad attached to the end of the Śatapatha Brāhmaṇa.

Bṛhaspati the name of the spiritual preceptor of the gods (who is incarnated as Droṇa).

Buddha ("the awakened one") the epithet of Siddhārtha Gautama considered by some Hindus to be an incarnation of Viṣṇu.

Chedi the name of a country located to the south of the Yamunā River.

Citraratha a celestial musician *(gandharva)* who taught Arjuna *cākṣuṣīvidyā*, "the art of seeing anything and everything in the three worlds."

Dakṣa one of the Prajāpatis (creators) who omitted to invite Śiva to a sacrifice performed to obtain a son. Śiva thereupon had Dakṣa killed and the sacrifice destroyed.

Devaka Kṛṣṇa's grandfather (father of Devakī).

Devakī Kṛṣṇa's mother.

Devasthana a great royal sage *(mahārṣi)* who gave spiritual advice to Yudhiṣṭhira after the war.

Devayānī the daughter of Śukra, the preceptor of the *asuras* (demons). She married Yayāti and had a son called Yadu, the progenitor of the Yādavas.

Devikā the second wife of Yudhiṣṭhira who bore him a son (Yaudheya). Also means "the bad player."

Dhanaṃjaya an epithet of Arjuna. "They call me Dhanaṃjaya because I stand in the midst of booty after conquering all the countrysides and plundering their entire wealth" (IV.39.11).

Dharmarāja the "king of dharma," an epithet of Yudhiṣṭhira.

Dharmaśāstra a form of religious text called *smṛti* ("recollected") dealing with domestic and social rules and duties. The "Laws of Manu" (Manusmṛti) is one of the most important.

Dhārtarāṣṭra the name for the hundred sons of Dhṛtarāṣṭra.

Dhātṛ a personification of the divine functions of bestowing, disposing, etc., the divine "Bestower." Similar to Śāstṛ ("the Ordainer").

Dhṛṣṭadyumna Draupadī's brother, born from the sacrificial fire complete with a crown on his head, armor on his body, and bow and arrows and sword in his hands.

Dhṛtarāṣṭra Ambikā's son and father of the Kauravas who was born blind. The prime "victim of fate" in the Mahābhārata.

Diti one of the wives of Kaśyapa and progenitor of the demons known as *daityas*.

Draupadī the daughter of King Drupada and wife in common of the five Pāṇḍavas. Often called "Pāñcalī" from the name of her birthplace in the kingdom of Pāñcala.

Droṇa the son of Bharadvāja and preceptor of both Kauravas and the Pāṇḍavas. He married Kṛpī and fathered Aśvatthāman. Although a Brahmin he obtained the entire armory of Paraśurāma (a famous warrior) and chose the life of a warrior (a "warrior-Brahmin"). He was partial to Arjuna but fought on the Kaurava side (supposedly because of financial dependence).

Drupada the king of Pāñcala and father of Draupadī and Dhṛṣṭadyumna. He fought on the Pāṇḍava side and was finally killed by his archenemy Droṇa.

Duḥśālā the only daughter of Dhṛtarāṣṭra by Gāndhārī. She married Jayadratha.

Duḥṣanta one of the progenitors of the Kurus; the father of King Bharata of the Lunar dynasty *(Candravaṁśa)* and husband of Śakuntalā (whom he had originally disowned).

Duḥśāsana one of the one hundred sons of Dhṛtarāṣṭra who is vilified for having dragged Draupadī into the assembly hall during the dice game and stripping her of her clothes.

Durvāsas an irascible sage believed to have been a portion of Śiva. He taught Kuntī a mantra that enabled her to obtain the favors of various gods to father Karṇa and three of the five Pāṇḍavas.

Duryodhana the eldest of the one hundred sons of Dhṛtarāṣṭra and Gāndhārī and incarnation of the demon Kali. His jealousy of the Pāṇḍavas was the main cause of the war between the cousins. Duryodhana was killed by Bhīma during a mace duel after the war, in which the latter dealt a low blow on a sign from Arjuna.

Dvaipāyana the epithet of Vyāsa ("he who is born on an island"); also the name of the lake in which Duryodhana takes refuge after the war.

Dvaitavana a forest with a lake in which the Pāṇḍavas lived in the Vanaparvan section of the Mahābhārata.

Dvārakā the abode of Kṛṣṇa and capital city of the Yādavas.

Dvijasattama or (**Dvijottama**) "best of the twice-born"—an epithet of Arjuna.

Dyaus one of the eight Vasus of whom Bhīṣma is an incarnation.

Earth see Bhūmidevī.

Ekalavya a *Śūdra* (lower-caste) forester who went to Droṇa to learn archery. Droṇa forced him to give his thumb as a preceptor fee so that he would never be as good as Arjuna.

Gāndhāra a kingdom ruled by Subala. Also the name of the king of that kingdom who was father to Gāndhārī and Śakuni.

Gāndhārī the daughter of Subala and wife of Dhṛtarāṣṭra. She was so devoted that she blindfolded herself with a silk shawl.

Gandharva a heavenly musician.

Gāṇḍīva the famous bow of Arjuna.

Gaṅgā the river Ganges personified as a goddess and the mother of Bhīṣma.

Gautamī a Brahmin lady whose son succumbed to a snakebite in a story in the Anuśāsanaparvan (Book XIII).

Ghaṭotkaca the son of Bhīma and the demon Hiḍimbā. He fought bravely for the Pāṇḍavas before being killed by Karṇa.

Girivraja the capital seat of King Jarāsandha, who had conquered and imprisoned one hundred kings before being killed by Bhīma.

Gītā see Bhagavadgītā

Gopis cowherds, and more specifically, the cowherd army that Kṛṣṇa lends to Duryodhana (known as the Nārāyaṇas) after Arjuna chooses Kṛṣṇa (as a non-combatant) to assist him.

Hari an epithet of Viṣṇu/Kṛṣṇa.

Hāstinapura ("city of the elephant") the capital city of the Kauravas.

Hayagrīva a saintly king of old who defeated his enemies but was finally killed for lack of allies.

Hiḍimbā a demon who fell in love with Bhīma and was the mother of Ghaṭotkaca.

Hīmavat the Himālaya mountain region.

Indra "King of the Gods" and the actual father of Arjuna. Also called Śakra, Maghavān, Jiṣṇu, Vṛṣā, etc. Indra had been preeminent in Vedic times but by the time of the Mahābhārata had been reduced to king of a heavenly pantheon subject to the supreme cosmic triumvirate of Brahmā, Viṣṇu, and Śiva.

Indraprastha ("the city of Indra") the capital city built by the Pāṇḍavas in the Khāṇḍava area. (= *Khāṇḍavaprastha* and *Śakraprastha*).

Īśvara the Lord, "God" in a personal sense.

Janaka the name of a famous king of Mithilā who reportedly made the claim that "Truly immense is my wealth, yet I have nothing. If the whole of Mithilā were reduced to ashes, nothing of mine would be burned" (Śāntiparvan. 17). He became a recluse in his old age.

Janamejaya the great-grandson of Arjuna who performed the great snake sacrifice at which the bard Vaiśaṃpāyana first recounted the story of the Mahābhārata that he had learned from the sage Vyāsa.

Janārdana an epithet of Viṣṇu/Kṛṣṇa.

Jarāsaṃdha a fierce king of Magadha who was created by the demoness Jarā by joining two halves of a child. He was killed by Bhīma.

Jayadratha the king of Sindhu and a bitter enemy of the Pāṇḍavas ever since he lost out to the five brothers for the hand of Draupadī. He was the brother-in-law of Duryodhana through his marriage to Duḥśālā. He was killed by Arjuna with an arrow that carried his head to the lap of his own father who was performing penance at a nearby holy spot.

Kāla the personified form of "Time."

Kali a demon of whom Duryodhana was the incarnation. Sin personified.

Kalkin the tenth avatar of Viṣṇu who is yet to come.

Kāma the personified form of desire.

Karṇa the eldest (illegitimate) son of Kuntī by the Sun god Sūrya. He was possessed by the demon Naraka and was a sworn enemy of the Pāṇḍavas. Karṇa was killed by Arjuna when his chariot-wheels sank into the ground in response to a curse by a Brahmin sage.

Kaṭhopaniṣad the title of a famous Upaniṣad reporting on the dialog between the boy Naciketas and the King of Death (Yama).

Kaśi the city of Banares *(Vārāṇasī).*

Kaśyapa an ancient sage alleged to be the progenitor of the gods and the demons.

Kauravas The "descendants of King Kuru." Though technically both the Pāṇḍavas and the supporters of Duryodhana are Kauravas, it is generally the name reserved for the latter.

Kauśika a Brahmin who is offered some needed spiritual guidance by a butcher (in Book III.198–200).

Keśava an epithet of Kṛṣṇa.

Khāṇḍavaprastha a tract of virgin forest in which the Pāṇḍavas build their capital city Indraprastha (or Śakraprastha).

Kirmīra a demon *(rākṣasa)* killed by Bhīma at the start of their twelve-year exile in the forest.

Krodha the personification of "Anger" a part of whom incarnates in Aśvatthāman.

Kīpa the first teacher of archery to the Pāṇḍava and Kaurava children.

Kṛṣṇa the son of Vasudeva and Devakī of the Yādava clan. Arjuna's friend and charioteer, but also the ninth incarnation of Viṣṇu as Supreme Deity *(paramātman, paramapuruṣa, ādideva, etc.).* In ancient times the *ṛṣi* Nārāyaṇa and companion to Nara *(Arjuna).* Kṛṣṇa showed his evenhandedness (that is, as "God") by morally supporting the Pāṇḍavas while lending his army to fight for the Kauravas. He was accidentally killed in the forest by a hunter named Jara (old age), in fulfillment of a curse by Gāndharī.

Kṛṣṇa/Nārāyaṇa a designation to emphasize Kṛṣṇa's connection with his earlier incarnation as Nārāyaṇa (tantamount to "God").

Kṛtavarman a king of the Vṛṣṇi dynasty and a famous archer who sided with the Kaurava forces. He accompanied Aśvatthāman when the latter attacked and killed the sleeping Pāṇḍavas in their camp.

Kubera the god of wealth. He comforted the Pāṇḍavas during their sojourn in the forest.

Kuntī the first wife of Pāṇḍu, mother of the Pāṇḍavas and Kṛṣṇa's aunt. Her real name was Pṛthā but she was brought up by Kuntibhoja—hence Kuntī. The sage Durvāsas taught her a mantra that allowed her to invoke whatever god she wished and to have children by them. She eventually perished in a forest fire along with Gāndharī and Dhṛtarāṣṭra.

Kurma ("Turtle") the second incarnation (avatar) of Viṣṇu.

Kuru a famous king of the Puru dynasty and progenitor of the epic protagonists.

Kurukṣetra (the field of the Kurus) the place of the battle between the Pāṇḍavas and Kauravas. The name derives from the fact that King Kuru had previously done penance there.

Kurus (the descendants of King Kuru) the name given to the lineage of the Pāṇḍavas and the Kauravas.

Lakṣmī the consort of Viṣṇu. She is the goddess of fortune and beauty; also known as Śrī.

Lomaśa a sage who was reported to be a great story teller. He comforts Yudhiṣṭhira when the latter was in exile in the forest.

Mādhava an epithet of Kṛṣṇa.

Madhva (1197–1276) a Vaiṣṇava philosopher who advocated a system of dualist *(dvaita)* Vedānta. For him the human soul is unique, even in the state of *mokṣa.*

Mādrī the daughter of the king of Madra and the second wife of Pāṇḍu. The mother of Nakula and Sahadeva and sister to King Śalya of Madra.

Magadha a famous city of ancient India known today as Rājagṛha. The king during the time of the Mahābhārata was the infamous Jarāsaṃdha.

Mahādeva an epithet of Śiva.

Mahārudra a form of Śiva who destroys the world by fire.

Maheśvara ("Great Lord") an epithet of Śiva.

Maṅki a sage whose loss of two bullocks finally led him to *mokṣa.* His lamentation is known as the Maṅkigītā.

Manu a name applied to fourteen successive mythical progenitors of the human race. They create and support the world through successive epochs or *manvantaras* (ages of Manu), each of which is one-fourteenth of a Day of Brahmā (thus of over three hundred million years duration). The first Manu *(Manu-svayambhū,* "the self-existent") is credited with producing the Manusmṛti, a highly respected code of Hindu conduct and law. The world is currently in the seventh *manvantara* of the present Brahmā cycle, presided over by Manu-Vaivasvata, often regarded as the Hindu Noah who built the ark as related in the "Purāṇa of the Fish" legend (Book III.185.)

Manu-prajāpati a name given to the creative aspect of a Manu.

Mārkaṇḍeya an ancient sage who recounted a number of legends to console the Pāṇḍavas in their misfortune.

Matsya name of the first of the ten avatāras of Viṣṇu, in the form of a fish. Also the name of the country in which the Pāṇḍavas spent a year incognito (at the court of King Virāṭa). The Sanskrit expression *matsyanyāya* also means the "law of the fish" (our "law of the Jungle").

Meru a famous mountain regarded as the central axis of the world *(axis mundi).* It is located somewhere in the Himalayas. The spinal column is its analogue in the human microcosm. The ground plan of Hindu temples are based on its cosmic geography.

Mīmāṃsā a ritualistic school that stresses the importance of karma (as ritual action) and dharma (duty). One of the six systems of Hindu philosophy, based on the Mīmāṃsā Sutra of Jaimini (composed around 400 B.C.). Often called Pūrva Mīmāṃsā to distinguish it from the Vedānta. *See* Vedānta.

Mithilā the capital of the country known as Videha, celebrated for its sāttvic virtues under the famed king Janaka. Its modern name is Tirhut.

Mitra a name for the Sun god *(Sūrya)*.

Mokṣadharmaparvan sections 168–353 of Book XII (see Śāntiparvan) dealing with the path of release from attachment to the world *(mokṣa)*.

Mṛtyu the personified form of Death who appears in the account of Gautāmī and the serpent (cf. Book XIII.1.43). The story is designed to purge Yudiṣṭhira of responsibility for the war by suggesting that it was brought about entirely by Duryodhana's own actions (karma).

Nakula the youngest son of Pāṇḍu and Mādrī and twin brother to Sahadeva. They are incarnations of the Aśvins (deities of the stars Castor and Pollux).

Namuchi a demon *(asura)* who is bested by Indra (cf. Book XII.219).

Nara Arjuna as the bosom friend of Nārāyaṇa in a former incarnation.

Nārada a great *ṛṣi* who is able to travel at will between the earth and heaven. He gives advice to the Pāṇḍavas on numerous occasions. It is he who later recounts the story of the Mahābhārata to the gods.

Naraka a name for hell. Also the name of a demon *(asura)* associated with Karṇa.

Narasiṁha the fourth of the ten avatars *(daśāvatāras)* of Viṣṇu as a man-lion (lion with a human head). He killed a great demon who had been terrorizing his devotees.

Nārāyaṇa a form of Viṣṇu. As Nara and Nārāyaṇa were inseparable companions in a former eon living in a hermitage at Badarī, currently incarnate as Arjuna and Kṛṣṇa.

Nārāyanīyaparvan a subsection of the Mokṣadharmaparvan that extols Nārāyana, Viṣṇu, or Vāsudeva (Kṛṣṇa) as the Supreme Godhead.

Nīlakaṇṭha a well-known seventeenth-century Vedāntic commentator of the Mahābhārata.

Niṣāda a tribe of forest dwellers.

Nivātakavacas an army of demons who were such a threat to heaven that Indra had to ask Arjuna for help in defeating them.

Pāñcāla a name of the kingdom ruled by Drupada. The inhabitants are called Pāñcālas.

Pāñcālī (the princess of Pāñcāla) an epithet of Draupadī.

Pāṇḍavas a name given to the descendants of King Pāṇḍu. Normally confined to the five brothers Yudhiṣṭhira, Bhīma, Arjuna, Nakula, and Sahadeva.

Pāṇḍu the legitimate heir to the Lunar dynasty *(Candravaṁśa)* at Hāstinapura. He was the "father" of the five Paṇḍava brothers.

Pāṇḍuputra ("the son of Pāṇḍu") a synonym for Yudhiṣṭhira.

Paramapuruṣa ("the Supreme Person") another designation of Kṛṣṇa/Viṣṇu in His highest aspect.

Paramātman ("the Supreme Self") another designation of Kṛṣṇa/Viṣṇu in His highest aspect as "the self of the self of all beings."

Parāśara the father of Vyāsa.

Paraśurāma ("Rāma-with-the-ax") *See* Rāma Jāmadagnya.

Parikṣit a son of Abhimanyu and the grandson of Arjuna who ruled at Hāstinapura for sixty years after the Mahābhārata war. He was killed by Aśvatthāman while in his mother's womb but was brought back to life by Kṛṣṇa. He was finally killed by a snake.

Pārtha ("the son of Pṛthā") a common epithet for Arjuna.

Pārvatī the wife of Śiva. The Mahābhārata also uses a number of synonyms for Pārvatī, for example, Umā, Devī, Durgā, and Gaurī.

Patañjali the compiler and editor of the basic text of classical Yoga known as the Yoga Sūtras.

Prabhu ("Lord") a name applied throughout the Mahābhārata to Kṛṣṇa, Viṣṇu, etc. as a kind of divine overseer (lit. "the boss"). Cf. Dhātṛ and Śāstṛ.

Prahlāda a demon *(asura)* king and grandfather of Bali. He once defeated Indra in a battle that lasted a hundred years.

Prajāpati (lit. "Lord of creatures") name given to a variety of Vedic gods as procreator, protector of life, etc. According to Book XII.384 of the epic there were twenty-five Creators or Prajāpatis, including Manu, Dakśa, Bhṛgu, and Dharma. He is also associated with Brahmā, Viṣṇu, or Śiva.

Pṛthā the real name of Kuntī.

Pūjani a smart bird who shows little faith in the assurances of King Brahmadatta.

Puruṣavyāghra ("Tiger among Men") a synonym for Arjuna.

Puruṣottama ("Supreme Person") Kṛṣṇa or Viṣṇu in their highest aspect.

Rādhā the mother of Karṇa. Also the name of Kṛṣṇa's favorite consort.

Rāma a famous king who is regarded as the seventh incarnation of Viṣṇu. He was the son of King Daśaratha and one of his three wives, Queen Kausalyā. Rāma's story is told in the second great Indian epic called the Rāmāyaṇa *(see* Rāmāyana). He is to be distinguished from Rāma Jāmadagnya. *See* Paraśurāma or Rāma-with-the-ax.

Rāma Jāmadagnya ("of the devouring fire") the patronymic of a famous Brahmin warrior, also known as "Rāma of the ax" (Paraśurāma). He killed the entire warrior caste twenty-one times over and stored their blood in five lakes.

Rāmānuja (1017–1137) a famous Vaiṣṇava saint and theologian and leading exponent of the Viśiṣṭadvaita (qualified nondualist) form of the Vedānta.

Rāmāyaṇa the story of Rāma, sometimes called Ādi Kāvya (First Epic) to indicate that it occurred and was written first.

Ṛgveda the first of the four Vedas of Hinduism containing 1,017 hymns of praise to various gods, etc. The word "Veda" comes from a Sanskrit root meaning "to know."

Rudra a form of Śiva.

Śacī ("the powerful") the daughter of the sage Puloman and the wife of Indra.

Sabhāparvan the title of Book II of the Mahābhārata dealing, among other things, with the notorious dice game in which Yudhiṣṭhira loses all.

Sahadeva the youngest of the sons of Pāṇḍu, by his second wife Mādrī. In reality he was the "son" of one of the Aśvins.

Śakra another name for Indra.

Śakuni the wily brother of Queen Gāndhārī and uncle of Duryodhana. His Machiavellian counsels were largely responsible for sowing the seeds of the conflict.

Śakuntalā the wife of King Duḥṣanta of the Lunar dynasty.

Śālva Demon king of Saubha who is finally killed by Kṛṣṇa after the latter managed to destroy his aerial chariot (the epic equivalent of the modern U.F.O.) with his discus.

Śalya a king of the Madra or Bālhīka kingdom and Mādrī's brother. However, he assisted the Kaurava forces and was finally killed by Yudhiṣṭhira.

Sāmba a Brahmin scholar.

Saṃjaya a *sūta* (a royal herald or bard) at the Kaurava court who narrates the course of the battle to the blind King Dhṛtarāṣṭra. Also the name of the weak-kneed son of Vidurā.

Śaṃkara (788–820 A.D.) an exponent of the *advaita* (nondual) Vedānta philosophy that allows no distinction between Brahman and the individual self. He was born at Kaladi in South India and wrote commentaries on the Brahmasūtras, the principal Upaniṣads, and the Bhagavadgītā.

Sāṃkhya one of the six main systems of Hindu philosophy. Some scholars see evidence of a form of "Proto-Sāṃkhya" in the Mahābhārata, specifically in the Bhagavadgītā.

Śaṃtanu the son of King Pratīpa of the Lunar dynasty *(Candravaṁśa)* and the father of Bhīṣma by the goddess Gaṅgā.

Sanatkumāra a Brahmin sage; one of four Kumāras regarded as mental sons of Brahmā.

Śāntiparvan the title of Book XII of the Mahābhārata. It contains three main sub-sections, the Rājadharmaparvan (treating of royal duties), the Āpaddharmaparvan (treating of rules to be followed in times of distress), and the Mokṣadharmaparvan (treating of release).

Sarasvatī the goddess of learning and also the name of a major tributary of the Ganges (considered as holy). It is mentioned in several places in the epic.

Sarveśvara ("Lord of All") an epithet of Śiva.

Śāstṛ a personification of the divine functions of commanding, chastising, etc.; the divine "Ordainer." Similar to Dhātṛ (the "Bestower").

Śatakratu (of the 100 sacrifices) an epithet of Indra.

Sātyaki (alias Yuyudhāna) a Yādava friend of Kṛṣṇa. He fought on the Pāṇḍava side and was responsible for decapitating Bhūriśravas on the twelfth day of the battle after Arjuna had saved him from certain death by cutting off Bhūriśravas' right hand. According to Biardeau, his name denotes the totality of things, and he is that aspect of the presence of Kṛṣṇa in the

Pāṇḍava camp by which he prepares for the renewal of the world and of the dharma by protecting a "remnant" of human existence.

Satyavatī the mother of Vyāsa by Parāśara.

Savyasācin an epithet of Arjuna.

Sindhu the name of a kingdom allied to the Kauravas. Jayadratha was king of Sindhu, whence he is sometimes called Saindhava (that is, "of Sindhu").

Śiśupala the king of Cedi who, in reality, was an incarnate demon. He was born with three eyes and four hands and brayed like an ass at birth. He refused to recognize the superiority of Kṛṣṇa, who finally killed him after agreeing to forgive a hundred of his crimes.

Śiva the third form of the Supreme Deity in His function as the destroyer of the universe at the end of each cosmic cycle *(kalpa)*. Śiva has two wives, Gaṅgā and Pārvatī and has appeared in several partial incarnations. In the Mahābhārata he appears in the form of the irascible sage Durvāsas and more importantly, in Aśvatthāman who destroys the Pāṇḍava camp after the war and attempts to kill the fetus of Parikṣit in the womb of Uttarā. *See also* Rudra.

Somadatta the father of Bhūriśravas. He fought on the Kaurava side and was also killed by Sātyaki.

Śrī the goddess of prosperity who is incarnate in Draupadī.

Subala the king of Gāndhāra and father of Śakuni and Gāndhārī.

Subhadrā Kṛṣṇa's sister who became Arjuna's second wife and was the mother of Abhimanyu.

Śuka Vyāsa son.

Śukra the Brahmin *(bhārgava)* preceptor to Vṛṣaparvan, Lord of the demons *(asuras)*. He also cursed King Yayāti to instant decrepitude. *See also* Devayānī.

Sūrya the Sun god who is called by Kuntī to be the father of Karṇa.

Suyodhana ("of good combat") an epithet of Duryodhana.

Svayaṃbhū the "self-existent." An epithet of Brahmā, Viṣṇu/Kṛṣṇa and Śiva.

Svetadvīpa (lit. "White Island") a mysterious island on the northern side of the Ocean of Milk. It is supposedly inhabited by a sinless people of white complexion who have no sense organs and do not take food.

Ulūpī a serpent *(nāga)* princess who had a son, Irāvat, by Arjuna.

Utanka a Brahmin sage.

Uttarā the daughter of King Virāṭa of Matsya, wife of Abhimanyu and mother of Parikṣit.

Vaiśaṃpāyana a prominent disciple of Vyāsa who recounts the story of the Mahābhārata to King Janamejaya during a great snake sacrifice.

Vaiṣṇavāstra a magical arrow "of [the power of] Viṣṇu" given to Bhagadatta by Viṣṇu. It was neutralized by Kṛṣṇa (incarnation of Viṣṇu).

Vaivasvata a patronymic of Manu and also of Yama.

Vanaparvan the title of Book III of the Mahābhārata dealing with the period of forest exile of the Pāṇḍavas.

Varāha ("boar") the third of the ten incarnations *(daśāvatāras)* of Viṣṇu.

Vāraṇāvata (endowed with elephants) the name of the town in which the Kauravas attempted to assassinate the Pāṇḍavas by burning them alive in a house made of lacquer.

Varuṇa the Vedic god of the sea. He is considered to be one of the twelve Āditya gods.

Vāsava ("accompanied by the Vasus") an epithet of Indra.

Vasiṣṭha a Brahmin hermit who had a lifelong quarrel with Viśvāmitra (a warrior-king who later became a hermit) over the cow of of plenty *(Kāmadhenu)*. To realize his desire to appropriate the cow Viśvāmitra abandoned his royal responsibilities to perform severe penance *(tapas)* in order to gain the necessary occult powers to defeat Vasiṣṭha. Viśvāmitra eventually succeeded in becoming a Brahmin.

Vasu the eight gods known as the Vasus *(aṣṭavasus)* were cursed to suffer a life on earth after one of their number also tried to steal Vasiṣṭha's cow. Seven of them were drowned at birth at their own request (since they wished to make their trip here below as short as possible). However, the Vasu called "Āpa" or "Dyaus," who had actually tried to steal the cow, was condemned to spend many long years here on earth as Bhīṣma.

Vasudeva the father of Kṛṣṇa, Balarāma, and Subhadrā. That is why Kṛṣṇa is often called "Vāsudeva" (son of Vasudeva).

Vāyu the god of the wind whose counterpart on earth is Bhīma, his "son" by Kuntī.

Vedānta one of the six systems of Indian philosophy. It is also known as Uttara Mīmāṃsā since it is based on the later portions of the Vedas (that is, in contrast to Pūva Mīmāṃsā based on the earlier ritualistic portions). The chief interpretations are three, the Advaita Vedānta of Śaṃkara, the Viśiṣṭādvaita of Rāmānuja, and the Dvaita of Madhva.

Vedāntasūtra a sutra of 555 verses written by Bādarāyaṇa between 500 and 200 B.C. It has been the subject of many commentaries by proponents of the Vedānta school of Indian philosophy.

Vedas a collection of hymns, rituals, regulations for religious sacrifices, and philosophical essays regarded as the basis of the Hindu religion. They are divided into *saṃhitas* (the fourfold collection of the Ṛg, Sama, Yajur, and Atharva Vedas), Brāhmaṇas, Āraṇyakas, and Upaniṣads. In practice, however, it is the more philosophical Upaniṣads that receive the most attention today, particularly in the form of commentaries by the various proponents of the Vedānta (end of the Veda).

Vidura the youngest of the "sons" of King Vicitravīrya; he is actually the result of the union of a śūdra (low-caste) servant-girl and Vyāsa, on the instigation of Queen Satyavatī. He is a sort of Cassandra figure, since his wise counsel to the Kauravas was never followed.

Vikarṇa the only one of Dhṛtarāṣṭra's sons who expressed any sympathy or support for the Pāṇḍavas.

Vikartana a name for the Sun. Karṇa is Vaikartana, that is, son of the Sun.

Viṣṇu "God" in His preservative function (in contrast to the functions of creation and destruction). *See also* Brahmā and Śiva. He is the Supreme Deity in the Mahābhārata.

Viṣṇu-Nārāyaṇa a designation of Viṣṇu, suggestive of a connection with Kṛṣṇa.

Viṣṇuyaśas another name for Kalkin.

Vṛddhakṣatra the father of King Jayadratha of the Sindhus.

Vṛṣṇi the clan descended from the famous Yādava king of the same name. Kṛṣṇa himself was a Vṛṣṇi.

Vṛtra a fierce and mighty demon *(asura)* who was killed in days of yore by Indra. An account of the "fall" and ascent of Vṛtra is told in the Vṛtragītā portion of the Śāntiparvan (Book XII).

Vyāsa the reputed sage and author of the Mahābhārata. Vyāsa is really the common grandfather of the Kauravas and the Pāṇḍavas. He fathered Dhṛtarāṣṭra, Pāṇḍu, and Vidura at the request of Queen Satyavatī.

Yādava a descendant of King Yadu. Kṛṣṇa's family were Yādavas.

Yadu the son of King Yayāti and Queen Devayānī, and founder of the Yadu lineage *(Yaduvaṁśa).*

Yājñavalkya an ancient sage and profound scholar who spent the major part of his life at the court of King Janaka of Mithilā.

Yama the King of the dead.

Yayāti an eminent king of the Lunar dynasty *(Candravaṁśa)* who had two rival wives, Devayānī and Śarmiṣṭhā. He had two sons by Devayānī: Yadu and Turvasu; and three sons by Śarmiṣṭhā: Druhyu, Anudruhyu, and Pūru. Though the youngest, the reign passed to Pūru as a reward for exchanging his youth for his father's old age.

Yogeśvara (lit. "Lord of Yoga") an epithet of Kṛṣṇa.

Yudhiṣṭhira the eldest son of King Pāṇḍu and his wife Kuntī. He is actually the "son" of the god Dharma (whom Kuntī had invoked for the purpose).

Glossary of Sanskrit Terms

The philosophical vocabulary of classical Sanskrit includes a large number of technical terms that have no exact equivalent in Western languages. This is, in large part, due to differences in philosophical orientation or religious practice and experience, leading to wide differences in the connotations of the closest analogues in the two languages, for example, it would be misleading to translate *puruṣakāra, svaceṣṭita, svayatna,* and other similar terms, as "free will" since none of these words are derived from root concepts that we would recognize as "freedom" or "will" in the modern sense. The difficulty is compounded when it comes to terms such as *mokṣa* or *samādhi* for which the closest English equivalents inevitably evoke the centuries of Christian religious tradition and experience with which they are charged. The meanings of Sanskrit words may also vary widely according to context, thus adding to the complexity.

With these caveats in mind in this section we offer a partial list of the more common Sanskrit words mentioned in the main text of this book, together with their most appropriate, though by no means exact, rendition, or paraphrase in modern English.

Abhimāna a term used in a technical sense by Rāmānuja to describe the false conception of oneself as the ego rather than as one's "true nature" as the *ātman.* Translated variously as "mistaken notion," "mistaken identity," "false identification," etc. In normal parlance indicates a tendency to present a false front (for example, vanity).

Abhyāsa the act of repetition (as an exercise of reading, study, etc.), disciplined study of the scriptures.

Abhyāsayoga the practice of the disciplined study of the scriptures.

Acit the objective world of "matter" (as opposed to spiritual substance or consciousness).

Adharma conduct not in accord with social or religious norms.

Adhikāra the qualifications regarded as necessary for a spiritual aspirant.

Adhvaryu a type of priest who chants hymns of the Yajurveda while preparing the ground for a Vedic sacrifice.

Adhyāsa "superimposition." The theory of Śaṃkara defined in his introduction to the Commentary on the Vedānta Sūtras as "the apparent presentation of the attributes of one thing in another thing." The example given is the mother-of-pearl that has the false appearance of being silver. Also a rope that looks like a snake.

Advaita (lit. "nondual") the notion that the universe is of one essence.

Aham (lit. "I am") the I or ego-sense.

Ahaṃkāra the ego or ego-sense.

Ahiṃsā nonviolence, the highest value of the Brahmin aspirant after spiritual insight.

Akarma (lit. "nonaction") the notion that to achieve liberation one should refrain from all social activities (denounced by Kṛṣṇa in the Gītā).

Anādi (lit. "having no beginning") existing from all eternity.

Anitya (lit. "not eternal") temporal.

Anuṣṭubh a class of metre used in the Sanskirt verses of the Mahābhārata. It consists of 4 × 8 syllables (four half lines of eight syllables each).

Apsaras a celestial maiden, often sent by the gods to test the sages.

Artha one of the four goals of life involving the various forms of material security, primarily wealth, power, and status.

Āśrama one of the four "stages of life" of the traditional Hindu (as student, householder, forest dweller, and renunciate at the very end of life). The word also connotes a hermitage; the abode of a saint, sage, holy man, or religious teacher (usually in the forest).

Āśramadharma the rules of conduct appropriate to each of the four "stages of life."

Asura the general term for a demon, who is in perpetual hostility to the gods. *See also* Daitya and Dānava.

Aśvamedha the horse sacrifice, an elaborate ritual performed by kings to legitimate their rule (or as an excuse to conquer others). It was performed for Yudhiṣṭhira after the war (after some preliminary conquests by Arjuna). A hundred such sacrifices was deemed sufficient to displace the king of heaven (Indra).

Atiprayatna great exertion, supreme effort.

Ātman the True Self (in contrast to the false ego-self).

Avatāra a human incarnation of the Divine.

Avidyā ignorance, the normal state of human existence.

Avyakta (lit. "not manifest") God, mind etc. in their unmanifested nature.

Bhaga one of the Āditya gods who presides over love and marriage. His eyes were destroyed by Rudra-Śiva.

Bhāgadheya share, portion, lot, good fortune.

Bhāgya (lit. "relating to Bhaga") good fortune, luck, happiness.

Bhakti devotion to a personal God.

Bhaktiyoga the practice of devotion to a personal God, in this case Kṛṣṇa.

Bhavitavyam that which "is to be," fate.

Bheda breach, split, division. The word is used in the Mahābhārata to describe the family breach between the two sets of cousins.

Bhoga worldly enjoyment.

Bhūrloka the abode or plane of the earth.

Bhūta spirit being, "ghost." Also means element (as one of the four elements of air, water, earth, and fire).

Bhuvarloka the abode or plane of the heavens or sky.

Brahmaloka the abode of Brahmā.

Brahman the impersonal Absolute; the unmanifested Source or "God" from which all things emanate.

Brāhmaṇa a Brahmin priest; the highest of the four traditional castes of Hinduism.

Brahmaśiras (lit. "head of Brahmā) cf. Brahmāstra.

Brahmāstra (Brahmā's missile) a celestial missile controlled by Brahmā, also known as the *brahmaśiras* (Brahmā's head) and the *pāśupata,* given to both Arjuna (by Droṇa and Śiva) and Aśvatthāman (by Droṇa). Arjuna and Aśvatthāman eventually use it against each other but the latter directed its power against the unborn Parikṣit, the only remaining heir to the Kuru dynasty.

Brahmin the English name for a Brāhmaṇa.

Buddhi intellect, the faculty that allows one to discriminate between truth and error, and right and wrong.

Cakra wheel (for example, of a chariot). Used in combination with a number of other words to suggest the cyclic nature of time (for example, *samsāra-cakra* = the "wheel of life").

Cakravartin (lit. "turner of the wheel") an emperor, great king.

Cit consciousness (in the sense of that from which the objective world arises), the ground of subject and object. The experience of *mokṣa* is often described as *sat-cit-ānanda* (reality-consciousness-bliss).

Daitya a demon descended from Kaśyapa-Prajāpati and his wife Diti. *See also* Asura and Dānava.

Daiva (lit. "of the gods") destiny, fate. Although this term is the most common Sanskrit also has many other words to convey the same idea (for example, *bhavitavyaṃ, daivatā, diṣṭa, iśvaranirdiṣṭa,* and *vidhātvihitaṃ*).

Daivatā destiny, fate.

Dāna generosity, gift giving, one of the cardinal virtues of Hinduism.

Dānava a demon descended from Kaśyapa-Prajāpati and his wife Danu. *See also* Asura and Daitya.

Daṇḍa rod, staff (carried by the king as a symbol of his executive powers).

Daṇḍanitī (lit. "application of the rod") the power of the king to administer justice, criminal justice, and punishment.

Daṇḍaśāstra the literature on criminal justice.

Darśana (lit. "view") philosophy; a "way of looking" at things. Traditional Hinduism offers six *darśanas.*

Dāya compassion (one of the cardinal virtues of Hinduism).

Deha body (generic).

Dehin an embodied being (human or otherwise).

Deva god. The multitudes of gods are in constant conflict with the demons for the control of the "Three Worlds" of heaven, earth, and the nether regions ("hell"). They are also wary of humans who seek spiritual or occult powers through various forms of self-denial *(tapas).*

Devaloka (lit. "abode of the gods") heaven.

Devayuga (lit. "divine *yuga*" or "*yuga* of the gods") a complete cycle of the four *yugas* (amounting to 4,320,000 solar years).

Dhana wealth, riches.

Dharma socially sanctioned conduct; duties ordained by religious tradition for each of the four castes *(varṇadharma)* and stages of life *(aśramadharma),* ethical behavior, and righteousness in general.

Dharmacakra (lit. "wheel of the dharma") the scope of the law.

Dharmakṣetra (lit. "field of the dharma") symbolic name for Kurukṣetra where the Mahābhārata war took place.

Diṣṭa fate.

Dvaita (lit. "dual") a term used to indicate that the human soul is completely separate from God.

Dvandva (lit. split or "dichotomy") a term used to indicate the dichotomy between subject and object.

Dvāparayuga the second of the four *yugas* or eons of Hinduism in which the dharma has been reduced by one-fourth. Also as a demon incarnated in Śakuni.

Dveṣa hatred (a cardinal vice of Hinduism).

Dvija "twice-born," a generic title applied to one of the three higher castes. Often compounded as an epithet, for example, *dvijottama* (best of the twice-born).

Gandharva a heavenly musician or singer who performs at the banquets of the gods. They are descended from Kaśyapa-Prajāpati and his wife Ariṣṭa.

Gāṇḍīva the name of Arjuna's divine bow, once owned by the god Soma.

Guṇa (lit. "strand") one of three properties or "qualities" *(sattva, rajas,* and *tamas)* of all material existence *(prakṛti)* according to the Sāṃkhya philosophy.

Guru preceptor, mentor, teacher. There are many types of guru for both spiritual and worldly pursuits (for example, Droṇa with regard to archery).

Gurudakṣina preceptor's fee (usually paid or given at the end of a course of study).

Gṛhasthāśrama the householder's stage of life (the second of the four stages of life).

Haṭha chance, luck, etc. Although this term is the most common Sanskrit also has many other words to convey the same idea (for example, *bhāgadheya, bhāgya, saṃgati,* and *yadṛcchā*).

Hiraṇyagarbha (lit. "golden womb") the golden womb or "egg" out of which the self-existent Brahmā was born.

Hotri a type of priest who invokes the gods at a sacrifice by reciting the ṚgVeda.

Icchā desire.

Indriyas the five senses (of hearing, sight, smell, taste, and touch).

Itihāsa legend, ancient history, story. The Mahābhārata is an *itihāsa.*

Jagat the Universe (of changing name and form), world.

Janmani birth, incarnation.

Jāti caste, class. *See also* Varṇa.

Jaya victory.

Jīva a living (embodied) being.

Jīvātman the Universal Self in its embodied state.

Jñāna true knowledge, the state of true knowing.

Kāla abstract time, name of a god (as the personified form of Time).

Kālacakra the "wheel of Time" (Time as eternally recurrent).

Kaliyuga the fourth of the four eons of Hinduism, in which the dharma has been reduced by three-fourths.

Kalpa the period of time between a secondary cycle of creation *(pratisarga)* that occurs at the dawn of each new "day of Brahmā" and the subsequent withdrawal of the Universe *(naimittikapralaya)* that accompanies the onset of His "night." It is equivalent to 4.32 billion years in human terms.

Kāma desire, lust.

Karma sacrificial action, action in a generic sense, the effects of a past action on the present and future life and behavior of an individual.

Karmabhūmi (lit. "plane of action") earth, the human world.

Karmastha (lit. "one standing [or 'who takes his stand'] in action") a technical term used to describe one who places his trust in actions that lead to worldly results.

Karmavid (lit. "knower of action") a technical term used to describe one who knows all the subtleties of action and its results.

Karmayoga the spiritual practice of acting in the world without being affected by it (that is, attached to the results).

Kartṛ actor, the one who acts.

Kirāta a member of a tribe of hunters considered to be outcaste *(mleccha).* Śiva opposes Arjuna in the forest as a Kirāta.

Krodha anger (a cardinal vice).

Kṛtayuga the first of the four eons, in which the dharma is followed in its entirety.

Kṣamā patience, forbearance, also forgiveness.

Kṣatriya warrior, the second of the four major castes in traditional Hinduism.

Kṣatriyadharma the warrior's code of conduct.

Kṣattṛ a mixed-caste son of a *kṣatriya* and a *śūdra* woman (or of a *śūdra* man and a *kṣatriya* woman). Vidura was a *kṣattṛ* since he was the son of a slave girl.

Kṣetra field, field of activity, objective world, etc.

Kṣetrajñā (lit. "knower of the field") one who knows the true nature of the objective world.

Kurukṣetra (lit. "field of the Kurus") the geographic locale of the Mahābhārata war.

Līlā "play" (as in a child's play). Since the Supreme Being can have no real motive (or "desire") for creating the world it can only be a product of "play" or "sport."

Lobha greed.

Loka abode, "world," locale.

Mahāmoha (lit. "Great Delusion") the condition of humanity prior to the destruction of the world by Śiva.

Mahārāja (lit. "Great King") the title of the monarch.

Mahāsamādhi (lit. "Great Ecstasy") the supreme state of meditation.

Mahāyuga (lit. "Great Eon") a period of one-thousand eons.

Mama me, mine, egocentricity.

Mamatā (lit. "the state of Me") possessiveness.

Manas "heart," the emotive mind (as compared to the dispassionate intellect).

Mantra a word or phrase considered to have magical or regenerative powers.

Mānuṣya manliness, initiative.

Māyā illusion, the world as a projection of Consciousness, the power of illusion (possessed by Kṛṣṇa).

Māyāvin one who possesses the power of *māyā.*

Mīmāṃsā one of the six systems of Hindu philosophy, concerned primarily with the correct interpretation of Vedic ritual. It is sometimes called the "Pūrvamīmāṃsā" (in contrast to the Uttaramīmāṃsā or Vedānta).

Moha delusion.

Mokṣa state of beatitude, bliss, freedom, the goal of existence.

Mokṣaśāstra literature dealing with the goal of existence.

Mokṣavid one who "knows" (that is, has experienced) the state of *mokṣa.*

Mṛtyu death, death personified.

Muni (lit. "dumb") a holy man, sage.

Nāga a race of beings descended from Kadrū inhabiting the city of Bhogavatī under the earth. They have a human face and a serpentlike lower body.

Naimittikapralaya (or **pratipralaya**) the destruction of the world that occurs at the end of a "Day of Brahmā," that is to say at the conclusion of each cycle of 1,000 *yugas* (= a *mahāyuga* or *kalpa*), equivalent to 4.32 billion years. It is essentially a periodic reabsorption of objective form initiated by Śiva.

Naiṣkarmya the state of being nonattached to the fruits of one's actions.

Nirdiṣṭa enjoined, ordered, determined (for example, by the gods).

Nirvikalpasamādhi the ultimate state of meditative absorption in which there is no consciousness of objective form.

Nītiśāstra a class of literature dealing with state administration.

Nivṛtti (lit. "introjection") the path of withdrawal from worldly activity; one of two paths that an aspirant may follow, equivalent to *saṃnyāsa.*

Nivṛttidharma conduct appropriate to the path of withdrawal.

Nyāya a universal rule or axiom; standard (for example, *matsyanyāya* is the "rule of the fish" in which the big fish eat the little fish). Also the name of one of the six systems of Indian philosophy dealing with logic and syllogistic argument.

Pāñcāla a member of the tribe of *pañcālas.* Draupadī is often called "Pañcālī."

Pāpa actions resulting in demerit or "sin."

Pauruṣa human initiative, drive.

Phala fruit, result (of action), "reward."

Piṇḍa ball of rice, description of Arjuna after he had been bested by Śiva in the form of a Kirāta hunter.

Piśāca a name for a class of demon known for their fondness for human flesh. Cf. I.1.35 for origins.

Pitāmaha (lit. "grandfather") an epithet of Bhīṣma. Also an epithet of Brahmā as "grandfather of the worlds."

Pitṛ ancestor, deceased member of the family that one sustains through ritual offerings of food, etc.

Prabhu lord, title attributed to Kṛṣṇa.

Pradhāna chief, essential, principal, primary (for example, primary or unevolved matter).

Prajñā wisdom, spiritual insight.

Prajñācakṣu (lit. "eye of wisdom") epithet of Dhṛtarāṣṭra (ironic).

Prakāśa visible, shining, bright. Also lucidity or mental alertness (clearness of mind).

Prakṛtapralaya the reabsorption of the Universe at the "death of Brahmā"; the end of the Universe that occurs after 100×360 "days of Brahmā" (that is, his "life"), equivalent to 155,520 billion human years.

Prakṛtasarga the creation of the Universe, the reappearance of a new Universe at the beginning of a new "life of Brahmā."

Prakṛti matter (as opposed to spirit), one of the two elements of existence according to the Sāmkhyā philosophy.

Pralaya (lit. "dissolution") a technical term applied to the universal dissolution or reabsorption of the Universe at the end of a *kalpa,* or a *mahākalpa. See naimittikapralaya, pratipralaya,* and *prakṛtapralaya.*

Prāṇa the "breath" of life, the life force, vital air, vitality.

Prarabdhakarma karma to be exhausted in the present life.

Prasāda God's favor or "Grace"; also the remnants of food left by a spiritual mentor, presented to disciples as a gift (symbolic of good fortune).

Pratipralaya *See* Naimittikapralaya.

Pratisarga the creation of the Universe at the beginning of each new "day of Brahmā."

Pravṛtti (lit. "projection") the path of participation in worldly activity, one of two paths that an aspirant may follow.

Pravṛttidharma conduct appropriate to the path of participation.

Prāyaścitta expiation, attonement (for a fault).

Prayatna effort, drive.

Pṛthivī the earth, the element earth.

Puṇya merit, good karma.

Purāṇa legend; story; a class of Hindu religious literature dealing with the stories of gods, demons, the creation of the world, etc.

Puruṣa man, human being.

Puruṣakāra human initiative, effort, drive. Although this term is the most common Sanskrit also has many other words to convey the same idea (for example, *dākṣya, īha, mānuṣya, pauruṣa, puruṣārtha, puruṣaprayatna, svaceṣṭita, svakarmatā, utsāha, utthāna, vyavasāya,* and *vyāyāma*).

Puruṣaprayatna human effort, drive, etc.

Puruṣarṣabha (lit. "tiger of men") an epithet of Arjuna.

Puruṣārtha human initiative; also a name for the four goals of human life (pleasure, wealth/power, morality, and liberation).

Puruṣasūkta a famous hymn from the Ṛgveda (X.xc.12).

Pūrvakarma karma accumulated as a result of past actions.

Pūrvapakṣa the opponent who expresses an erroneous view in philosophical debate.

Pūrvaprayatna prior effort.

Rāga passion (usually associated with hate).

Rāgadveṣau passion and hatred.

Rājā king.

Rājadharma code of conduct for a king.

Rajas passion, activity, one of the three *guṇas* (with *sattva* and *tamas).*

Rājasūya a great sacrifice performed by the king at his coronation (in this case Yudhiṣṭhira).

Rākṣasa a giant, a class of superhuman inhabitant of the forest (who disturb sacrifices and is generally antagonistic to humans).

Ṛṣi a sage, saint, holy man. Three types are featured in the Mahābhārata, a *rājarṣi,* for example, Viśvamitra (a *Kṣatriya* with superhuman powers attained through years of severe austerities); a *brahmarṣi,* for example, Vasiṣṭha (a similar example from the Brahmin caste); and a *devarṣi* or "celestial" sage, for example, Nārada (who moves at will between heaven and earth).

Ṛta the moral order in its cosmic aspect.

Sabhā an assembly or council hall, place for public meetings.

Sādhana religious or spiritual practice.

Sādhu a holy man, sage.

Śakti power; initiative; name for the female consort of a god, thought to embody the power of the god.

Samadarśin (lit. "equal seeing" or "same seeing") thus "seeing everywhere the same" or (in our translation) "looking upon all things with an equal eye."

Samādhi bliss, meditative exhaltation.

Samaṣṭi the macrocosm.

Samatva the condition of being indifferent to the pairs of opposities (heat/cold, pleasure/pain, etc.).

Saṃdhya morning or evening twilight; Also used to describe the shoulder periods between successive *yugas*.

Saṃkalpa intention, volition, desire, purpose, "will."

Sāmkhya one of the six traditional systems of Indian philosophy involving the dualism of *puruṣa* and *prakṛti*.

Saṃnyāsa renunciation of worldly ties.

Saṃnyāsin one who has taken a vow of *saṃnyāsa*.

Saṃsāra the eternal cycle of birth and death from which one should attempt to free oneself by achieving *mokṣa*.

Saṃsāracakra the wheel of birth and death.

Saṃskāra the name given to the traces of past action that accumulate in the unconscious (*See also* Vāsana); also the name for the major passages of life (for example, birth, marriage, and death).

Sanātana eternal. Hinduism is often described as the *sanātana dharma* (eternal truth).

Śānti peace, an attitude of total tranquility and bliss.

Śāpa a curse (opposite of a boon. cf. Vara).

Sarga creation.

Śāstra a class of religious literature.

Sat according to context can mean being, existence, essence, reality, truth as the "really real," etc.

Sattva according to context can mean being, existence, truth, wisdom, purity, etc. Also the highest of the three *guṇas* of *sattva* (spiritual acumen), *rajas* (energy, ambition) and *tamas* (sloth, inertia).

Sattvastha (lit. "one standing, [or 'who takes his stand'] in the truth") a term indicative of one who has realized the true nature of things, one established in the truth.

Satya truth, reality.

Siddhi spiritual power that is achieved through *tapas*. Also worldly success.

Śila character.

Śraddhā faith.

Sukha pleasure.

Sukhaduḥkhau pleasure and pain (the two prime opposities of human experience).

Sūta a mixed-caste son of a *Kṣatriya* and a Brahmin woman (or of a Brahmin with a *Kṣatriya* woman). They often worked as grooms or charioteers. Karṇa is perjoratively called "son of a *sūta*" referring to the fact that he was brought up by a *sūta* (called Adhiratha).

Svabhāva (lit. "own nature") innate disposition or nature; personality; also used in the sense of human initiative, ability, and drive.

Svaceṣṭita human initiative, ability, drive.

Svadharma (lit. "one's own dharma") one's own task or function in the present life, largely determined by one's caste affiliation.

Svakarma one's own karma.

Svarga heaven (also called *svargaloka* or *svarloka*); the abode of the lesser gods and a place of respite after death for deserving souls.

Svayaṃvara a public contest of suitors in which a princess chooses her own bridegroom (for example, Draupadī).

Svayatna one's own efforts or abilities.

Tamas inertia, sloth (one of the three *guṇas*).

Tapas self-denial, "penance," a term describing various strenuous practices thought to lead to an increase in one's spiritual powers (cf. *siddhi*).

Tattva principle, element of reality.

Tattvavid (lit. "one who knows the *tattvas*") a realized being.

Tejas fiery aura, a term used to describe the appearance of one in command of certain spiritual powers. The spiritual "heat" obtained as a result of fierce austerities. The word has no real equivalent in English.

Tretāyuga the third of the four *yugas,* in which the dharma has been reduced by one-half.

Trimedhā (lit. "three sacrifices") the birth of Arjuna was marked by the announcement of a celestial voice that he would accomplish three sacrifices. These reportedly include the *rājasūya* sacrifice performed by his elder brother Yudhiṣṭhira and the *aśvamedha* sacrifice performed at the end of the war. According to Biardeau, the third was the symbolic "sacrifice" of the dharma during the dice game.

Trimūrti (lit. "having three forms") the three forms of the Absolute or "God" in His functions of creation, preservation, and destruction, traditionally allocated to Brahmā, Viṣṇu, and Śiva, respectively.

Triṣṭubh a class of metre of 4 × 11 syllables (four half lines of eleven syllables each). This metre is often used to convey emphasis (as we now do with underlining or italics).

Upādhi a technical term used by the nondualist *(advaita)* philosophers to indicate the form of anything which, in reality, is not what it seems. The "snake" one might see in a piece of rope is thus the *upādhi* of the rope. All the forms in the Universe are, in this view, the *upādhis* of the One Reality of Brahman.

Upakhyāna subsidiary stories, legends, homilies, etc. that are not part of the main plot.

Upaniṣad class of about one-hundred fifty religio-philosophical works, in either prose or verse form, concerning the relationship of the human soul with the Supreme Reality. Some are called *araṇyakas* (forest texts) since they were traditionally taught by sages living in the forest.

Upāya subterfuge, ruse, "skillful means," perceptual or mental trickery, magical illusion. The manner in which Kṛṣṇa is able to turn events to His advantage, "miracle."

Utsāha determination, initiative, drive.

Uttamapuruṣa "Supreme Person." Another name for God in His highest aspect.

Utthāna effort, drive.

Vairāgya an attitude of dispassion or indifference toward the opposites of pain and pleasure, etc., a necessary condition for the achievement of spiritual insight (though sufficient only when combined with *viveka).*

Vara a boon offered by a god or a sage.

Varṇa caste. The four main castes were traditionally the Brahmins, warriors *(Kṣatriyas),* merchants *(Vaiṣyas),* and workers *(Śūdras).* These are considered to have sprung from the head (brains), arms, belly, and legs of a "Primal Man" mentioned in the *Puruṣasūkta* hymn of the Ṛgveda. *See also* Puruṣasūkta.

Varṇadharma the rules of conduct appropriate to one's caste.

Varṇāśramadharma the rules of conduct appropriate to one's caste and stage of life.

Vāsana a name given to the mental results or "traces" of past actions that motivate one to perform present and future actions, the mental constituents of karma. *See also* Saṃskāra.

Vāyu wind, wind personified, the wind god.

Veda a class of religious literature considered to be eternal truth. The four Vedas that are traditionally regarded as constituting the foundations of the Hindu religion are the Ṛg, Sama, Yajur, and Atharva Vedas.

Vedānta (lit. "the end of the Veda") a class of philosophical literature that includes the Upaniṣads and their commentaries by recognized authorities, for example, Śaṃkara, Rāmānuja, and Madhva. Also a generic name for the philosophies based on such authorities. Sometimes called the "Uttaramīmāṃsā."

Vedāntasūtra a name given to a work by Bādarāyaṇa.

Vidhi a Vedic injunction, an act one must do or perform.

Vidyā body of knowledge, a "science."

Vīrya heroism, bravery.

Viśiṣṭādvaita the philosophy of "qualified nondualism" proposed by Rāmānuja, an eleventh-century Vaiṣnava saint.

Viveka intellectual discrimination, the ability (or power) to distinguish truth from error, and right from wrong, a necessary condition for the achievement of spiritual insight (though sufficient only when combined with *vairāgya*).

Vyaṣṭi the microcosm.

Vyavasāya human initiative, effort, drive.

Yadṛcchā chance, accidental happening.

Yajña sacrifice. Also worship, devotion.

Yakṣa a class of spirit or sprite inhabiting the forest, generally regarded as inoffensive. cf. I.1.35 for origins.

Yama Lord of Death.

Yantra a mystical diagram used as an aid to meditation.

Yatna effort, energy, drive.

Yoga the act of "yoking" or joining together. Employed to describe one of the six systems of Indian philosophy sponsored by Patañjali. Any system or practice that purports to lead the aspirant toward union with God or the Supreme Spirit.

Yogakṣema (lit. "union and preservation") the secure possession of what one has acquired (a major goal of worldly existence).

Yoganīdrā the meditative state of Brahmā during the period between the annihilation and creation of the Universe.

Yogayukta (lit. "yoked to Yoga") one who is well-versed in the practice of Yoga.

Yogi (or yogin) a practitioner of Yoga.

Yuga an eon or age of the world. There are four *yugas* of varying lengths with an aggregate of 4,320,000 years (cf. Kṛtayuga, Dvāparayuga, Tretāyuga, and Kaliyuga).

Yugacakra (lit. "wheel of the *yugas*") the complete cycle of the four *yugas*.

Yugānta (lit. "end of the yuga") the condition of the world at the end of an eon.

Bibliography

Bedekar, V. M. 1961. "The Doctrines of Svabhāva and Kāla in the Mahābhārata and Other old Sanskrit Works." *Journal of the University of Poona (Humanities),* **13**, 17–28.

———. 1969. "Principles of Mahābhārata Textual Criticism: The Need for Restatement." *Purāṇa,* **11**(12), 210–228. (Followed by a brief "Rejoinder" by Madeleine Biardeau in *Purāṇa,* 12[1], January 1970, pp. 160–161.)

Belvalkar, S. K. 1962. "The Bhagavad-gītā: A General Review of Its History and Character," chapter 9, pp. 135–157 of Vol. II ("Itihāsas, Purāṇas, Dharma, and other Śāstras") of Haridas Bhattacharyya et al. (1953–1962).

Bharadwaj, Dr. Saroj. 1992. *The Concept of "Daiva" in the Mahābhārata.* Nag Publishers, Delhi.

Bhattacharji, Sukamari. 1995. *Fatalism in Ancient India.* Baulmon Prakashan, Calcutta, India.

Bhattacharyya, Haridas et al., eds. 1953–1962. *The Cultural Heritage of India.* 2nd Edition (4 Vols.). Ramakrishna Mission, Institute of Culture, Calcutta.

Bhattacharyya, Kalidas. 1971a. "The Indian Concept of Freedom." *Bulletin of the Ramakrishna Mission, Institute of Culture,* **22**(9), 348–360.

———. 1971b. "The Status of the Individual in Indian Metaphysics," chapter 14, pp. 299–319 in Moore (1967).

Biardeau, Madeleine. 1968a. "Some More Contributions about Textual Criticism." *Purāṇa,* **10**(7), 115–123.

———. 1968b. "Études de mythologie hindoue (I): Cosmogonies purāṇiques." *Bulletin de l'École française d'Extrême-Orient (BEFEO),* **54**, 19–45.

———. 1969. "Études de mythologie hindou (II): Cosmogonies purāṇiques (Suite)." *Bulletin de l'École française d'Extrême-Orient (BEFEO),* **55**, 59–105.

———. 1970. "The Story of Arjuna Kārtavīrya without Reconstruction." *Purāṇa,* **12**(7), 286–303.

———. 1971a. "Brāhmanes et potiers." In *Annuaire de l'École pratique des Hautes Études,* Vième section-Sciences religieuses, vol. LXXIX (1971–1972), pp. 29–55.

———. 1971b. "Études de mythologie hindoue (III): Cosmogonies purāṇiques (Suite)." *Bulletin de l'École française d'Extrême-Orient (BEFEO),* **57**, 17–89.

———. 1972. *Clefs pour la pensée hindou.* Seghers, Paris.

———. 1973. "Le sacerdoce dans l'hindouisme classique." *Studia Missionalia,* **22**, 187–200.

———. 1976. "Études de mythologie hindoue (IV): Bhakti et Avatāra." *Bulletin de l'École française d'Extrême-Orient (BEFEO),* **63**, 111–263.

———. 1977. "Mythe épique et hindouisme d'aujourd'hui." *Indologica Taurinensia,* **5**, 43–53.

———. 1978. "Études de mythologie hindoue (V): Arjuna, le roi idéal; et les deux Kṛṣṇa." *Bulletin de l'École française d'Extrême-Orient (BEFEO),* **65**, 87–237.

———. 1981a. *Dictionnaire des Mythologies.* Flammarion, Paris.

———. 1981b. *L'hindouisme: anthropologie d'une civilisation.* Flammarion [Champs], Paris.

———. 1981c. "The Salvation of the King in the Mahābhārata." *Contributions to Indian Sociology.* New Series, **15**(1–2), 75–97.

———. 1981d. *Études de mythologie. Tome I. Cosmogonies purāṇiques*: reprise légèrement modifiée des trois premiers articles des "Études de mythologie hindoue" parus dans le BEFEO. Vol. 128 of the Series *Publications de l'École française d'Extrême-Orient.* École française d'Extrême-Orient, Paris.

———. Annual. *Annuaire de l'École pratique des Hautes Études, Vième section-Sciences religieuses.* École pratique des Hautes Études, Paris.

Biardeau, Madeleine and Charles Malamoud. 1976. *Le sacrifice dans l'Inde ancienne.* Bibliothèque de l'École des Hautes Études, Section des Sciences Religieuses, vol. LXXIX. Presses universitaires de France, Paris.

Biardeau, Madeleine and Jean-Michel Péterfalvi. 1985–1986. *Le Mahābhārata: extraits traduits du Sanscrit par Jean-Michel Péterfalvi.* Introduction et commentaires par Madeleine Biardeau (2 Vols.). G/F Flammarion, Paris.

Chaitanya, Krishna. 1985. *The Mahābhārata: A Literary Study.* Clarion Books, New Delhi.

Chapple, Christopher. 1986. *Karma and Creativity.* SUNY Series in Religion. State University of New York Press, Albany, N.Y.

Cromwell, Crawford S. 1974. *The Evolution of Hindu Ethical Ideals.* Firma K. L. Mukhopadhyay, Calcutta.

Dandekar, R. N., ed. 1942. *Progress of Indic Studies 1917–1942.* Bhandarkar Oriental Research Institute, Poona, India.

———. 1962. "Man in Hindu Thought." *Annals of the Bhandarkar Oriental Research Institute,* **43**(1–4), 1–57.

De Smet, R. V. 1972. "Early Trends in the Indian Understanding of Man." *Philosophy East and West,* **22**(3), 259–268.

Divanji, P. C. 1946. "Puruṣārtha, Daiva and Niyati." *Annals of the Bhandarkar Oriental Research Institute,* **26**(1–2), 142–151.

Dumézil, Georges. 1968. *Mythe et épopée: l'ideologie des trois fonctions dans les épopées des peuples indo-européens.* (3 Vols.). Éditions Gallimard, Paris.

Eliade, Mircea. 1974. *The Myth of the Eternal Return or Cosmos and History,* trans. Willard R. Trask. Bollingen Series, 46 (reprint). Princeton University Press, Princeton.

Farquhar, J. N. 1920. *An Outline of the Religious Literature of India* (first Indian reprint, 1967). Motilal Banarsidass, Delhi.

Gadamer, Hans-Georg. 1972. *Wahrheit und Methode: Grundzüge einer philosophischen Hermeneutik* (3 Vols., erweiterte Auflage). J. C. B. Mohr, Tübingen, Germany.

Ganguli, Kesari Mohan. 1952–1962. *The Mahabharata of Krishna Dwaipayana Vyasa* (12 Vols.). Published by P. C. Roy. Oriental Publications Co., Calcutta, second edition.

Gehrts, Heino. 1975. *Mahābhārata: das Geschehen und seine Bedeutung.* Bouvier Verlag Herbert Grundmann, Bonn.

Gode, P. K., ed. 1944. *Critical Studies in the Mahābhārata.* Vol. I of Sukthankar Memorial Edition. Karnatak Publishing House, Bombay.

Gokhale, Dinkar Vishnu, ed. 1950. *The Bhagavad-Gītā with the Commentary of Śrī Śaṃkarācārya.* Oriental Book Agency, Poona, India.

Gupta, Ananda Svarupa. 1970. "A Problem of Purāṇic Text-Reconstruction." *Purāṇa,* **12**(7), 304–321.

Gupta, S. P. and K. S. Ramachandran eds. 1976. *Mahābhārata: Myth and Reality: Differing Views.* Agam Prakashan, Delhi.

Hacker, Paul. 1978a. *Kleine Schriften.* Franz Steiner Verlag Gmbh, Wiesbaden, Germany.

——— 1978b. "Śaṃkara's Conception of Man." In Hacker (1978a), pp. 243–251.

——— 1978c. "Dharma im Hinduismus." In Hacker (1978a), pp. 496–509.

Hamilton, Edith and Huntingdon Cairns, eds. 1973. *The Collected Dialogues of Plato.* Bollingen Series. LXXI, trans. Paul Shorey. Princeton University Press, Princeton.

Hartmann, Nicolai. 1951. *Ethics* (3 Vols.). George Allen & Unwin, London.

Hiltebeitel, Alf. 1972. "The Mahābhārata and Hindu Eschatology." *History of Religions,* **12**(2), 95–135.

———. 1973. "Gods, Heroes and Kṛṣṇa: A Study of the Mahābhārata in Relation to Indian and Indo-European Symbolisms." Ph.D. diss., University of Chicago, Chicago.

———. 1976. *The Ritual of Battle: Krishna in the Mahābhārata.* Cornell University Press, Ithaca.

———. 1980. "Śiva, the Goddess, and the Disguises of the Pāṇḍavas and Draupadī." *History of Religions,* **20**(1–2), 147–174.

Hiriyanna, M. 1952. *Popular Essays in Indian Philosophy.* Kavyalaya Publishers, Mysore, India.

Hopkins, E. Washburn. 1906. "Modifications of the Karma Doctrine." *Journal of the Royal Asiatic Society,* **38**, 581–593.

Jain, Ram Chandra. 1979. *Jaya: The Original Nucleus of Mahabharata.* Agam Kala Prakashan, Delhi.

James, William. 1956. *The Will to Believe and Other Essays in Popular Philosophy.* Dover Publications, New York.

Jauhari, Manorama. 1968. *Politics and Ethics in Ancient India.* Bharatiya Vidya Prakashan, Varanasi, India.

Kalghatgi, T. G. 1972. *Karma and Rebirth.* L. D. Institute of Indology, Ahmedabad, India.

Kane, P. V. 1968–1977. *History of Dharmaśāstra* (5 Vols.). Bhandarkar Oriental Research Institute, Poona, India.

Kane, R. 1985. *Free Will and Values.* State University of New York Press, Albany.

Karmarkar, R. D., ed. 1964. *Śrībhāṣya of Rāmānuja,* edited with a complete English translation, introduction, notes, and appendixes (3 Vols.). University of Poona Sanskrit and Prakrit Series, Poona, India.

Katz, Ruth Cecily. 1989. *Arjuna in the Mahabharata: Where Krishna Is, There Is Victory.* University of South Carolina Press, Columbia.

Kaveeshwar, G. W. 1971. *The Ethics of the Gītā.* Motilal Banarsidass, Delhi.

Kinjawadekar, Pandit Ramchandrashastri, ed. 1979. *The Mahābhāratam: With the Bharata Bhawadeepa Commentary of Nīlakaṇṭha* (6 Vols.). Oriental Books Reprint Corporation, New Delhi.

Klaes, Norbert. 1975. *Conscience and Consciousness: Ethical Problems of Mahābhārata.* Dharmaram College, Bangalore, India.

Lal, P. 1980. *The Mahabharata of Vyasa.* Vikas Publishing House, Delhi.

Long, J. Bruce. 1980. "The Concepts of Human Action and Rebirth in the Mahābhārata," chapter 2, pp. 38–60 in O'Flaherty (1980).

Mainkar, T. 1969. *A Comparative Study of the Commentaries on the Bhagavadgītā* (2nd Ed.). Motilal Banarsidass, Delhi.

Malkani, G. R. 1968. "Philosophy of the Will." In Singh (1968), pp. 195–204.

May, Rollo. 1981. *Freedom and Destiny.* Norton, New York.

Moore, Charles. A., ed., with the assistance of Aldyth V. Morris. 1967. *The Indian Mind: Essentials of Indian Philosophy and Culture.* East-West Center Press and University of Hawaii Press, Honolulu.

Müller, F. Max. 1984. *The Laws of Manu,* trans. G. Büler. Vol. XXV of the Sacred Books of the East (reprint). Motilal Banarsidass, Delhi.

O'Flaherty, Wendy Doniger, ed. 1980. *Karma and Rebirth in Classical Indian Traditions.* University of California Press, Berkeley.

Prabhakar, C. L. 1975. "The Idea of Pāpa and Puṇya in the Ṛgveda." *Journal of the Oriental Institute of the University of Baroda,* **24**(3–4), 269–283.

Prabhavananda, Swami. 1979. *The Spiritual Heritage of India.* Vedanta Press, Hollywood.

Pusalkar, A. D. 1942. "Twenty-five Years of Epic and Puranic Studies." In Dandekar (1942).

———. 1962. "The Mahābhārata: Its History and Character," pp. 56–70 in Vol. II of Haridas Bhattacharyya et al. (1953–1962).

Rāmānuja. 1968. *Śrīmadbhagavadgītā śrīmadbhagavadrāmānujācāryakṛta bhāṣya.* Amaramudragālaya [kāśī gośāla] ṭājanahāla, Vārāṇasī, India.

Ray, Benoy Gopal. 1973. *Gods and Karma in Indian Religions.* Visva-Bharati University, Satiniketan, India: Center of Advanced Study in Philosophy.

Reagan, Charles E. and David Stewart, eds. 1978. *The Philosophy of Paul Ricoeur: An Anthology of His Work.* Beacon, Boston.

Ricoeur, Paul. 1966. *Freedom and Nature: The Voluntary and the Involuntary,* trans. Erazim V. Kohak. Northwestern University Press, Evanston, Ill.

———. 1978a. "Philosophy of Will and Action," chapter 4, pp. 61–74 in Reagan and Stewart (1978).

———. 1978b. "The Unity of the Voluntary and the Involuntary as a Limiting Idea," chapter 1, pp. 3–19 in Reagan and Stewart (1978).

Śaṃkarācārya. 1964. *Brahmasūtra with Śaṃkarabhāṣya. Works of Śaṃkarācārya in Original Sanskrit.* Vol. III. Motilal Banarsidass, Delhi.

Sharma, Arvind. 1984. "Fate and Free Will in the Bhagavadgītā." *Religious Studies,* **15**, 531–537.

———. ed. 1991. *Essays on the Mahābhārata*. E. J. Brill, Leiden, Netherlands.

Singh, Balbir. 1976. *The Conceptual Framework of Indian Philosophy*. Macmillan Co. of India, Delhi.

Singh, Ram Jee, ed. 1968. *World Perspectives in Philosophy, Religion and Culture: Essays Presented to Professor Dhirendra Mohan Datta*. Bharati Bhawan, Bombay.

Sircar, D. C., ed. 1969. *The Bhārata War and Purāṇic Genealogies*. University of Calcutta, Calcutta.

Sukthankar, V. S. 1957. *On the Meaning of the Mahābhārata*. Asiatic Society of Bombay, Bombay.

Sukthankar, Vishnu Sitaram et al., eds. 1933–1966. *The Mahābhārata for the First Time Critically Edited* (19 Vols. plus 6 Vols. of Indexes). Bhandarkar Oriental Research Institute, Poona, India.

Thompson, George. 1974. *Aeschylus: The Oresteia Trilogy*, trans. George Thompson. Dell Publishing Company, New York.

van Buitenen, J. A. B. 1972. "On the Structure of the Śabhāparvan of the Mahābhārata." *India Maior*. Festschrift J. Gonda, pp. 68–84.

———. ed. 1973–1978. *The Mahābhārata* (3 Vols.). University of Chicago Press, Chicago.

———. 1981. *The Bhagavadgītā in the Mahābhārata*. University of Chicago Press, Chicago.

van Nooten, Barend A. 1971. *The Mahābhārata Attributed to Kṛṣṇa Dvaipāyana Vyāsa*. Twayne Publishers, New York.

von Simson, Georg. 1977. "Die Einschaltung der Bhagavadgītā im Bhīṣmaparvan des Mahābhārata." *Indo-Iranian Journal*, **11**, 159–174.

Walli, Koshalya. 1977. *Theory of Karma in Indian Thought*. Bharata Manisha, Varanasi, India.

Whitney, William Dwight. 1973. *Sanskrit Grammar: Including Both the Classical Language, and the Older Dialects, of Veda and Brahmana*. Harvard University Press, Cambridge, Mass.

Woods, Julian F. 1988–1989. "The Doctrine of Karma in the Bhagavadgītā." *Journal of Studies in the Bhagavadgītā*, **8–9**, 47–81.

———. 1998. "Fatalism: Indian." In Vol. 3 of the *Routledge Encyclopedia of Philosophy*, Edward Craig, General Editor. Routledge: London and New York, pp. 564–568.

Index